Debrett Goes to Hollywood

Debrett Goes to Hollywood

Charles Kidd

Weidenfeld and Nicolson · London

For my parents

PICTURE ACKNOWLEDGEMENTS

Photographs are reproduced by kind permission of the following:

British Film Institute and the
Weidenfeld Archive.

Published in Great Britain by
George Weidenfeld & Nicolson Limited
91 Clapham High Street
London SW4 7TA

ISBN 0 297 78968 6

Printed in Great Britain by
Butler & Tanner Ltd
Frome and London

Contents

List of Family Trees

SYMBOLS

PARENT/
CHILD

⟶

MARRIAGE

————

LOVERS

♥

SIBLINGS

————

LIST OF ABBREVIATIONS

Acad	Academy	**ed**	educated/editor	**NY**	New York
acc	accident	**eng**	engineer	**OBE**	Officer of the Order of the British Empire
Apr	April	**exec**	executive		
assist	assistant	**Feb**	February	**Oct**	October
assoc	association	**Fla**	Florida	**Penn**	Pennsylvania
Aug	August	**Fl-Lieut**	Flight Lieutenant	**Pres**	President
b	born	**FRS**	Fellow of the Royal Society	**prod**	producer/produced
BA	Bachelor of Arts			**ptnr**	partner
bapt	baptised	**G/Capt**	Group Captain	**R**	Royal
bn	battalion	**HM**	His/Her Majesty	**RAF**	Royal Air Force
bro	brother	**HMS**	His/Her Majesty's Ship	**RCAF**	Royal Canadian Air Force
Bt	Baronet	**Inc**	Incorporated/including		
bur	buried	**Inst**	Institute	**Regt**	Regiment
B'way	Broadway			**rep**	repertory
c	*circa*	**Jan**	January	**Revd**	Reverend
Calif	California	**Jr**	Junior	**Rt Hon**	Right Honourable
Capt	Captain	**Jul**	July		
Co	Company/County	*k*	killed	**Sch**	School
Col	Colonel/Colorado	**KBE**	Knight Commander of the British Empire	**Sec**	Secretary
Conn	Connecticut			**Sep**	September
cr	created	**KG**	Knight of the Garter	**Soc**	Society
Cttee	Committee	**LA**	Los Angeles	**Sr**	Senior
d	died	**LLB**	Bachelor of Laws	**Supt**	Superintendent
d(s)	daughter(s)	*m*	married	**Treas**	Treasurer
Dec	December	**Mar**	March	**Trin**	Trinity
Dep Commr	Deputy Commissioner	**Mass**	Massachusetts	**Univ**	University
DFC	Distinguished Flying Cross	**MC**	Military Cross	**US**	United States
		mgr	manager	**USNR**	United States Naval Reserve
dir	director/directed	**mil**	military		
div	divorced/division	**MP**	Member of Parliament	**Va**	Virginia
DSC	Distinguished Service Cross	**MS**	Master of Science (USA)	**Vice Pres**	Vice President
DSc	Doctor of Science	**NJ**	New Jersey	**W**	West
DSO	Companion of the Distinguished Service Order	**Nov**	November	**WW**	World War
		NW	North West	**yr**	younger
				yst	youngest

Preface

꙰

This is the first attempt to chart the family trees of some of the great and glamorous names of Hollywood's Golden Era.

In some cases it has been possible to make extensive and original research into the ancestry of the stars, particularly Tyrone Power and the Bennett sisters, whose antecedants include a remarkable number of actors and musicians; also Gloria Grahame, who descends from King Edward III, one of the most powerful of the Plantagenet kings; and Howard Hawks and Humphrey Bogart, both of whom descend from American pioneer stock. Other family articles trace the wide-reaching network of blood and marriage connections that still dominate and influence the film industry.

A feature of *Debrett Goes to Hollywood* is the new style of genealogical table – the 'lateral' family tree. This is one that runs sideways rather than the traditional father-to-son style, and it relies mainly upon multiple marriages for its direction. The astonishing incidence of divorce in the movie colony, and the stars' propensity for attracting mates from the upper echelons of society, make it possible to link up the most unlikely names, e.g. Sir Winston Churchill and Groucho Marx (see table 21), and one might be surprised to find that both Brooke Shields and Blake Edwards can both be connected to the Fairbanks dynasty (see table 13), on the traditional tree.

The choice of family for inclusion has been somewhat arbitrary, and rests largely upon their genealogical interest to the author. Many may be disappointed to find that their favourite star has not been included, but the general rule is that each family treated contains several members who have made some significant contribution to the American cinema of the Golden Era. It is hoped that a similar book devoted to some of the famous British families of actors might follow *Debrett Goes to Hollywood*, thus such eminent names as Chaplin, Redgrave, Gielgud and Mills and so forth, will not be found in these pages. The inclusion of Richard Greene, a British actor, would seem to contradict this, but his alliances with two prominent American dynasties make his genealogy of relevance to this study.

Debrett Goes to Hollywood was originally intended as a 'Hollywood Dynasties' book, but this subject has been recently covered by Stephen Farber and Marc Green in their excellent volume of the same name. In order not to duplicate this work, the families of Fonda, Garland/Minnelli, Mayer/Selznick, etc, have not been included. The only family that is covered by both books is that of Alan Ladd, but the author believes this is qualified by the previously unmentioned link between the Ladds and the Thalberg/Shearer family.

Genealogical research is never ending, and there are still some puzzles to be sorted out. For example, the precise link between the LeRoy and Lasky families has not been uncovered, and a note in the archives of the British Film Institute states that Tom Neal (see table 17) is a great nephew of John Drew (see table 1), but no evidence has been found so far to authenticate this kinship. If there is anyone who might have knowledge of this connection, or could put the author in touch with the late Mr Neal's son (Thomas Patrick Neal, last heard of in Palm Springs in 1972), he would be grateful.

Very many people have helped in the compilation of the family trees, and the author is especially indebted to Patric Dickinson (Rouge Dragon Pursuivant at the College of Arms), David Williamson, Hugh Montgomery-Massingberd, Frances-Jane French, and Hugh St Clair for their generous contributions. Thanks also to Robert Jarman (managing director of Debrett's Peerage Ltd), David Roberts, Ed Hanson, Gary Boyd Roberts, Dorothy M. Lower, Peter Watson, Katie Ekberg, Malcolm Green, Robin Cross and Juan Balansó.

Every family contacted cooperated to a greater or lesser degree (with the notable exception of the Ladds), but particular thanks are due to Diana Anderson, Shelley Wanger, Patricia Leigh-Wood, Romina Power, Deborah Power Loew, Deborah Thalberg, Douglas Fairbanks Jr, Jesse Lasky Jr, Jean Owens Hayworth, Suzanne Cansino Beaber, Marylyn Thorpe Roh, Pascal Franchot Tone, Kitty Hawks, Elsie Fernández Castelló, Lorinda Roland and the late Bessie Love.

Apart from the selected bibliography, acknowledgement and thanks are given to *Variety*, *The Stage*, *Time Life Magazine* and *People Magazine*; also thanks to the staffs of the British Film Institute, the British Library (Colindale), and the India Office Library and Records.

1 The Barrymore Dynasty

✿✿✿

At a banquet in 1982, seven-year-old Drew Barrymore celebrated the centenary of her grandfather John Barrymore's birth. In that year too she made her film début in *ET* and became the latest member of the 'family business'. Both her names represent famous figures of the stage and screen – the Barrymore (previously Blyth) family and the Drews have been associated with the performing arts since the middle of the last century. Her great grandfather Maurice Barrymore was a very successful theatre actor and her great grandmother Georgiana (Georgie) Drew, a famous comedienne, and of course their children were the extraordinarily talented trio, Lionel, Ethel and John (or Jack).

Unlike so many actors whose careers were made in Hollywood, Lionel, Ethel and John Barrymore were established Broadway stars before they went West. After seeing Edward Sheldon's adaptation of the Italian play 'The Jest' co-starring John and Lionel, critics enthused. 'To the future of such actors it is impossible to set any limits.'

The Barrymores made a huge contribution to the cinema – they were pioneers who helped turn motion pictures from a gimmick to an art form. Unlike the unfortunate John Gilbert, they successfully transferred to talkies and Lionel showed himself to be a capable director in a number of films between 1929 and 1931, including the well-received *Confession* (1929). John Gilbert's first talkie to be released, *His Glorious Night* (1929), was directed by Lionel, and has gone down in legend as perhaps the most disastrous talkie début ever (it was one of the principal causes of the Great Lover's downfall).

Lionel can also be credited with persuading Irv-ing Thalberg that Clark Gable was a valuable commodity, despite what Thalberg called his batlike ears. The Barrymores were versatile actors. Jack played everything from Shakespeare to Captain Ahab in *The Sea Beast* (1926) and *Moby Dick* (1930). He was an actor who gave vigour to every part. Selznick deemed his portrayal of insanity in *Bill of Divorcement* (1932), 'as the greatest all-time performance on any motion picture screen.'

By their own admission the Barrymores were drawn to Hollywood by the money. In the theatre they could expect to earn $500 a week, whereas in the movie *The Nightingale*, Ethel was offered $15,000 for two weeks' work and later $60,000 to do five films between 1915 and 1917 by Metro Pictures. In 1931 John earned $460,000 from films.

The two Barrymore brothers settled in Hollywood. Lionel lived there for five decades, making a total of 182 films between 1912 and 1953, and still holds the record for the artist longest contracted to MGM. He won an Oscar in 1931 for *A Free Soul*, coincidentally the film that made Clark Gable a star. However, Ethel determinedly stuck to her stage career, making occasional dashes out West for a picture then immediately hurrying back to New York. She was always disparaging about films. 'I have always belonged to the theatre,' she said and claimed never to have seen any of her films. She called John and Lionel 'mere factory hands' for giving their lives to Hollywood.

The Barrymores were dubbed the Royal Family of Hollywood, a legend perpetuated when all three of them acted in *Rasputin and the Empress* in 1932. Anne Shirley, who played Princess Anastasia to

Ethel's Empress, recalls that Miss Ethel was queenly not only in her role. 'When the three Barrymores swung into action at Metro, Hollywood forgot all about its Garbos, Dietrichs and Gables,' wrote gossip columnist Louella Parsons. It is surprising that in such a competitive profession, fuelled by egos, there seemed to be little resentment of the Barrymores. Laraine Day said, 'I can't think of anyone who disliked Lionel,' and Frank Capra pronounced, 'In any actors, hall of fame, Lionel Barrymore's name deserves top billing among the immortals, yet he was the humblest most cooperative actor I have ever known.' But Lionel was not as versatile as his siblings, and latterly confined himself to variations on the 'crusty patriarch' theme, notably as Dr Gillespie in the long running 'Dr Kildare' series. From the mid-1930s he was increasingly crippled by arthritis, hence the desk- and chair-bound nature of his work in those years.

Lionel called acting the family curse and in the early years tried to break away from it by going to live in Paris and study art. He was quite an accomplished artist – after his death his nautical etchings were some of the most reproduced work of an American artist. But unfortunately his art could not support his lifestyle, particularly when he married Irene Fenwick. His friends said that he probably wouldn't have made films at such a rate, and given more time to his painting if it were not for her. She made him buy a huge mansion in Beverly Hills in which she gave lavish parties, asking guests with gold-engraved invitations. If someone she wanted was having a party or attending another she just asked all the guests to hers. But Lionel was devoted to her and never really got over her premature death, from anorexia, when she was only forty-nine.

Jack didn't settle permanently in Hollywood until the mid-1920s when he was well into his forties. His sprawling home, 'Bella Vista' boasted two swimming pools, a trout pond, a bowling green, a skeet-shooting range and an aviary of exotic birds (including his not-so-exotic pet vulture, Maloney). Here he entertained his many pals with an endless supply of liquor and tales of dissipation.

Jack was also a competent artist but acting was sadly not his only curse – he was afflicted by the demon alcohol, associating drinking with manliness and camaraderie. It was to prove his undoing.

In the early 1930s alcohol tightened its grip on Jack and his acting suffered. A crisis came in 1933 during the filming of *Counsellor-at-Law*, when his memory entirely deserted him causing fifty-six hopeless takes before filming was packed up for the day. Next day he was word perfect, but the writing was on the wall. The last great flaring of his sardonic talent to mock his own image of bravura was in *Twentieth Century* (1934), with Carole Lombard. She insisted on him again for *True Confession* (1937), though this time as a supporting player not as co-star.

Jack was haunted by his father's total mental collapse and death in Bellevue Hospital, and often feared for his own sanity. His wife, Dolores Costello, found his drinking turned him into a monster at home; she bravely tried to cure him, but his determination to drink proved more than she could stand, and she eventually left him. Whereas Ethel and Lionel were venerated in their old age, Jack became an object of pity. He was also prey to an unscrupulous manager, Henry Hotechenor.

Jack's third and last wife was Elaine Barrie, twenty-one years his junior. They first met when she interviewed him for her school magazine. The article never appeared, and their marriage was nothing more than a four year term of trial separations and reconciliations. Elaine took up acting and together they set out on a grisly tour with a feeble comedy, 'My Dear Children', which opened in New York in January 1940.

Incredibly, Jack could still steal scenes without even trying, notably in *The Great Man Votes* (1939), and in *Midnight* (1939). His performance in *The Great Profile* (1940), a bitter self-parody, reveals behind his bleary eyes a cynical amusement at the thought of the 'great actor' presiding at his own disintegration.

Jack's last film was the abysmal *Playmates* (1941) where, when the time came to film a scene in which he recited Hamlet's soliloquy, his memory again failed him. Turning his back on the crew he mumbled, 'It's been a long time.' One of the saddest of the many descriptions of his decline comes from Mary Astor, with whom he had had a brief affair at the height of his career, and who says she once spotted him alone in a radio studio corridor, sagging against a wall 'like someone who just couldn't walk another step.'

The drama critic John Mason Brown also remembered the John Barrymore of his youth as Hamlet in 1923 in New York, 'John Barrymore, with his slim, proud figure, the lean, Russian wolfhound aquilinity of his profile, and the princely beauty of his full face, continues for me to be the embodiment of the Dane. His Hamlet had a withering wit. It had scorn at its command; passion too. Though undisciplined, it crackled with the lightning of personality.'

Jack eventually died of a combination of cirrhosis of the liver and pneumonia. His character was never as stable as Lionel or Ethel's. He once confessed that he was only happy hiding behind a film or play part and was wary of anyone, even his wives, getting too close to him. Dolores Costello recalled that on one of their pleasure cruises on Jack's luxury yacht *Infanta* they met a guide who had lived with his wife for ten idyllic years in the wilderness without ever seeing another human being, and on hearing this Jack gave a look of utter amazement and disbelief.

Elaine's acting career has not been successful since Jack's death. In 1964 she returned to writing with a book entitled *All My Sins Remembered*. It is not polite about Ethel, Lionel, Dolores and Jack's friends.

Unfortunately, Jack's daughter Diana by his second wife Blanche Oelrichs – an authoress who called herself Michael Strange and was apt to dress in men's clothes – also had a drink problem. The title of her book *Too Much Too Soon* is a sad reflection on her life. As the daughter of John Barrymore she was accorded a talent she could not live up to. Said Tennessee Williams, 'She had great talent but no control, like an engine running away.' The result was a trail of broken love affairs and drunken brawls, which eventually ended in her death at thirty-nine among empty liquor and pill bottles.

John and Dolores' pampered and adored son

John Jr was hailed a heart-throb at seventeen in his first films *The Sundowners* (1950) and *High Lonesome* (1950) – but he realized that it was not enough just being the son of Jack Barrymore. He walked out of the play 'Hasty Heart' in which he acted opposite his cousin Ethel Colt because he felt that he was

John Barrymore holding his son, John Blyth Barrymore. In the group are his third wife, Dolores Costello, with their elder child, Ethel Dolores, and the children of Ethel Barrymore, Ethel Colt and Samuel Colt.

Lionel Barrymore, eldest of 'The Fabulous Barrymores', left the Broadway stage in 1925 and turned exclusively to films. He became one of Hollywood's foremost character stars in the 1930s and 40s.

me the name Barrymore means drink and when he drinks he is a different person altogether.'

After a period of hibernation in the Californian desert he now sports a mane of white hair and takes occasional film parts. His son John Blyth Barrymore III, now thirty-one, studied music and does lucrative television work periodically.

Lionel and his brother John's attitudes to children were rather paradoxical. They took great interest in everyone else's – Lionel once sent a 5ft cross of white roses to a little girl who died trapped down an abandoned pipe shaft – but they were distant towards their own. Lionel lost two babies yet never became close to his nieces and nephews. The Wheeler family who looked after him in his old age supplanted his real family – Florence Wheeler was the sole beneficiary of his will. John Jr quarrelled badly with his parents and was taken in by Ethel, and Diana never knew her father either. One month after her birth Jack renounced guardianship of her in case his marriage to Michael Strange should collapse.

Ethel, after her divorce from Russell Colt, asked for no child support and maintained her children's luxurious lifestyle herself – this meant periods when they were separated. Her son, Jackie Colt, made a brief foray into acting with his mother in *School for Scandal* but preferred pleasure to hard work and lived quietly on the Colt fortune, made by his inventor great grandfather, until his death. Her other son Sammy also made a few films but then devoted his energies to looking after his mother. 'He never married,' said his sister Ethel, 'because he could never find a woman to equal his mother.'

Ethel Colt made a great contribution to theatre. She once said, 'Theatre shouldn't be an end in itself. We can get the greatest pleasure from it as a tool to achieve even better things in all fields.' Ethel worked for the Family Service Association of America, and collaborating closely with writers she helped to create instructive plays on child care, drug abuse, alcoholism and women in industry until her untimely death from cancer.

So the 'Barrymore Company' goes on, and hopefully future generations of cinema and theatre goers will continue to enjoy their work.

not ready. He certainly had talent, though, but he was wild. The breakdown of his marriage to Cara Williams and the notoriety he achieved through his drunken and disorderly behaviour forced him to flee to Rome. He made quite a few films there even recreating his father's role as the Prince in *The Night They Killed Rasputin* (1960). His second marriage to Gabriella Palazzoli also foundered. On their divorce she commented, 'It's Hollywood's influence and John's friends that have been breaking up our marriage. John is a genius, I married him because I loved him not because his name is Barrymore. To

TABLE 1 THE DREW AND BARRYMORE DYNASTIES

JOHN DREW (*b* 1827, Dublin; *d* 1862, Philadelphia, = USA), son of an Irish artisan; emigrated with parents to New York 1837, where father became treas. at Niblo's Garden; went to sea, jumped ship at Liverpool; returned to USA; actor; 1st New York success as Dr O'Toole in 'The Irish Tutor'; best at comic Irish character parts; ran Arch Street Theatre, Philadelphia, with wife from 1853; *d* as the result of a fall, aged 35

1850, LOUISA LANE (1818–97), da of THOMAS FREDERICK LANE (1796–1825), actor; brought to USA by mother; theatrical début 1827 playing Duke of York to Junius Brutus Booth's Richard II; continued to act for the next 70 years, most famous role being Mrs Malaprop in 'The Rivals'; tyrannical but highly successful lessee of Arch Street Theatre, which she ran single-handed 1861–92. She *m* (1) 1836 (div.) HENRY BLANE HUNT (1796–1854), English opera singer; (2) 1848 GEORGE MOSSOP (1814–49), Irish actor/singer

FRANK NELSON DREW (1831–1903), actor =

FANNY GRIBBLES (*b* 1831), American actress

JOHN DREW (1853–1927); actor; 1st appearance at Arch Street Theatre 1873; joined Augustin Daly, New York 1875; renowned as a comedian, particularly drawing-room comedies; later with Charles Frohman =

1880, JOSEPHINE BAKER (1851–1918), actress, da of JOHN LEWIS BAKER, of Philadelphia, actor/manager, by his wife ALEXINA FISHER, actress

GEORGIANA (GEORGIE) DREW (1856–93), actress; 1st appearance at Arch Street Theatre 1872 in 'The Ladies' Battle'; moved to New York and worked with Augustin Daly; tall, versatile and blue-eyed her promising career was cut short by her early death =

1876, MAURICE BARRYMORE (1849–1905) (né HERBERT ARTHUR CHAMBERLAYNE HUNTER BLYTH), 2nd son of WILLIAM EDWARD BLYTH, surveyor for East India Co. and Dep. Commr. for Jhelum 1873; *b* in an underground chamber at Fort Agra, NW India, during the troubles; called to English bar; champion boxer, won Queensberry Cup; US stage début 1875 for Augustin Daly; greatest role was Rawdon Crawley in 'Becky Sharp' 1899, opposite Mrs Fiske; suffered complete mental collapse due to syphilis

LOUISE DREW (*d* 1894), actress =

CHARLES MENDRUM, actor

GEORGIANA DREW MENDRUM, actress (Mrs R.L. STOKES)

SIDNEY DREW (1864–1919); son of Louisa Drew, but not by John Drew who *d* 2 years before Sidney was *b*); appeared with 1st wife on stage as part of a comedy team, and with 2nd wife in films for Vitagraph Co., as 'Mr & Mrs Sidney Drew'; *d* in New York =

(1) GLADYS RANKIN (1870–1914), actress (see table 3)

(2) LUCILLE McVEY (1890–1925), former Lyceum actress (as June/Jane Morrow)

LOUISE DREW (*d* 1954) (only child) =

1917, JOHN DEVEREAUX, actor in Triangle Films (*d* 1958, New York, aged 76)

LIONEL BARRYMORE (1878–1954); actor =

(1) 1904 (div. 1922) DORIS RANKIN; sister of his uncle SIDNEY DREW's 1st wife; by whom he had 2 das, ETHEL and MARY, both of whom *d* in infancy

(2) 1923, IRENE FENWICK (*d* 1936), actress, formerly wife of JAY O'BRIEN, stockbroker

ETHEL BARRYMORE (1879–1959); actress =

1909 (div. 1923), RUSSELL GREENWOOD COLT (*d* 1960, aged 78), son of Col. SAMUEL COLT, Chm. US Rubber Co.

JOHN BARRYMORE (1882–1942); actor (see table 2)

SIDNEY RANKIN DREW (1892–1918); *k* in action while flying over France

---

JOHN DREW DEVEREAUX, actor (has issue, a da, *b* 1955)

ETHEL BARRYMORE COLT (1912–77), actress

= 1944, ROMEO MIGLIETTA, Italian petroleum and mining eng.

JOHN DREW COLT (1913–75); actor =

MARJORIE DOW, actress, formerly wife of HUGH BANCROFT

SAMUEL COLT, actor

JOHN DREW MIGLIETTA (*b* 1947)

TABLE 2 THE JOHN BARRYMORE DYNASTY

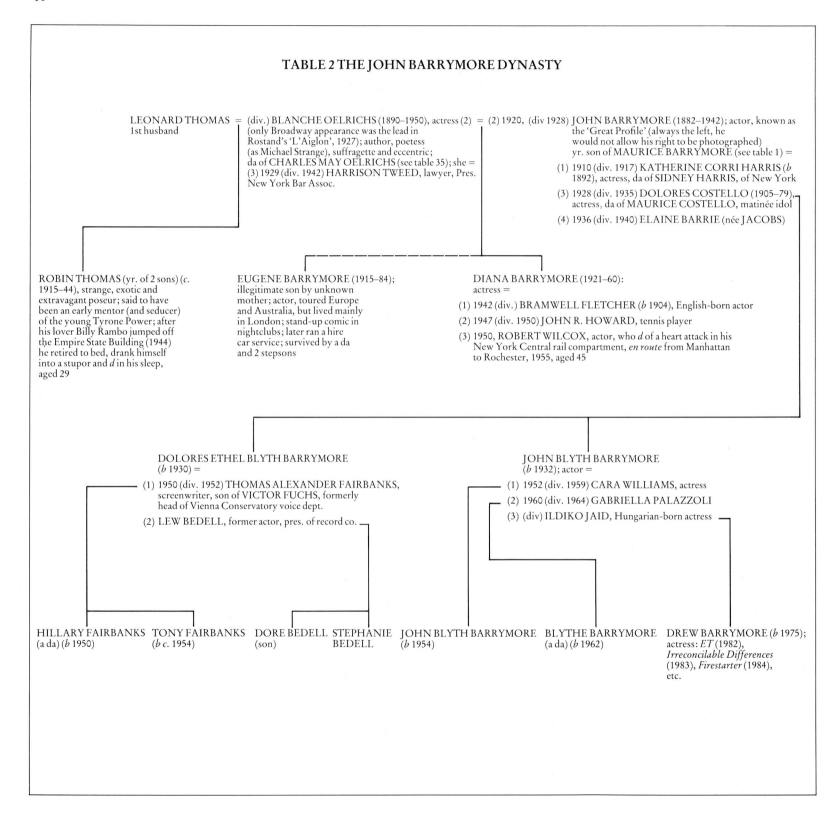

LEONARD THOMAS = (div.) BLANCHE OELRICHS (1890–1950), actress (2) = (2) 1920, (div 1928) JOHN BARRYMORE (1882–1942); actor, known as
1st husband (only Broadway appearance was the lead in the 'Great Profile' (always the left, he
Rostand's 'L'Aiglon', 1927); author, poetess would not allow his right to be photographed)
(as Michael Strange), suffragette and eccentric; yr. son of MAURICE BARRYMORE (see table 1) =
da of CHARLES MAY OELRICHS (see table 35); she =
(3) 1929 (div. 1942) HARRISON TWEED, lawyer, Pres. (1) 1910 (div. 1917) KATHERINE CORRI HARRIS (b
New York Bar Assoc. 1892), actress, da of SIDNEY HARRIS, of New York

(3) 1928 (div. 1935) DOLORES COSTELLO (1905–79),
actress, da of MAURICE COSTELLO, matinée idol

(4) 1936 (div. 1940) ELAINE BARRIE (née JACOBS)

ROBIN THOMAS (yr. of 2 sons) (c. | EUGENE BARRYMORE (1915–84); | DIANA BARRYMORE (1921–60):
1915–44), strange, exotic and | illegitimate son by unknown | actress =
extravagant poseur; said to have | mother; actor, toured Europe
been an early mentor (and seducer) | and Australia, but lived mainly | (1) 1942 (div.) BRAMWELL FLETCHER (b 1904), English-born actor
of the young Tyrone Power; after | in London; stand-up comic in
his lover Billy Rambo jumped off | nightclubs; later ran a hire | (2) 1947 (div. 1950) JOHN R. HOWARD, tennis player
the Empire State Building (1944) | car service; survived by a da
he retired to bed, drank himself | and 2 stepsons | (3) 1950, ROBERT WILCOX, actor, who d of a heart attack in his
into a stupor and d in his sleep, | New York Central rail compartment, en route from Manhattan
aged 29 | to Rochester, 1955, aged 45

DOLORES ETHEL BLYTH BARRYMORE JOHN BLYTH BARRYMORE
(b 1930) = (b 1932); actor =

(1) 1950 (div. 1952) THOMAS ALEXANDER FAIRBANKS, (1) 1952 (div. 1959) CARA WILLIAMS, actress
screenwriter, son of VICTOR FUCHS, formerly
head of Vienna Conservatory voice dept. (2) 1960 (div. 1964) GABRIELLA PALAZZOLI

(2) LEW BEDELL, former actor, pres. of record co. (3) (div) ILDIKO JAID, Hungarian-born actress

HILLARY FAIRBANKS TONY FAIRBANKS DORE BEDELL STEPHANIE JOHN BLYTH BARRYMORE BLYTHE BARRYMORE DREW BARRYMORE (b 1975);
(a da) (b 1950) (b c. 1954) (son) BEDELL (b 1954) (a da) (b 1962) actress: ET (1982),
Irreconcilable Differences
(1983), Firestarter (1984),
etc.

TABLE 3 THE RANKIN AND DAVENPORT DYNASTIES

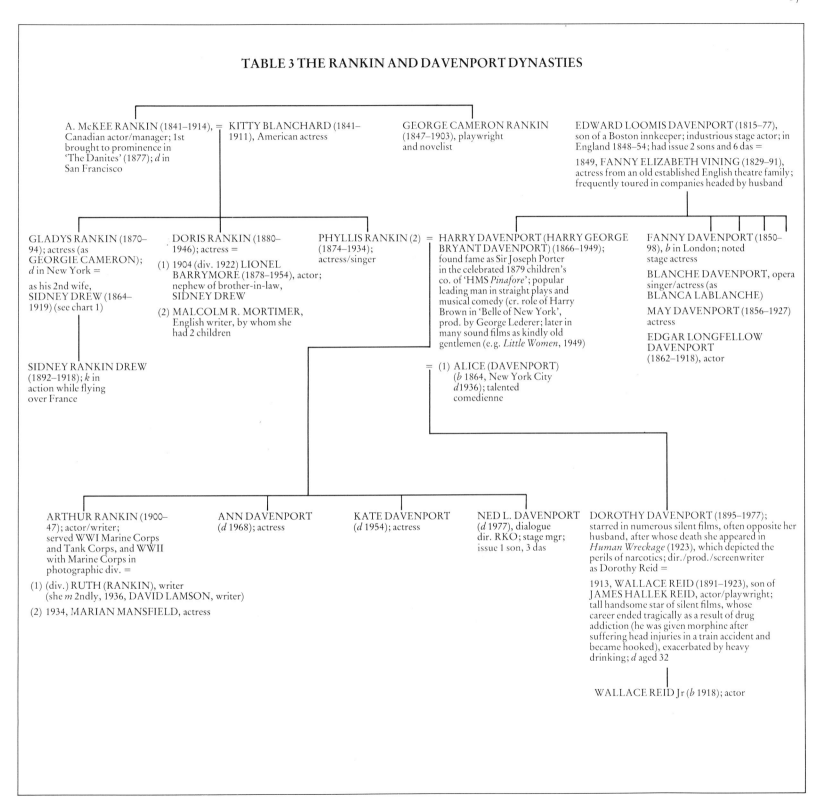

A. McKEE RANKIN (1841–1914), = **KITTY BLANCHARD** (1841–
Canadian actor/manager; 1st 1911), American actress
brought to prominence in
'The Danites' (1877); *d* in
San Francisco

GEORGE CAMERON RANKIN
(1847–1903), playwright
and novelist

EDWARD LOOMIS DAVENPORT (1815–77),
son of a Boston innkeeper; industrious stage actor; in
England 1848–54; had issue 2 sons and 6 das =

1849, **FANNY ELIZABETH VINING** (1829–91),
actress from an old established English theatre family;
frequently toured in companies headed by husband

GLADYS RANKIN (1870–
94); actress (as
GEORGIE CAMERON);
d in New York =

as his 2nd wife,
SIDNEY DREW (1864–
1919) (see chart 1)

DORIS RANKIN (1880–
1946); actress =

(1) 1904 (div. 1922) LIONEL
BARRYMORE (1878–1954), actor;
nephew of brother-in-law,
SIDNEY DREW

(2) MALCOLM R. MORTIMER,
English writer, by whom she
had 2 children

PHYLLIS RANKIN (2) =
(1874–1934);
actress/singer

**HARRY DAVENPORT (HARRY GEORGE
BRYANT DAVENPORT)** (1866–1949);
found fame as Sir Joseph Porter
in the celebrated 1879 children's
co. of 'HMS *Pinafore*'; popular
leading man in straight plays and
musical comedy (cr. role of Harry
Brown in 'Belle of New York',
prod. by George Lederer; later in
many sound films as kindly old
gentlemen (e.g. *Little Women*, 1949)

FANNY DAVENPORT (1850–
98), *b* in London; noted
stage actress

BLANCHE DAVENPORT, opera
singer/actress (as
BLANCA LABLANCHE)

MAY DAVENPORT (1856–1927)
actress

**EDGAR LONGFELLOW
DAVENPORT**
(1862–1918), actor

SIDNEY RANKIN DREW
(1892–1918); *k* in
action while flying
over France

= (1) **ALICE (DAVENPORT)**
(*b* 1864, New York City
d 1936); talented
comedienne

ARTHUR RANKIN (1900–
47); actor/writer;
served WWI Marine Corps
and Tank Corps, and WWII
with Marine Corps in
photographic div. =

(1) (div.) RUTH (RANKIN), writer
(she *m* 2ndly, 1936, DAVID LAMSON, writer)

(2) 1934, MARIAN MANSFIELD, actress

ANN DAVENPORT
(*d* 1968); actress

KATE DAVENPORT
(*d* 1954); actress

NED L. DAVENPORT
(*d* 1977), dialogue
dir. RKO; stage mgr;
issue 1 son, 3 das

DOROTHY DAVENPORT (1895–1977);
starred in numerous silent films, often opposite her
husband, after whose death she appeared in
Human Wreckage (1923), which depicted the
perils of narcotics; dir./prod./screenwriter
as Dorothy Reid =

1913, WALLACE REID (1891–1923), son of
JAMES HALLEK REID, actor/playwright;
tall handsome star of silent films, whose
career ended tragically as a result of drug
addiction (he was given morphine after
suffering head injuries in a train accident and
became hooked), exacerbated by heavy
drinking; *d* aged 32

WALLACE REID Jr (*b* 1918); actor

2 *The Bennett Sisters and Gloria Swanson*

The Bennett family typifies the best of Hollywood in the Golden Era. The two sisters, Constance and Joan, both made many movies which enjoy re-runs on television, but it is their life-styles that recall an age of glamour never to return. Constance and Joan, and their lesser-known sister Barbara, totalled twelve husbands, eight divorces and twelve children. Their stories include an unsolved mystery, the tragedy of mental illness, and a scandal that nearly ended a career. Also revealed for the first time is a family link with Gloria Swanson, and a love-affair, which for once has a happy ending.

Although Bennett is a familiar surname to film and theatre historians, it is, in fact, the female line that connects Constance and Joan Bennett to a deep-rooted theatrical past. Their earliest traceable ancestor, William Wood, was a strolling player who migrated from Wales to London. His original surname was Wodin or Woodin, and it is possible that he belonged to a gypsy family. Both his son and daughter were associated with the theatre. His son William performed at the popular London theatres before emigrating to the USA, and his daughter Sarah married the most famous costumier of his day, Frederick Vokes (this branch of the Vokes family became extinct a generation later).

In America, William Wood (II) had three sons and one daughter. The eldest, another William Wood, born 23 January 1833, enlisted as a three-month volunteer in the Union Army and died of influenza at Philadelphia aged twenty-eight. The second son, Albert Wood, born 1836, became a musician in New York; and the youngest son, Frank Wood, born 1844 (New York City), became an actor and pantomimist. It is from William Wood's only daughter, Rosabel Wood, that the Bennett sisters descend.

Rosabel was a dancer, known as Rose Wood, when she met and married Lewis Morrison, a well-known actor-manager. He was of English parentage, born in Kingston, Jamaica, 4 September 1845. They married in New Orleans in 1865, but were eventually divorced in 1890. She was a formidable matriarch, and lived to see her three grand-daughters' names in lights.

The Morrisons' younger daughter, Adrienne (born 1 March 1883), became a stage actress. At the age of twenty she married Richard Bennett, an actor who was groomed by Charles Frohman as a successor to John Drew. He was handsome and had a particularly good speaking voice; two of his great successes were in J. M. Barrie's 'What Every Woman Knows' (1908), and in Eugene Brieux's 'Damaged Goods' (1913–14) – a controversial play about syphilis – in which Adrienne Morrison also appeared. He was a highly-strung man, tyrannical with his daughters, quarrelsome with his wife and contemptuous of the drama critics, but he also had a tremendous love of his art. He became one of the leading matinée idols of his day, but appeared only infrequently in films (including *Bought* (1931), with daughter Constance). He also served as a technical director on a number of silent films.

Richard Bennett was born on 21 May 1873, at Deacon's Mills, Indiana. His first marriage was in 1901 (divorced 1903), to Grena Heller. She was born in San Francisco, where she studied music, and was a concert pianist prior to becoming the music critic on the *Journal American* and the *New York American* (before the merger of the two) for over forty years. She died on 4 April 1946 (New York City) aged sixty-two, survived by an adopted son. There were no children from this marriage.

Richard Bennett married secondly, 8 November 1903, Adrienne Morrison (as above). They had three daughters and were divorced in 1925. He married thirdly (11 July 1927) Mrs Aimee Raisch Hastings. She was the daughter of A. J. Raisch, and was previously married to Harry Hastings, a polo player. She met Bennett when they were both in a play 'Creoles' in which she had a minor role. They were divorced 1937; she died on 18 October 1955 (San Francisco) aged sixty.

Richard Bennett died of a heart attack on 21 October 1944 (Los Angeles) aged seventy-one, and was buried in the family plot at Old Lyme, Connecticut.

Adrienne Morrison married secondly, 19 June 1927, Eric Seabrook Pinker, a British-born literary agent, son of James Brand Pinker (who established the firm in 1897). She and Pinker ran the agency together until the company had to be dissolved (largely due to his embezzlements, for which he served time in Sing Sing Prison). She died on 20 November 1940.

The three daughters of Richard Bennett and Adrienne Morrison had a stimulating but unstable childhood. The middle daughter, Barbara, who became a dancer, was an early friend and champion of the actress Louise Brooks. In her book *Lulu in Hollywood* the late Miss Brooks describes the three sisters with her customary perception.

> Barbara's beautiful older sister, Constance, had just started her career, but her reputation as the best-dressed and haughtiest actress in movies was already established. All the girls had Richard Bennett's wide cheekbones and finely set eyes, but in character the three daughters did not resemble one another in any way. Constance loved money. During a career that continued to her death, in 1965, she demanded and received a salary equal to that of the top star. Yet beauty, great acting ability and a lovely voice could not compensate for the lack of the one attribute without which the rest did not matter; she did not have that generosity, that love of her audience, which makes a true star. What Joan loved was security. Her marriages to men powerful in films guaranteed a successful career. Barbara made a career of her emotions. Periods of work or marriage were terminated by her frightening, abandoned laughter of despair and failure. Only her death, in 1958, achieved in her fifth suicide attempt, could be termed a success.

The mental problems suffered by Barbara Bennett reappeared in later generations, first with her only daughter, Lorelle Downey, who died in a mental institution in 1977, and then with Joan Bennett's granddaughter, Lisa Anderson, who showed great artistic promise at a very early age, but who was diagnosed a schizophrenic at the age of sixteen. As Constance Bennett's daughter, Lorinda Roland, a sculptress, says, 'In creativity/talent there's always a close battle between insanity and productive use of the same resources ... in our family it's a six and a half-dozen choice ... though fortunately the productive space does seem to hold fort over the other.'

CONSTANCE BENNETT
Eldest daughter of Richard Bennett and Adrienne Morrison

Born on 22 October 1904, in New York City and educated privately in New York and Paris, Constance was the archetypal glamorous blonde. She was as self-willed as her father and set the Bennett girls' marital pace at sixteen by eloping with an eighteen-year-old pre-law student (while her mother was planning her coming-out party in Washington, DC). A honeymoon was forbidden, she was packed off to Europe, and the marriage was annulled. On returning home she began a long and successful film career – first in melodramas and later in sophisticated comedies, where her sharp wit and high spirits were a natural advantage. She never had the ruthless drive of a Davis or Crawford and regarded her career more as a support for her extravagant life-style – perhaps at its height during her second marriage to Philip Plant, the railroad and steamship heir. Her large fortune was the result of the quantity rather than the quality of her work.

In 1931 Constance Bennett was second only to Garbo in a poll of US exhibitors, and in the same year her agent, Myron Selznick, got her a record salary of $30,000 a week from Warner Bros., while she was making *Bought*. Some of her best films were made during the 1930s: *The Common Law* (1931) with Joel McCrea; *Lady With a Past* (1932), a comedy with Ben Lyon; *What Price Hollywood?* (1932), a comedy–melodrama directed by George Cukor (said to be based on the lives of silent film players John Bowers and Marguerite de la Motte; loosely remade as *A Star is Born*; *Topper* (1937) with Cary Grant; and *Merrily We Live* (1938) with Brian Aherne.

Constance's tough but casual attitude to her film career – 'Hollywood is pretty painful, even in small doses' – was in sharp constrast to her vigorous work for the British War Relief Fund – to which she and Douglas Fairbanks Jr were two of the first Hollywood stars to commit themselves; she was also chairman of the International Committee for Refugees of England. She was a close friend of Marion Davies, and was a hardened poker-player (as recounted by David Niven in *Bring on the Empty Horses*). Of Marilyn Monroe she is said to have remarked, 'there's a broad who's got a future behind her!' Like her father she loathed the Press.

In the early 1950s Constance left films for the stage, mostly playing in touring productions (including 'Auntie Mame' and 'Toys in the Attic'); she also did some television work; in 1965 she had a good part in *Madame X* as Lana Turner's mother. She died on 24 July 1965, at the Fort Dix Hospital, New Jersey, of a cerebral haemorrhage. Her fifth husband, Colonel (later Brigadier-General) John Coulter, to whom she had been married for twenty years, and her three children were there. As none of her children have issue of their own her line will eventually become extinct.

CHESTER MOOREHEAD
First husband of Constance Bennett. Married 6 June 1921, Greenwich, Connecticut; annulled 1923

Son of Frank Moorehead, Professor of Pathology at the University of Illinois, Chester was a pre-law student at the University of Virginia when he eloped with Constance Bennett. The marriage was annulled on grounds that parental permission had not been obtained, and that she refused to live with him. Later he became an advertising man and committed suicide on 12 December 1945, aged forty-two, by swallowing poison in a hotel room in Chicago. There were no children from this marriage.

PHILIP MORGAN PLANT
Second husband of Constance Bennett. Married 3 November 1925, Greenwich, Connecticut; divorced December 1929

Philip Morgan Plant was the son of Seldon B. Manwaring, of Hartford, Connecticut, by his wife Mae, daughter of Martin Cadwell, also of Hartford. A resourceful woman, Mae (Maisie), born *c.* 1880, was first married to Seldon Manwaring, who, according to her step-granddaughter Brooke Hayward's family memoir *Haywire*, 'managed a restaurant in a small town near New London, Connecticut, where Maisie helped him by waiting on tables.' They had one son, Philip, born *c.* 1901. She divorced Manwaring in 1914 and married the fabulously rich Commodore Morton F. Plant, the railroad and steamship owner and developer of the west coast of Florida. Her son was legally adopted by Morton Plant, whose surname he took. Plant died in 1918 leaving a fortune reported to be $50,000,000. In 1919 his widow married Colonel William Hayward, soldier and lawyer (and father of Leland Hayward, see table 6). He died in 1944 and ten years later she married for the fourth and final time, John E. Rovensky, an industrialist. The *New York Times* observed that she had a Lillian Russell type of beauty.

The Morton Plants' lavish style of life was reminiscent of the great days of Fifth Avenue. In 1916

Constance Bennett's husky voice, worldly manner and gutsy humour made her a natural star in the comedies of the 1930s. She eloped at sixteen, married the heir to a railroad and steamship fortune six years later, and her third husband, the Marquis de la Falaise, was formerly married to Gloria Swanson.

TABLE 4 THE MATERNAL ANCESTRY OF CONSTANCE, BARBARA AND JOAN BENNETT

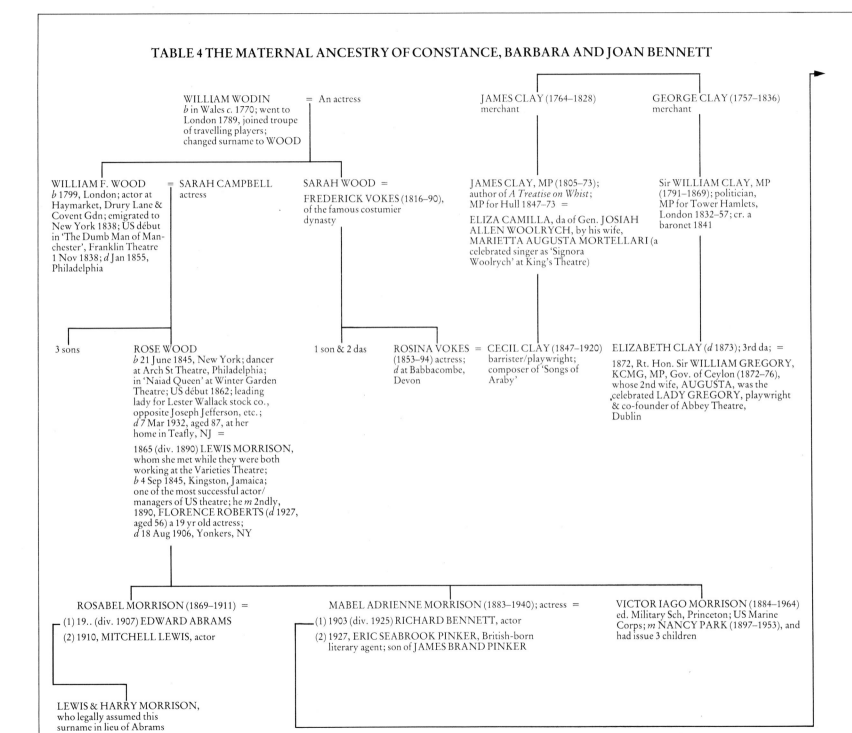

WILLIAM WODIN
b in Wales *c.* 1770; went to
London 1789, joined troupe
of travelling players;
changed surname to WOOD   = An actress

JAMES CLAY (1764–1828)
merchant

GEORGE CLAY (1757–1836)
merchant

WILLIAM F. WOOD
b 1799, London; actor at
Haymarket, Drury Lane &
Covent Gdn; emigrated to
New York 1838; US début
in 'The Dumb Man of Man-
chester', Franklin Theatre
1 Nov 1838; *d* Jan 1855,
Philadelphia   = SARAH CAMPBELL
actress

SARAH WOOD =
FREDERICK VOKES (1816–90),
of the famous costumier
dynasty

JAMES CLAY, MP (1805–73);
author of *A Treatise on Whist*;
MP for Hull 1847–73 =
ELIZA CAMILLA, da of Gen. JOSIAH
ALLEN WOOLRYCH, by his wife,
MARIETTA AUGUSTA MORTELLARI (a
celebrated singer as 'Signora
Woolrych' at King's Theatre)

Sir WILLIAM CLAY, MP
(1791–1869); politician,
MP for Tower Hamlets,
London 1832–57; cr. a
baronet 1841

3 sons

ROSE WOOD
b 21 June 1845, New York; dancer
at Arch St Theatre, Philadelphia;
in 'Naiad Queen' at Winter Garden
Theatre; US début 1862; leading
lady for Lester Wallack stock co.,
opposite Joseph Jefferson, etc.;
d 7 Mar 1932, aged 87, at her
home in Teafly, NJ =

1865 (div. 1890) LEWIS MORRISON,
whom she met while they were both
working at the Varieties Theatre;
b 4 Sep 1845, Kingston, Jamaica;
one of the most successful actor/
managers of US theatre; he *m* 2ndly,
1890, FLORENCE ROBERTS (*d* 1927,
aged 56) a 19 yr old actress;
d 18 Aug 1906, Yonkers, NY

1 son & 2 das

ROSINA VOKES =
(1853–94) actress;
d at Babbacombe,
Devon

CECIL CLAY (1847–1920)
barrister/playwright;
composer of 'Songs of
Araby'

ELIZABETH CLAY (*d* 1873); 3rd da; =
1872, Rt. Hon. Sir WILLIAM GREGORY,
KCMG, MP, Gov. of Ceylon (1872–76),
whose 2nd wife, AUGUSTA, was the
celebrated LADY GREGORY, playwright
& co-founder of Abbey Theatre,
Dublin

ROSABEL MORRISON (1869–1911) =
(1) 19.. (div. 1907) EDWARD ABRAMS
(2) 1910, MITCHELL LEWIS, actor

MABEL ADRIENNE MORRISON (1883–1940); actress =
(1) 1903 (div. 1925) RICHARD BENNETT, actor
(2) 1927, ERIC SEABROOK PINKER, British-born
literary agent; son of JAMES BRAND PINKER

VICTOR IAGO MORRISON (1884–1964)
ed. Military Sch, Princeton; US Marine
Corps; *m* NANCY PARK (1897–1953), and
had issue 3 children

LEWIS & HARRY MORRISON,
who legally assumed this
surname in lieu of Abrams

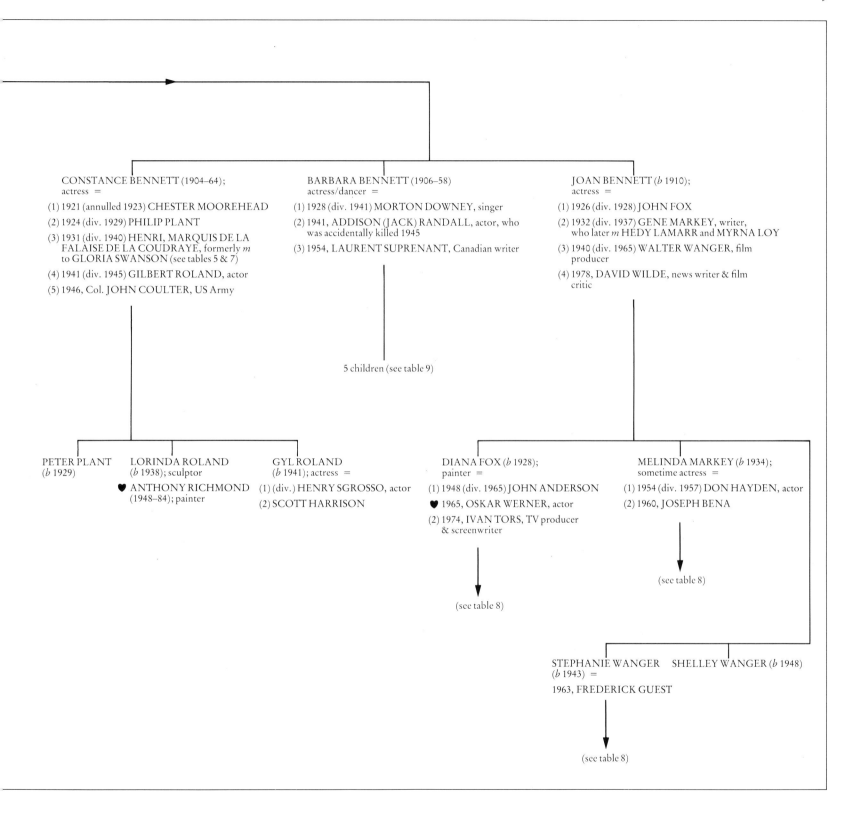

CONSTANCE BENNETT (1904–64);
actress =

(1) 1921 (annulled 1923) CHESTER MOOREHEAD

(2) 1924 (div. 1929) PHILIP PLANT

(3) 1931 (div. 1940) HENRI, MARQUIS DE LA
FALAISE DE LA COUDRAYE, formerly *m*
to GLORIA SWANSON (see tables 5 & 7)

(4) 1941 (div. 1945) GILBERT ROLAND, actor

(5) 1946, Col. JOHN COULTER, US Army

BARBARA BENNETT (1906–58)
actress/dancer =

(1) 1928 (div. 1941) MORTON DOWNEY, singer

(2) 1941, ADDISON (JACK) RANDALL, actor, who
was accidentally killed 1945

(3) 1954, LAURENT SUPRENANT, Canadian writer

JOAN BENNETT (*b* 1910);
actress =

(1) 1926 (div. 1928) JOHN FOX

(2) 1932 (div. 1937) GENE MARKEY, writer,
who later *m* HEDY LAMARR and MYRNA LOY

(3) 1940 (div. 1965) WALTER WANGER, film
producer

(4) 1978, DAVID WILDE, news writer & film
critic

5 children (see table 9)

PETER PLANT
(*b* 1929)

LORINDA ROLAND
(*b* 1938); sculptor

♥ ANTHONY RICHMOND
(1948–84); painter

GYL ROLAND
(*b* 1941); actress =

(1) (div.) HENRY SGROSSO, actor

(2) SCOTT HARRISON

DIANA FOX (*b* 1928);
painter =

(1) 1948 (div. 1965) JOHN ANDERSON

♥ 1965, OSKAR WERNER, actor

(2) 1974, IVAN TORS, TV producer
& screenwriter

(see table 8)

MELINDA MARKEY (*b* 1934);
sometime actress =

(1) 1954 (div. 1957) DON HAYDEN, actor

(2) 1960, JOSEPH BENA

(see table 8)

STEPHANIE WANGER
(*b* 1943) =

1963, FREDERICK GUEST

SHELLEY WANGER (*b* 1948)

(see table 8)

they exchanged their Fifth Avenue house with Cartier for two Oriental pearl necklaces, then valued at $1,500,000. They then built a forty-room, limestone and marble mansion on the north east corner of Fifth Avenue and Eighty-Sixth Street, where they amassed an amazing collection of pictures, furniture, panelling, tapestries and Georgian silver. Following her death in 1956 the mansion and contents were sold for an eventual sum of $2,438,980 – then the highest amount ever made at a public auction.

Philip M. Plant inherited a fortune from his stepfather, said to be about $15,000,000. He was a well-known socialite and big-game hunter. At the age of twenty-four he married Constance Bennett in the lobby of the Pickwick Arms Hotel, Greenwich; they spent their honeymoon in Florida and Cuba, and then moved to Europe, where he had homes in Biarritz, the Swiss Alps and Paris. Among their smart set was Gloria Swanson, whose husband the Marquis de la Falaise became Constance Bennett's next spouse. The Plant/Bennett life-style was just too fast and they divorced on bad terms four years later. Constance received a $500,000 cash settlement. While married to Plant, Constance had one son, Peter Bennett Plant.

Philip M. Plant retired to his estate at Oswegatchie Farm, Waterford, Connecticut, where he reared pheasants and rare fowl; he was president of the Ornamental Pheasant Society of America in 1936. He married secondly, 11 April 1934 (Clearwater, Florida), Mrs Edna Dunham, a sportswoman, formerly wife of Ernest F. Dunham, a broker; and thirdly, 15 December 1938 (New York City), Marjorie King, a former showgirl (in 'Showboat' 1936, etc.), daughter of Mrs Leslie Robinson, of Beverly Hills, California. He died on 18 June 1941, and was buried at New London. He was survived by his mother (who left the Explorers Club $25,000 in his memory), and his wife.

PETER BENNETT PLANT
Only son of Constance Bennett

The paternity of Peter Plant has long been disputed. Constance Bennett (and, subsequently, Peter Plant

himself) maintained that he was her son by Philip Plant (and therefore heir to the Plant fortune), but the family executors when dealing with Philip Plant's estate stated that he died without issue. Constance Bennett disputed the will and won $150,000 as 'attorney expenses', which only confused the matter still further.

Peter Plant and his sisters agree that he was born on 3 January 1929 at the Royal Free Hospital, London. It seems odd, however, that Constance, who loathed any invasion of her privacy, should choose not to have her son born in a private nursing home. There is no record of Philip Plant ever officially recognizing the child as his. The child's existence was not made public until three years later (by which time the Plants were divorced and Constance married to the Marquis de la Falaise), when, in November 1932, a news item appeared stating that Miss Bennett was attempting to adopt, by English law, a three year old English boy, Dennis A. Armstrong. There is a birth certificate registered for a boy of this name (born on 21 January 1929 – eighteen days after Peter's alleged birth date – at the Royal Free Hospital), son of a Sarah Savina Armstrong, by a father unknown. Another contemporary report suggested that Miss Armstrong was a cousin of the Bennetts.

Whatever his paternity, Peter Plant is an advertising and sales promotion specialist with Farmer's Insurance, Los Angeles. He has been married four times and has no children.

HENRI, MARQUIS DE LA FALAISE DE LA COUDRAYE
Third husband of Constance Bennett. Married 22 November 1931, Beverly Hills; divorced 1940

Born on 11 February 1898, Henri was the son and heir of Comte Gabriel Louis de la Falaise, of Paris (see table 5). He was the European representative for Pathé Films, but never took a prominent role in the film world. He married first, 28 January 1925 (divorced 1930), Gloria Swanson, the film star (see below); and thirdly, 21 December 1940 (Neuilly-sur-Seine), Emma Rodriguez Restrepo,

TABLE 5 THE FAMILY OF HENRI, MARQUIS DE LA FALAISE

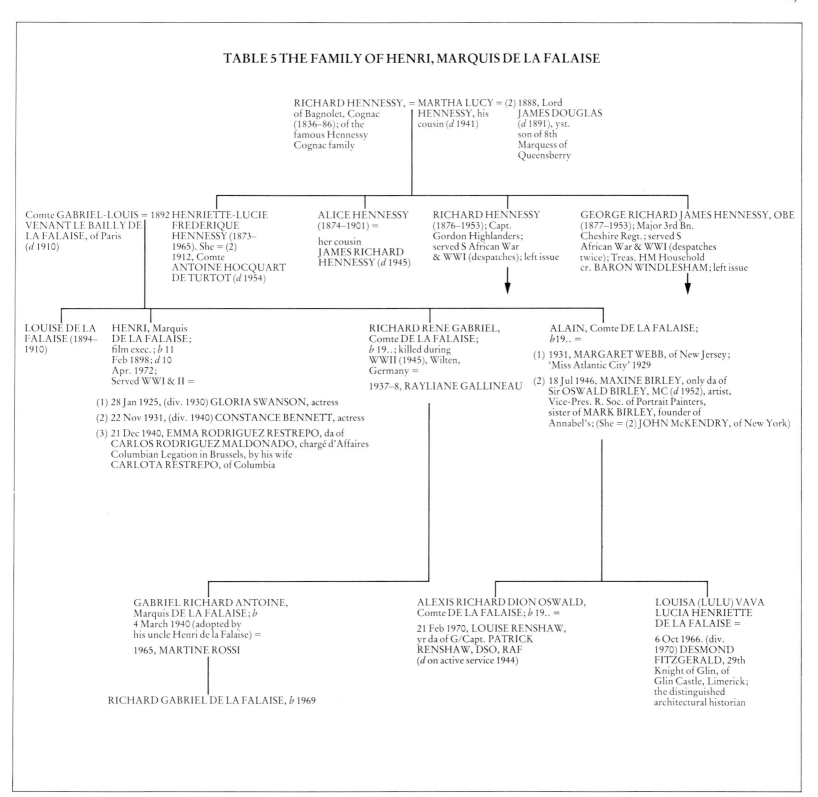

RICHARD HENNESSY, = MARTHA LUCY = (2) 1888, Lord
of Bagnolet, Cognac   HENNESSY, his   JAMES DOUGLAS
(1836–86); of the   cousin (*d* 1941)   (*d* 1891), yst.
famous Hennessy   son of 8th
Cognac family   Marquess of
Queensberry

Comte GABRIEL-LOUIS = 1892 HENRIETTE-LUCIE
VENANT LE BAILLY DE   FREDERIQUE
LA FALAISE, of Paris   HENNESSY (1873–
(*d* 1910)   1965). She = (2)
1912, Comte
ANTOINE HOCQUART
DE TURTOT (*d* 1954)

ALICE HENNESSY
(1874–1901) =

her cousin
JAMES RICHARD
HENNESSY (*d* 1945)

RICHARD HENNESSY
(1876–1953); Capt.
Gordon Highlanders;
served S African War
& WWI (despatches); left issue

GEORGE RICHARD JAMES HENNESSY, OBE
(1877–1953); Major 3rd Bn.
Cheshire Regt.; served S
African War & WWI (despatches
twice); Treas. HM Household
cr. BARON WINDLESHAM; left issue

LOUISE DE LA
FALAISE (1894–
1910)

HENRI, Marquis
DE LA FALAISE;
film exec.; *b* 11
Feb 1898; *d* 10
Apr. 1972;
Served WWI & II =

(1) 28 Jan 1925, (div. 1930) GLORIA SWANSON, actress

(2) 22 Nov 1931, (div. 1940) CONSTANCE BENNETT, actress

(3) 21 Dec 1940, EMMA RODRIGUEZ RESTREPO, da of
CARLOS RODRIGUEZ MALDONADO, chargé d'Affaires
Columbian Legation in Brussels, by his wife
CARLOTA RESTREPO, of Columbia

RICHARD RENE GABRIEL,
Comte DE LA FALAISE;
b 19..; killed during
WWII (1945), Wilten,
Germany =

1937–8, RAYLIANE GALLINEAU

ALAIN, Comte DE LA FALAISE;
b 19.. =

(1) 1931, MARGARET WEBB, of New Jersey;
'Miss Atlantic City' 1929

(2) 18 Jul 1946, MAXINE BIRLEY, only da of
Sir OSWALD BIRLEY, MC (*d* 1952), artist,
Vice-Pres. R. Soc. of Portrait Painters,
sister of MARK BIRLEY, founder of
Annabel's; (She = (2) JOHN McKENDRY, of New York)

GABRIEL RICHARD ANTOINE,
Marquis DE LA FALAISE; *b*
4 March 1940 (adopted by
his uncle Henri de la Falaise) =
1965, MARTINE ROSSI

ALEXIS RICHARD DION OSWALD,
Comte DE LA FALAISE; *b* 19.. =

21 Feb 1970, LOUISE RENSHAW,
yr da of G/Capt. PATRICK
RENSHAW, DSO, RAF
(*d* on active service 1944)

LOUISA (LULU) VAVA
LUCIA HENRIETTE
DE LA FALAISE =

6 Oct 1966. (div.
1970) DESMOND
FITZGERALD, 29th
Knight of Glin, of
Glin Castle, Limerick;
the distinguished
architectural historian

RICHARD GABRIEL DE LA FALAISE, *b* 1969

Gloria Swanson with her younger daughter Michelle Farmer (now Mme Robert Amon, of Paris). In her autobiography, Swanson laments her decision to abort the child she conceived by the Marquis de la Falaise. Two of her least favourite contemporaries were Mary Pickford and Constance Bennett.

daughter of Carlos Rodriguez Maldonado, Chargé d'Affaires at the Colombian Legation in Brussels. He died without issue on 10 April 1972, having adopted his nephew, Gabriel Richard Antoine, son of his younger brother, Richard de la Falaise, who was killed in the Second World War.

GLORIA SWANSON
First wife of Henri, Marquis de la Falaise.
Married 28 January 1925, Paris; divorced 1930

Gloria Swanson was born on 27 March 1899, Chicago, of Swedish/Polish descent. Her father being in the army, she spent much of her childhood on various military posts in Key West, Texas and Puerto Rico. She first had hopes of being a singer and was taken to Chicago by an aunt to visit the Embassy Studios where she was given small parts. She left high school after one year and moved to Hollywood where she was directed in two Essanay films by Wallace Beery, whom she married in 1916. She was seventeen and the marriage lasted little over a month. Cecil B. De Mille saw her potential and starred her in six pictures – all clever comedies of sex and manners, not the epics of his later years.

In 1919 she married Herbert K. Somborn, a motion picture distributor, and owner of the Brown Derby restaurant, which flourished in Hollywood on Vine Street from 1929–85 (the original site was opposite the Ambassador Hotel). He was a nephew of S. W. Straus of the Straus investment house. In 1920 they bought a twenty-four-room mansion in Beverly Hills; their daughter Gloria Somborn was born later that year, and, when the marriage was deteriorating, she adopted a son, Joseph, in February 1923. Having divorced Somborn in 1923, she moved from Hollywood to New York (bought a twenty-five-acre estate in Croton-On-Hudson), and insisted on making all her films in New York.

Gloria went to France in 1924 to appear in *Madame Sans-Gêne* and there met and married Henri, Marquis de la Falaise. She was now a major star, earning $20,000 a week at Paramount, and was not only the first of her calibre to appear in a foreign film, but was also the first to marry a (genuine) European nobleman. She played the part to perfection. 'Am arriving Monday with Marquis. Arrange ovation,' was her wired command to her studio. Her arrival in New York, and then Hollywood, in March 1925, as the Marquise de la Falaise created scenes of unprecedented public adulation. Walter Wanger later recalled, 'We gave her a great ball in the Crystal Room at the Ritz, which was *the* chic place in New York at that time, and we sent her across the country in a private train, not just a private car; when she arrived at Los Angeles, there was a terrific hullabaloo – as there had been all across the country.'

After a long contract with Paramount, Gloria finally left in 1926 to form her own production company, backed by an Eastern syndicate headed by Joseph P. Kennedy (father of the late President), who was later, in Swanson's autobiography, *Swanson on Swanson*, revealed to have been her lover. Her best film to date, *Sadie Thompson*, based on Somerset Maugham's 'Rain' was released in 1928, and made over $1,000,000 at the box office.

The Kennedy affair ended Gloria Swanson's marriage to Falaise; after their divorce in 1930 he married Constance Bennett the following year. In her autobiography, Miss Swanson states adamantly that as his marriage to Constance took place in the USA (at the home of George Fitzmaurice, the director, in Beverly Hills) it was not recognized by the French courts, and therefore Constance was never really the Marquise. This silly claim is repeated by Falaise's last wife. It is interesting to note, however, that despite the Swanson–Bennett rivalry, Miss Swanson's Anderson grandchildren are first cousins to Joan Bennett's Anderson grandchildren, thus uniting two major Hollywood families (see table 7).

Gloria's next husband, Michael Farmer, was always referred to by the Press as an 'Irish sportsman', although there is no evidence of his athletic prowess – unless his frequent betrothals are considered 'sport'. However, he was certainly Irish, being born on 9 May 1902, in Cork. His father, Michael William Farmer, was a newspaper printer, and his mother, Mary Jane, was the daughter of Joseph Good, a baker. Somehow or another,

Michael Farmer was unofficially adopted by a wealthy American, Mrs Hubbard, and through her reached Hollywood. Following his divorce from Swanson, Farmer gradually sank into alcoholism and obscurity, ending his days in a hostel in Chester, England, in June 1975, aged seventy-three.

By Michael Farmer, Gloria Swanson had another daughter, Michelle Bridget, born in 1932. Her next marriage was to William N. Davey, an investment broker, which lasted only forty-four days.

Miss Swanson's most striking film role, and finest performance, as the spectral Norma Desmond – faded star of the silent era – in *Sunset Boulevard* (1950), won her renewed acclaim and a third Oscar nomination (she lost to Judy Holliday in *Born Yesterday*). The private film preview on the Paramount lot was made more memorable when, following the screening, Barbara Stanwyck knelt in tribute at Miss Swanson's feet and kissed the hem of her silver lamé dress. Astonishingly, Gloria Swanson was under 5 ft tall.

Gloria was an accomplished sculptor and painter, and an ardent nutritionist. Noël Coward recalled taking a drive with Miss Swanson during which they discussed dentistry almost exclusively. In 1976 she was married for the sixth and last time, to William Dufty, seventeen years her junior. She died after a brief illness, on 4 April 1983, in New York, aged eighty-four.

GILBERT ROLAND
Fourth husband of Constance Bennett. Married 20 April 1941, Yuma, Arizona; divorced 1945

Born Luis Antonio Damaso de Alonso, 11 December 1905, Chihuahua, Mexico; son of a bull fighter of Spanish descent. He originally intended to follow his father into the ring, but he became a dashing leading man in silent and sound films (notably as Armand in the silent version of *Camille* (1927), opposite Norma Talmadge). During the Second World War he was a Second Lieutenant in the US Air Force. He and Constance Bennett had two daughters: Lorinda and Gyl, the elder being

born three years before their marriage (another well-kept Constance Bennett secret). After his divorce he married secondly, 12 December 1954 (Yuma, Arizona), Guillermina Cantu, then described as a twenty-nine-year-old 'Mexican socialite and tennis champion'.

Gloria Swanson and Cecil B. DeMille in one of the all-time greats, Sunset Boulevard *(1950), in which as Norma Desmond, one time star, she declares 'I am big – it's the pictures that got smaller'; directed by Billy Wilder and co-written by Wilder and Charles Brackett.*

LORINDA ROLAND
Elder daughter of Constance Bennett and Gilbert Roland

Born on 21 April 1938, New York City. Lorinda was educated at the Art Students League, New York, Skowhegan School of Painting and Sculpture, Maine and Cranbrook Academy of Art, Michigan; BFA 1960. She taught sculpture, painting and ceramics to the elderly at the New York City Department of Welfare 1962–4, and was awarded the Guggenheim Fellowship for 1963–4. She then moved from New York to Los Angeles, where she converted an old garage, built by the Selznick Studios in the 1940s for their antique fire engines,

TABLE 6 CONSTANCE BENNETT'S CHILDREN AND THE LINK TO LELAND HAYWARD

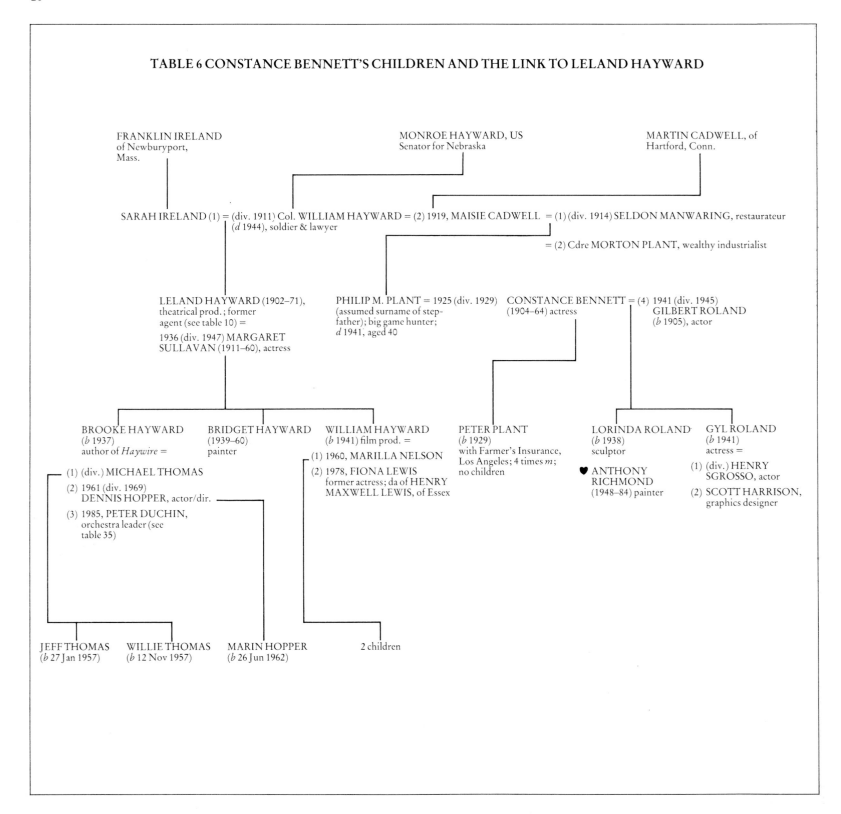

FRANKLIN IRELAND
of Newburyport,
Mass.

MONROE HAYWARD, US
Senator for Nebraska

MARTIN CADWELL, of
Hartford, Conn.

SARAH IRELAND (1) = (div. 1911) Col. WILLIAM HAYWARD = (2) 1919, MAISIE CADWELL = (1) (div. 1914) SELDON MANWARING, restaurateur
(d 1944), soldier & lawyer

= (2) Cdre MORTON PLANT, wealthy industrialist

LELAND HAYWARD (1902–71),
theatrical prod.; former
agent (see table 10) =

1936 (div. 1947) MARGARET
SULLAVAN (1911–60), actress

PHILIP M. PLANT = 1925 (div. 1929)
(assumed surname of step-
father); big game hunter;
d 1941, aged 40

CONSTANCE BENNETT = (4) 1941 (div. 1945)
(1904–64) actress
GILBERT ROLAND
(b 1905), actor

BROOKE HAYWARD
(b 1937)
author of *Haywire* =

(1) (div.) MICHAEL THOMAS

(2) 1961 (div. 1969)
DENNIS HOPPER, actor/dir. ●

(3) 1985, PETER DUCHIN,
orchestra leader (see
table 35)

BRIDGET HAYWARD
(1939–60)
painter

WILLIAM HAYWARD
(b 1941) film prod. =

(1) 1960, MARILLA NELSON

(2) 1978, FIONA LEWIS
former actress; da of HENRY
MAXWELL LEWIS, of Essex

PETER PLANT
(b 1929)
with Farmer's Insurance,
Los Angeles; 4 times m;
no children

LORINDA ROLAND
(b 1938)
sculptor

♥ ANTHONY
RICHMOND
(1948–84) painter

GYL ROLAND
(b 1941)
actress =

(1) (div.) HENRY
SGROSSO, actor

(2) SCOTT HARRISON,
graphics designer

JEFF THOMAS
(b 27 Jan 1957)

WILLIE THOMAS
(b 12 Nov 1957)

MARIN HOPPER
(b 26 Jun 1962)

2 children

TABLE 7 THE GLORIA SWANSON DYNASTY AND THE LINK TO JOAN BENNETT

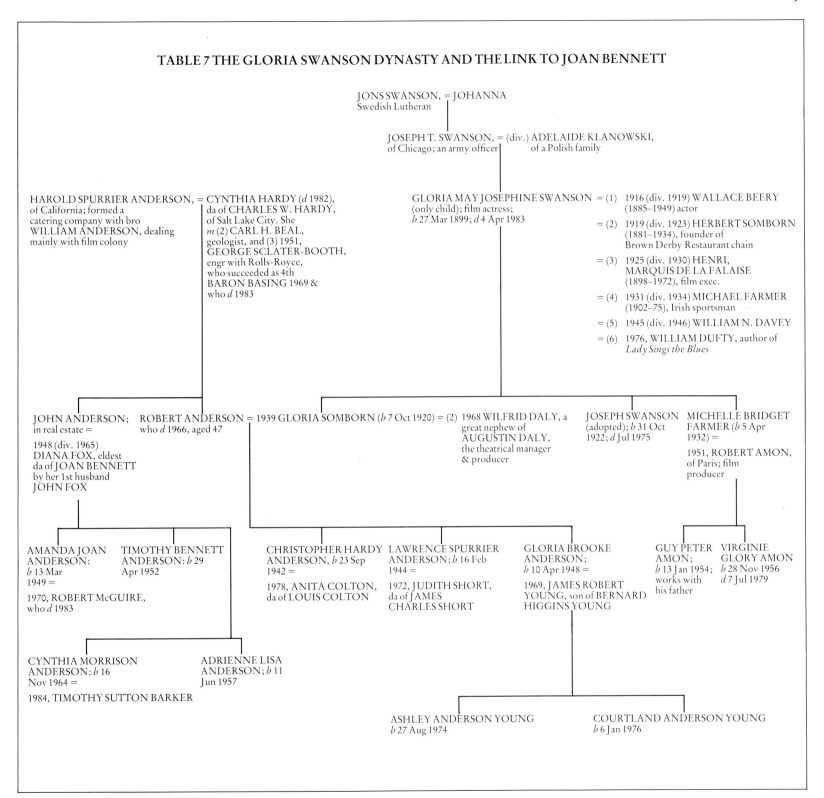

JONS SWANSON, = JOHANNA
Swedish Lutheran

JOSEPH T. SWANSON, = (div.) ADELAIDE KLANOWSKI,
of Chicago; an army officer   of a Polish family

HAROLD SPURRIER ANDERSON, = CYNTHIA HARDY (*d* 1982),
of California; formed a   da of CHARLES W. HARDY,
catering company with bro   of Salt Lake City. She
WILLIAM ANDERSON, dealing   *m* (2) CARL H. BEAL,
mainly with film colony   geologist, and (3) 1951,
    GEORGE SCLATER-BOOTH,
    engr with Rolls-Royce,
    who succeeded as 4th
    BARON BASING 1969 &
    who *d* 1983

GLORIA MAY JOSEPHINE SWANSON = (1) 1916 (div. 1919) WALLACE BEERY
(only child); film actress;   (1885–1949) actor
b 27 Mar 1899; *d* 4 Apr 1983

= (2) 1919 (div. 1923) HERBERT SOMBORN
    (1881–1934), founder of
    Brown Derby Restaurant chain

= (3) 1925 (div. 1930) HENRI,
    MARQUIS DE LA FALAISE
    (1898–1972), film exec.

= (4) 1931 (div. 1934) MICHAEL FARMER
    (1902–75), Irish sportsman

= (5) 1945 (div. 1946) WILLIAM N. DAVEY

= (6) 1976, WILLIAM DUFTY, author of
    Lady Sings the Blues

JOHN ANDERSON;   ROBERT ANDERSON = 1939 GLORIA SOMBORN (*b* 7 Oct 1920) = (2) 1968 WILFRID DALY, a   JOSEPH SWANSON   MICHELLE BRIDGET
in real estate =   who *d* 1966, aged 47   great nephew of   (adopted); *b* 31 Oct   FARMER (*b* 5 Apr
            AUGUSTIN DALY,   1922; *d* Jul 1975   1932) =
1948 (div. 1965)   the theatrical manager
DIANA FOX, eldest   & producer   1951, ROBERT AMON,
da of JOAN BENNETT   of Paris; film
by her 1st husband   producer
JOHN FOX

AMANDA JOAN   TIMOTHY BENNETT   CHRISTOPHER HARDY   LAWRENCE SPURRIER   GLORIA BROOKE   GUY PETER   VIRGINIE
ANDERSON: ANDERSON: *b* 29   ANDERSON, *b* 23 Sep   ANDERSON; *b* 16 Feb   ANDERSON;   AMON;   GLORY AMON
b 13 Mar   Apr 1952   1942 =   1944 =   *b* 10 Apr 1948 =   *b* 13 Jan 1954;   *b* 28 Nov 1956
1949 =   works with   *d* 7 Jul 1979
        1978, ANITA COLTON,   1972, JUDITH SHORT,   1969, JAMES ROBERT   his father
1970, ROBERT McGUIRE,   da of LOUIS COLTON   da of JAMES   YOUNG, son of BERNARD
who *d* 1983   CHARLES SHORT   HIGGINS YOUNG

CYNTHIA MORRISON   ADRIENNE LISA
ANDERSON: *b* 16   ANDERSON; *b* 11
Nov 1964 =   Jun 1957

1984, TIMOTHY SUTTON BARKER

ASHLEY ANDERSON YOUNG   COURTLAND ANDERSON YOUNG
b 27 Aug 1974   *b* 6 Jan 1976

into a studio. Her first one-woman show was at Silvan Simone Gallery, Los Angeles, in 1966; she was subsequently a sculpture teacher at Studio Watts, California, 1968–9, and at Otis Art Institute 1974–6. She has many works in private collections and has done a number of commissions for public buildings and corporations. Unmarried, she lived with (from 1974 until his death) Anthony Richmond, a painter (born 30 September 1948, Yokohama, Japan), who was killed in a motorcycle accident in Los Alamos, California, 22 July 1984. She has no issue.

GYL ROLAND
Younger daughter of Constance Bennett and Gilbert Roland

Born Christina Gyl Consuelo Roland, 9 December 1941 (two days after Pearl Harbor), Beverly Hills, California; educated at the Academy of Dramatic Arts, New York. Gyl is a film and stage actress, whose film credits include *Black Gunn* (1972), *Terror Circus* (1976), *Day of the Locust* (1976), *Barn of the Living Dead* (1977) and *Body Heat* (1982); and also a wardrobe and 'image consultant'. She married first, Henry Sgrosso, an actor (divorced); and secondly, Scott Harrison, a graphics designer with a computer company (separated). She has no issue.

BRIG. GEN. JOHN THERON COULTER
Fifth husband of Constance Bennett. Married 22 June 1946, Riverside, California

Brigadier-General (retired) US Army. After Constance Bennett's death he married 14 February 1972 (Palm Springs), Virginia Pine (*née* Peine), a former girlfriend of the late actor George Raft (who had wanted to marry her, but whose wife would not consent to a divorce). She was formerly the wife of Quentin James Reynolds (died 17 March 1965) the writer.

JOAN BENNETT
Youngest daughter of Richard Bennett and Adrienne Morrison

In contrast to Olivia de Havilland and Joan Fontaine, there seems to have been little rivalry between sisters Constance and Joan Bennett – certainly no hostility was ever aired in public. The only wry comment passed by Joan Bennett was that although the youngest Bennett girl, according to Constance her seniority gradually rose from junior, the middle, and finally eldest sister.

Born on 27 February 1910, in Palisades, New Jersey, Joan Bennett was educated at a private boarding school in Connecticut and at a finishing school in Versailles. Like Constance, she married at sixteen, to a man she had met on the boat when sailing to France. They skipped over to London and were married in Chelsea. They lived at 22 Carlyle Square (since 1983 the home of David and Lady Carina Frost). Their daughter, Adrienne (later known as Diana) was born in February 1928. The pressures of motherhood at seventeen, combined with an irresponsible and hard-drinking husband, proved intolerable, and she returned to the fold. Her father, initially opposed to all his daughters' acting careers, got her a supporting role in his production of 'Jarnegan' at the Longacre Theatre, New York. Joan eventually had to enlist her mother's help in order to leave the show. She had her young child to look after, and realized that the advent of sound made a trained stage actor a valuable property in Hollywood. So there she went, her first starring role being *Bulldog Drummond* (1929), with Ronald Colman, and she subsequently had little difficulty in finding screen work. She served a valuable apprenticeship in relatively undistinguished films, playing a wide variety of roles from ingenue to temptress. In 1931 she signed a two-year contract with Fox at $2,000 per week (compared with Constance's $30,000 per week).

In 1932 Joan married again, this time to Gene Markey, a screenwriter. Although she received increasingly good reviews for her work, Fox dropped her and she went free-lance. As Amy in *Little Women* (1934), a good part in an above average production, she was spotted by Walter Wanger, an independent producer who had previously dismissed her as 'very sweet ... but will never photograph.' Her performance improved with such films as *The Man Who Reclaimed His Head* (1935), with Claude Rains, and *She Couldn't Take It* (1935), with George Raft. Having had another daughter, Melinda, born in 1934, she divorced Markey in 1937.

In 1939 her screen image went through a complete reversal when, for the film *Trade Winds*, she was obliged to assume a disguise. At the suggestion of director Tay Garnett she donned a black wig, and the transformation from blonde to dark was so startling she decided to stay dark. It was also noted by the gossips that she now bore a marked likeness to Hedy Lamarr, whom her ex-husband, Gene Markey, married in 1939 – the year *Trade Winds* was released and *Life* magazine ran a picture story on Misses Bennett, Lamarr and Vivien Leigh as triple Hollywood look-alikes. This new look, combined with her 1940 marriage to Walter Wanger, brought her a number of much stronger and interesting roles – particularly in the four directed by Fritz Lang: *Man Hunt* (1941), *The Woman in the Window* (1944), *Scarlet Street* (1946), and *The Secret Beyond the Door* (1948).

Joan Bennett's marriage to Walter Wanger lasted a quarter of a century, the longest of all three sisters, and produced two more daughters, Stephanie and Shelley. In 1952, however, a drama occurred which hit the headlines, for Wanger was convinced his wife was having an affair with her agent Jennings Lang. One day Miss Bennett met Lang for lunch, and they were talking in a car park, when suddenly Wanger appeared brandishing a gun. Lang was hit in the groin, and Wanger was sent to trial and eventually to jail (for fifteen weeks).

Joan Bennett, the youngest and only surviving daughter of Richard Bennett, with her two-year-old daughter, Melinda Markey, at Palm Springs in 1936. She now has twelve grandchildren, including Oskar Werner's only son, Felix.

Happily the marriage survived the scandal, although the Wangers were eventually divorced on grounds of incompatiblity in 1965. More immediately, the film studios, having perfected their double standards, reacted in their familiar puritanical way and were reluctant to employ Miss Bennett. One person who spoke up for her was Humphrey Bogart, who insisted on using her in *We're No Angels* (1955), and she continued to appear in stage plays throughout the 1950s and early 1960s. In 1978 she married David Wilde, a film critic, to whom she is still married. They live in Scarsdale, New York.

Miss Bennett's film roles varied from scheming villainy in *The Woman in the Window* (1944), to maternal forbearance in *Father of the Bride* (1950), as Spencer Tracy's wife. She had the light touch required for comedy, but was at her best when tackling malevolent and mercenary females.

JOHN MARION FOX
First husband of Joan Bennett. Married 15 September 1926, Chelsea, London; divorced 1928

Son of Robert Ralston Fox, a Seattle lumberman, he was about ten years older than Miss Bennett. He married three more wives and had four more children.

DIANA ANDERSON
Only daughter of Joan Bennett and John Fox

Born on 20 February 1928, Hollywood; she was originally called Adrienne Ralston Fox, but she later assumed the first name of Diana, and her surname was successively changed to Markey (1936) and Wanger (1945) in keeping with her mother's marriages. She is a painter, traveller and self-confessed gypsy; also the librarian for the Southern California Palaeontology Society. She married first, 8 May 1948 (Hollywood) (divorced 1965), John Hardy Anderson, real estate agent, and former brother-in-law of Gloria Swanson's elder daughter, Gloria. Diana Anderson has issue, Amanda Joan Anderson, born 13 March 1949; in real estate: married 1970, Robert McGuire (born 1950; TV manager and technician for Channel Seven), who died in 1983, of cancer; Timothy Bennett Anderson, born 29 April 1952; wood carver and cabinet maker; studied film writing at UCLA; Cynthia Morrison Anderson, born 16 November 1954; trained as a photographer at the Arts Center, Los Angeles; campaigner for human rights: married 8 December 1984, Timothy Sutton Barker; Adrienne Lisa Anderson, born 11 June 1957; mentally ill.

Diana Anderson also has issue by Oskar Werner: Felix Florian Werner, born 6 June 1966.

OSKAR WERNER
Had a love-affair with Diana Anderson from 1965–8

Born Oskar Josef Bschliessmayer, 13 November 1922, Vienna. He was an intelligent and versatile stage and screen actor, perhaps best remembered as the young German in love with Jeanne Moreau in Truffaut's *Jules et Jim* (1961); also noted for his performances in *Ship of Fools* (1965), for which he was nominated for a Best Actor Oscar, and in *Fahrenheit 451* (1966). His career was diminished by alcoholism, and he lived as a recluse at Triesten, Liechtenstein, for the last ten years of his life. He married first, 1944 (divorced), Elisabeth Kallina, an actress, by whom he had issue, Eleanora Werner, born *c.* 1944; violinist: married Adelbert Skocic, violinist with Vienna Philharmonic, and has issue, Andrea, born *c.* 1966, and Lise, born *c.* 1968.

Oskar Werner married secondly, 1954 (divorced 1968), Anne Power, daughter of Annabella, the French film actress (see table 31), and adopted daughter of Tyrone Power. He had no issue from this marriage.

Werner died on 23 October 1984, aged sixty-one, in Marburg, West Germany, having had further issue by Diana Anderson, Felix Florian Werner, born 6 June 1966; educated at Harvard High School, where he majored in German.

With this formidable theatrical tradition on both

sides of his family, it is interesting to speculate what Felix Werner's future might be. His cousin, Lorinda Roland, writes: 'Felix Florian Werner is something else; extremely bright, good looking, tall like his mother, sensitive like his father. Should (I hope) do something phenomenal in his lifetime . . .'

IVAN TORS
Second husband of Diana Anderson. Married 24 September 1974, Nairobi, Kenya

Born on 12 June 1916, Budapest. He was a playwright in Europe before emigrating to the US in the early 1930s. He served in the Second World War with the US Army Air Force, and was later a successful producer of children's TV animal series, notably *Daktari* and *Flipper*. He founded a 260-acre wildlife reserve, 'Africa, USA' near Los Angeles. He married first, 25 February 1953, Constance Dowling, an actress, who died on 28 October 1969 (sister of Doris Dowling, also an actress, and the seventh wife of Artie Shaw), by whom he had issue, Steven Tors, born 28 December 1954, an animal translocator in Namibia, also leads camera safaris; Peter Tors, born 26 January 1957, a stuntman in Hollywood; and David Tors, born 14 April 1961, with US Air Force in Germany. He also left a foster son, Alfred Ndwego, of Kenya. Ivan Tors died on 4 June 1983, aged sixty-seven, of a heart attack, while location hunting in Brazil.

GENE MARKEY
Second husband of Joan Bennett. Married 12 March 1932, Hollywood; divorced 1937

Born on 11 December 1895, Jacksonville, Michigan; son of Eugene Lawrence Markey by his wife Alice White. Educated at Dartmouth. He was the author of more than a dozen novels and also wrote plays and film scripts for romantic Hollywood productions of the 1930s. He served as a Lieutenant in the US Army after the First World War, and as liaison officer with Lord Mountbatten in the South East Asia Command in the Second World War. He

retired as Admiral in the US Naval Reserve. After his divorce from Miss Bennett he married secondly, 4 March 1939 (Mexicali, Mexico) (divorced 1940), Hedy Lamarr, film actress, with whom he adopted a son; thirdly, 2 January 1946 (San Pedro, California) (divorced 1950), Myrna Loy, the noted actress; and fourthly, 1952, Mrs Lucille Parker Wright, owner of Calumet Farm, Kentucky, a leading racehorse breeder, including eight Kentucky Derby winners and two Triple Crown (she died on 24 July 1982, aged eighty-five). He died on 1 May 1978 (Miami), aged eighty-four.

MELINDA MARKEY
Only daughter of Joan Bennett and Gene Markey

Born on 27 February 1934 (she shares her birthday with her mother). Briefly an actress, Melinda Markey appeared with her mother in 'Susan and God' at Westport, Connecticut, in 1951, and also appeared in the following films: *Titanic* (1953), *The Other Woman* (1955), *The Adventures of Hajj Baba* (1955) (produced by her step-father Walter Wanger), *Prince of Players* (1955), with Richard Burton as Edwin Booth and John Derek as John Wilkes Booth, and *Crashout* (1955). She married first, 1954 (divorced 1957), Donald Hayden, a former actor (born 1926), son of Harry Hayden, actor (died 1955), by his wife Lela Bliss, actress (died 1980), founders of the Bliss Hayden miniature theatre in Hollywood (now defunct), and has issue, Markey Hayden Bena, born 29 August 1956, educated at Hobart College, Geneva, New York, and at the Herbert Berghof Studio, New York; an actor; has assumed his step-father's surname.

Melinda Markey married secondly, 25 October 1960, Joseph Bena, and has further issue, Parker Joseph Bena, born 31 March 1962, and Samantha Joan-Louise Theresa Bena, born 3 March 1967.

WALTER WANGER
Third husband of Joan Bennett. Married 12 January 1940, Phoenix, Arizona; divorced 1965

Born on 11 July 1894, San Francisco, as Walter

Feuchtwanger. His father, a wealthy knitted-goods manufacturer, died a year before the great fire, and the family moved to New York. Walter Wanger was an unusually well-educated and cultivated man in the early days of Hollywood. He was brought up by a family of clever women, three of his aunts were highly gifted: a painter, a linguist and a philosopher. He was educated in New York, Switzerland and at Dartmouth, and was widely travelled. He left college prematurely in order to join Granville Barker's New Theatre in New York, as an assistant, and then spent time in London just prior to the outbreak of the First World War (he had a place at Oxford University). As a result of the war he became very interested in the medium of film as means of propaganda (a study he carried through to the Second World War); he served as an officer with the US Army Intelligence in the First World War, and was on President Wilson's staff at the Paris Peace Conference.

His first motion picture work was with Zukor and Lasky at Paramount, where he had virtually free-range in production. In his opinion the films Paramount was turning out were second-rate, and he constantly strove to improve their standards by employing top writers, designers, and photographers. 'This experience convinced me at an early age that there's very little difference between statesmanship and showmanship,' he later commented.

Wanger was a shrewd manipulator of the Hollywood system. He plucked Louise Brooks out of a Ziegfeld chorus line, bobbed her hair, and started a world-wide craze. He appreciated the power of the press and freely admitted exploiting the Swanson/Falaise marriage 'to the hilt' to garner publicity for MGM. He was friendly with William Randolph Hearst and Marion Davies (his first wife, actress Justine Johnstone, to whom he was married from 1919 to 1938, shared a dressing room with Davies on Broadway), and he described Hearst and Davies as taking over the social leadership of Hollywood from Fairbanks and Pickford, only to be replaced in turn by David Selznick and his wife Irene Mayer.

Walter Wanger produced pictures for Paramount, Columbia and MGM, including *The*

Sheik (1921), *Queen Christina* (1934), *Algiers* (1938), *Foreign Correspondent* (1940), *Smash-Up* (1947), *Joan of Arc* (1948), unfortunately timed apropos the Ingrid Bergman/Roberto Rossellini affair which 'didn't exactly help project her image as a saint', and which lost Wanger a considerable sum, *Invasion of the Body Snatchers* (1956), *I Want To Live* (1958), for which Susan Hayward won a Best Actress Oscar, and the disastrous *Cleopatra* (1963).

In 1952 Wanger was convicted of shooting and wounding his wife's agent, Jennings Lang, and was sentenced to fifteen weeks on a penal farm (mainly as a librarian). His experiences in prison inspired one of his later films, *Riot in Cell Block 11* (1954). He died on 17 November 1968, aged seventy-four, in Manhattan.

STEPHANIE WANGER
Elder daughter of Joan Bennett and Walter Wanger

Born 26 June 1943 (Los Angeles). A portrait painter and restaurateur; she opened the 'Brighton Grill' in New York in 1985. She married on 21 August 1963 (Manhattan), Frederick Edward Guest, an investment banker, second son of the late Winston Frederick Churchill (a great grandson of the 7th Duke of Marlborough). Among the guests was the Maharajah of Jaipur; Prince Juan Carlos (now King Juan Carlos of Spain) was an usher. Mrs Guest has issue, Victoria Woolworth Guest, born 23 October 1966; Vanessa Wanger Guest, born 1973; Frederick Edward Churchill Guest, born 1975; and Andrew Churchill Guest, born 1976.

SHELLEY ANTONIA WANGER
Younger daughter of Joan Bennett and Walter Wanger

Born 4 July 1948 (Hollywood). Miss Wanger formerly worked on the *New York Review of Books*, and is now the articles editor of *House and Garden*.

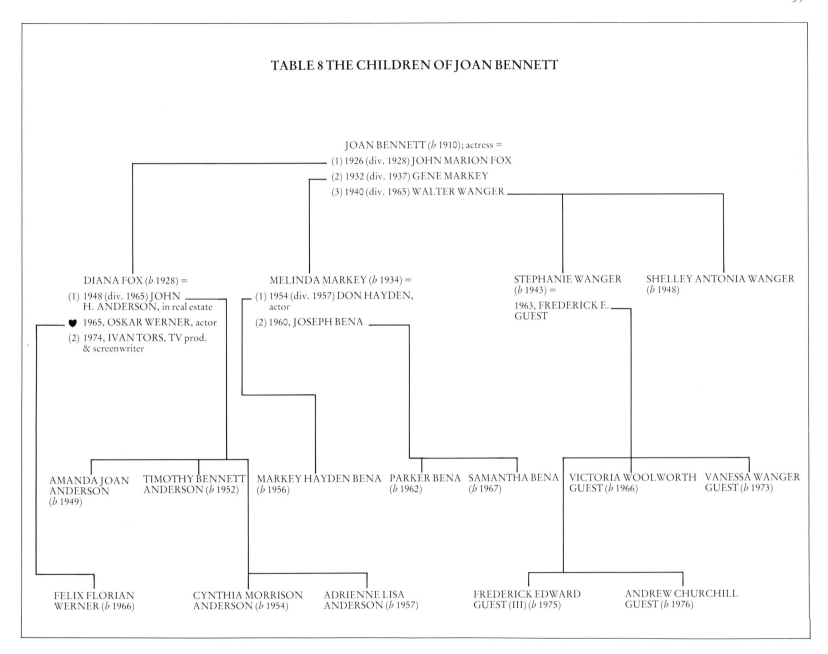

TABLE 8 THE CHILDREN OF JOAN BENNETT

JOAN BENNETT (*b* 1910); actress =
(1) 1926 (div. 1928) JOHN MARION FOX
(2) 1932 (div. 1937) GENE MARKEY
(3) 1940 (div. 1965) WALTER WANGER

DIANA FOX (*b* 1928) =
(1) 1948 (div. 1965) JOHN H. ANDERSON, in real estate
1965, OSKAR WERNER, actor
(2) 1974, IVAN TORS, TV prod. & screenwriter

MELINDA MARKEY (*b* 1934) =
(1) 1954 (div. 1957) DON HAYDEN, actor
(2) 1960, JOSEPH BENA

STEPHANIE WANGER (*b* 1943) =
1963, FREDERICK E. GUEST

SHELLEY ANTONIA WANGER (*b* 1948)

AMANDA JOAN ANDERSON (*b* 1949)

TIMOTHY BENNETT ANDERSON (*b* 1952)

MARKEY HAYDEN BENA (*b* 1956)

PARKER BENA (*b* 1962)

SAMANTHA BENA (*b* 1967)

VICTORIA WOOLWORTH GUEST (*b* 1966)

VANESSA WANGER GUEST (*b* 1973)

FELIX FLORIAN WERNER (*b* 1966)

CYNTHIA MORRISON ANDERSON (*b* 1954)

ADRIENNE LISA ANDERSON (*b* 1957)

FREDERICK EDWARD GUEST (III) (*b* 1975)

ANDREW CHURCHILL GUEST (*b* 1976)

DAVID WILDE

Fourth husband of Joan Bennett. Married 14 February 1978

Born 13 November 1917 (New York City); educated at Yale. Formerly with Pan Am; owner and editor of Westchester weekly newspaper and public relations magazine; film critic. Mr Wilde was formerly married to Mary Jane Scott, of Memphis, Tennessee, by whom he has issue, Amanda Dess Wilde, born 16 March 1952, and Jennifer Jane Wilde, born 29 July 1954: married 22 October 1985, Tom Lovejoy.

36

TABLE 9 THE CHILDREN OF BARBARA JANE BENNETT, MIDDLE DAUGHTER OF RICHARD BENNETT

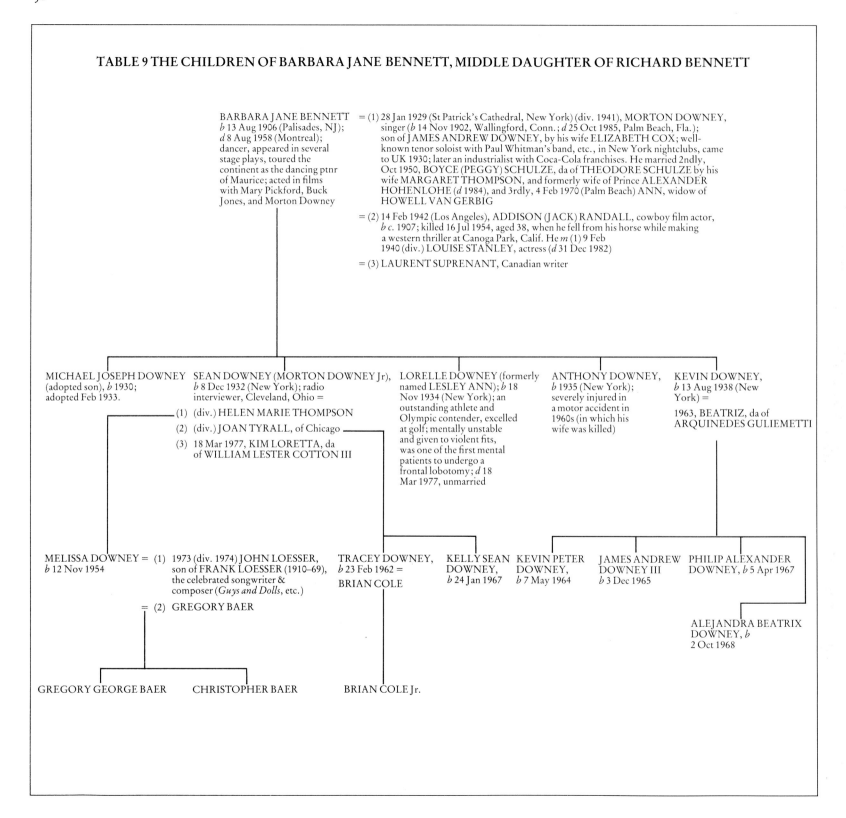

BARBARA JANE BENNETT
b 13 Aug 1906 (Palisades, NJ);
d 8 Aug 1958 (Montreal);
dancer, appeared in several
stage plays, toured the
continent as the dancing ptnr
of Maurice; acted in films
with Mary Pickford, Buck
Jones, and Morton Downey

= (1) 28 Jan 1929 (St Patrick's Cathedral, New York) (div. 1941), MORTON DOWNEY, singer (*b* 14 Nov 1902, Wallingford, Conn.; *d* 25 Oct 1985, Palm Beach, Fla.); son of JAMES ANDREW DOWNEY, by his wife ELIZABETH COX; well-known tenor soloist with Paul Whitman's band, etc., in New York nightclubs, came to UK 1930; later an industrialist with Coca-Cola franchises. He married 2ndly, Oct 1950, BOYCE (PEGGY) SCHULZE, da of THEODORE SCHULZE by his wife MARGARET THOMPSON, and formerly wife of Prince ALEXANDER HOHENLOHE (*d* 1984), and 3rdly, 4 Feb 1970 (Palm Beach) ANN, widow of HOWELL VAN GERBIG

= (2) 14 Feb 1942 (Los Angeles), ADDISON (JACK) RANDALL, cowboy film actor, *b c.* 1907; killed 16 Jul 1954, aged 38, when he fell from his horse while making a western thriller at Canoga Park, Calif. He *m* (1) 9 Feb 1940 (div.) LOUISE STANLEY, actress (*d* 31 Dec 1982)

= (3) LAURENT SUPRENANT, Canadian writer

MICHAEL JOSEPH DOWNEY (adopted son), *b* 1930; adopted Feb 1933.

SEAN DOWNEY (MORTON DOWNEY Jr), *b* 8 Dec 1932 (New York); radio interviewer, Cleveland, Ohio =
(1) (div.) HELEN MARIE THOMPSON
(2) (div.) JOAN TYRALL, of Chicago
(3) 18 Mar 1977, KIM LORETTA, da of WILLIAM LESTER COTTON III

LORELLE DOWNEY (formerly named LESLEY ANN); *b* 18 Nov 1934 (New York); an outstanding athlete and Olympic contender, excelled at golf; mentally unstable and given to violent fits, was one of the first mental patients to undergo a frontal lobotomy; *d* 18 Mar 1977, unmarried

ANTHONY DOWNEY, *b* 1935 (New York); severely injured in a motor accident in 1960s (in which his wife was killed)

KEVIN DOWNEY, *b* 13 Aug 1938 (New York) =
1963, BEATRIZ, da of ARQUINEDES GULIEMETTI

MELISSA DOWNEY = (1) 1973 (div. 1974) JOHN LOESSER, *b* 12 Nov 1954 son of FRANK LOESSER (1910–69), the celebrated songwriter & composer (*Guys and Dolls*, etc.)
= (2) GREGORY BAER

TRACEY DOWNEY, *b* 23 Feb 1962 = BRIAN COLE

KELLY SEAN DOWNEY, *b* 24 Jan 1967

KEVIN PETER DOWNEY, *b* 7 May 1964

JAMES ANDREW DOWNEY III *b* 3 Dec 1965

PHILIP ALEXANDER DOWNEY, *b* 5 Apr 1967

ALEJANDRA BEATRIX DOWNEY, *b* 2 Oct 1968

GREGORY GEORGE BAER   CHRISTOPHER BAER

BRIAN COLE Jr.

TABLE 10 THE BENNETT FAMILY MARRIAGE WEB

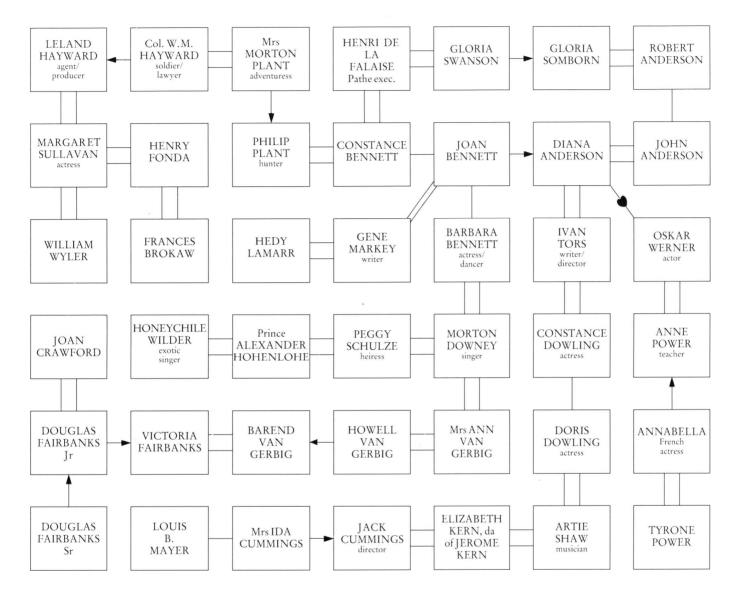

See page 7 for key to symbols.

3 The Fairbanks Dynasty

For an entire generation of Americans, Douglas Fairbanks Sr was the 'All-American Hero', and, moreover, with Mary Pickford and Charlie Chaplin, could claim to be one of the three truly international film stars. For silent films had a universal appeal that the 'talkies', with their inevitable language barrier, could not equal. For the following generation he was additionally recognized as the founder of the first cinema 'dynasty'; until the rise of the second generation Fondas in the 1960s, Fairbanks was the most familiar family name of the silver screen.

Fairbanks was actually an adopted surname, their original patronymic being the less lyrical sounding Ulman. Doug's father, Charles Ulman, born on 15 September 1833, at Berrysburg, Pennsylvania, was the son of Lazarus Ulman, a well-to-do half-Jewish mill owner; he was the fourth child of a family of six sons and four daughters. Charles Ulman, a formidable-looking, dark-haired man, qualified as a barrister in 1856 and moved to New York, where he eventually became head of the law firm, Ulman, Gazzam and Remington. At the height of his legal career he founded and was president of the United States Law Association. He married a beautiful Southern belle, Ella.

Ella Adelaide Marsh, gently reared in the traditional style of the Plantation families of the South, had already had a chequered matrimonial career. She was a Catholic, and her first husband was the handsome and suitable John Fairbanks, a plantation and mill owner from the New Orleans area. They had a son, John Fairbanks, after whose birth Fairbanks the elder died of tuberculosis. In need of support, Ella's choice of second husband was an unhappy one. He was Edward Wilcox, of Georgia, an unreliable character and a heavy drinker, by whom she had a second son, Norris Wilcox.

Although she faced financial ruin and certain social disgrace, Ella decided to obtain a divorce. Leaving her younger son in the care of a Wilcox relation named Lottie Barker, she took herself and her elder boy to New York, where she applied to Charles Ulman to dissolve her marriage. By this time Ulman was a successful and attractive man of about forty-nine, and a bachelor. He must have found the distressed young divorcée appealing, for, having effected her divorce, Ulman became her third husband. They had two sons, Robert, born 13 March 1882, and Douglas, born 23 May 1883. The trouble started when Ulman made quite substantial investments in silver mines at Denver, Colorado, and later decided to give up his law practice and move the family out there. His investments were disastrous; he lost all his money, and finally deserted his family in 1887. With her customary fortitude, Ella obtained a second divorce and resumed the surname of her first husband. Oddly, she never returned to Georgia to collect her Wilcox son, but he did reappear in the family history decades later when he worked for his half-brother, Douglas Fairbanks Sr, as office manager for the New York bureau of United Artists. (A relation described Norris Wilcox as handsome and charming; he was twice divorced, and in the early 1920s married Frances, about twenty years his junior; they had no issue but a happy marriage; she lives in New York City.)

The two Ulman boys were expensively educated

*Douglas Fairbanks in a look-alike atti-
tude with his only child, Douglas Fairbanks Jr. The younger Fairbanks later
recalled, however, that he was seldom
asked to 'Pickfair' – and never stayed
overnight until invited by Mary Pickford
long after his father's death.*

at the Jervis Military Academy, East Denver High
School, and at the Colorado School of Mines. Douglas and his brother Robert legally assumed the
surname of Fairbanks in 1900, and the following
year he joined Frederick Warde's touring company,
Doug making his first Broadway appearance a
couple of years later in 'Her Lord and Master'.
Doug then abruptly changed direction and for a
very short time became a clerk in a firm of New
York stockbrokers, followed by a job with a hard-
ware company. His one constant preoccupation was
physical training, boxing and wrestling in a local
gymnasium (when he was twelve his mother urged
him to sign a pledge of abstinence from liquor – a
pledge he kept for many years).

Fairbanks returned to the stage in 1902, and got
his first real break from William A. Brady, the
Broadway producer, who put him under a five-year
contract, later extended to seven years. Before the

First World War he established himself as a popular
leading man and then a star in light comedies. He
grinned rather too much for the critics' taste – his
public loved it – but he was good at his job, and
on the strength of his popularity was approached
by a film studio, Triangle (D. W. Griffith, Thomas
Ince and Mack Sennett), to work for them at a
salary of $2,000 a week. The money was an obvious
attraction, but equally appealing to Fairbanks was
the challenge of a new career.

Griffith found his comedy technique and off-set
practical jokes over-powering, and more or less
handed him over to Franks Woods, who realized
that Fairbanks' magic lay in his vigour and physical
presence. Alistair Cooke in his Museum of Modern
Art monograph (1940) said that Fairbanks, like
Gary Cooper, created an impression that his screen
image was the man himself, and that he could 'mate
actor and audience to produce a type of pleasure

which is closer to old-time vaudeville . . . than to an audience contemplating a painting or a play.'

Most of Fairbanks' films at this time were conventional comedy–melodramas, laced with daring acrobatic feats – a high dive from an Atlantic liner, a leap from a train, and so forth. He used a double only on the rarest occasions, and kept himself fit by playing some sport or other every day for over twenty years (his relatively early death can in part be attributed to this self-imposed physical regime). He was an expert horseman and swimmer, his fencing was fast and furious, and he developed a responsiveness that gave poise and rhythm to his every movement. Many of his stunts were timed to a metronome (which also helped the later musical scoring) and Fairbanks privately described himself more a dancer than an actor.

Altogether Doug made eleven films at Triangle. His association with the writers John Emerson and Anita Loos produced good results, and with them and director Allan Dwan, Fairbanks established the Douglas Fairbanks Pictures Corporation. This enabled him to take a greater share of the profits and also to write and direct. His breezy social satires won him much popularity: *American Aristocracy* (1916), *In and Out Again* (1917), and *Down to Earth* (1917), in which he knocked social climbing, pacifism and hypochondria respectively. In 1919 he went into partnership with Chaplin, Griffith and Mary Pickford to form United Artists – a coup which prompted Adolph Zukor to remark, 'So now the lunatics want to take over the asylum.'

This gave Fairbanks an ideal opportunity to break with his comedies in favour of heroic swashbucklers, for which, of course, he will always be renowned.

In 1920 Fairbanks was voted the most popular male film star in national polls in the USA, Britain and France. On 28 March 1920, in Hollywood, he married Mary Pickford, 'America's Sweetheart', and in Alistair Cooke's apt and oft-quoted phrase became 'a living proof of America's chronic belief in happy endings'. Fairbanks had, in fact, been first married thirteen years before to Beth Sully, and had an eleven-year-old son, Douglas Fairbanks Jr, and

Pickford had recently been divorced from a heavy-drinking Irish actor named Owen Moore. The Fairbanks/Pickford marriage was childless and ended in divorce in 1935.

For fifteen years the Fairbanks were Hollywood's golden couple. They lived at 'Pickfair', a twenty-two-room converted hunting lodge, imposingly positioned on a hillside behind Beverly Hills, where they enhanced their prestige by entertaining the glitterati of the time – an invitation to 'Pickfair' was considered in Hollywood the ultimate seal of approval. Names in the 'Pickfair' visitors' book included Lord and Lady Louis Mountbatten (who spent a part of their honeymoon there, and made an atrocious amateur film), Albert Einstein, William Randolph Hearst and Marion Davies. (Fairbanks Jr was seldom asked, and never stayed overnight, until invited by Mary Pickford many years after his father's death). Although generous, their soirées were somewhat staid, in fact, Gloria Swanson (who seems to have disliked Pickford) described their parties as 'deadly'. Swanson particularly remembered one evening when the guest of honour, the Duke of Kent (later killed in a flying accident on active service), expressed a wish to see Fatty Arbuckle's beach club. Only too willing to oblige, by clever use of the telephone Swanson managed to spirit the Duke and a handful of other bright sparks (including Chaplin and Aileen Pringle) away from the party without creating a diplomatic incident, and even had several cases from her own supply of champagne – in the days of prohibition – sent on ahead. Arbuckle wasn't there, but his orchestra was, and they danced until 3 a.m. and then went back to Swanson's 'in a whole string of cars'.

Staid or not, 'Pickfair' did more to make Hollywood socially acceptable than any other establishment, before or since.

In the early years of his second marriage, Fairbanks made his best-loved films: *The Mark of Zorro* (1920), *The Three Musketeers* (1921), *Robin Hood* (1922), *The Thief of Baghdad* (1924), *Don Q Son of Zorro* (1925), *The Black Pirate* (1926), *The Gaucho* (1927) and *The Iron Mask* (1929). After the New York premier of *Robin Hood*, a second showing had to be held at public insistence. This film had the biggest sets and cast of any Hollywood production up to that time, but it still made a profit and marked the apogee of Fairbanks' popularity.

Towards the end of the decade Fairbanks lost some of his enthusiasm for his work. His marriage was jeopardized by his casual philandering and by Mary Pickford's heavy drinking. Although they did quite genuinely still seem to love one another, the divorce was depressingly inevitable, and took place in January 1935. He made no further films of comparable significance, although he had a brief flirtation with the talkies. When he recorded the spoken prologue to the silent *Iron Mask* the bravura of his delivery forced the removal of the microphone to a distance of 30ft, but he had sufficiently mastered the technique for his only teaming with Pickford, in the unsuccessful *Taming of the Shrew* (1929). This was followed by *Reaching for the Moon* (1931), and *The Private Life of Don Juan* (1934).

Fairbanks married thirdly, 7 March 1936, Sylvia, Lady Ashley, a former Cockney chorus-girl, with whom he spent much time in Europe. He died in his sleep of a heart attack on 11 December 1939, at his beach house in Santa Monica, aged fifty-six.

BETH SULLY
First wife of Douglas Fairbanks Sr. Married 11 July 1907; divorced May 1919

Born Anna Beth Sully, 1888. Daughter and heiress of Daniel J. Sully, the cotton financier, of Fifth Avenue, New York, and Providence and Watch Hill, Rhode Island, by his wife Emma Frances Thompson, whose family began the cotton empire in Rhode Island. She married secondly, 1920 (divorced 1924), James Evans, a Pittsburgh stockbroker; and thirdly, 27 June 1929 (New York), Jack Whiting, musical comedy singer and dancer, who died on 15 February 1961, New York. She had issue one child, Douglas Fairbanks Jr, by her first husband, and died in 1967.

Fairbanks and Pickford – she still sporting her famous blonde curls, which were not shorn until 1928 when she was 35.

42

TABLE 11 THE FAIRBANKS FAMILY (I)

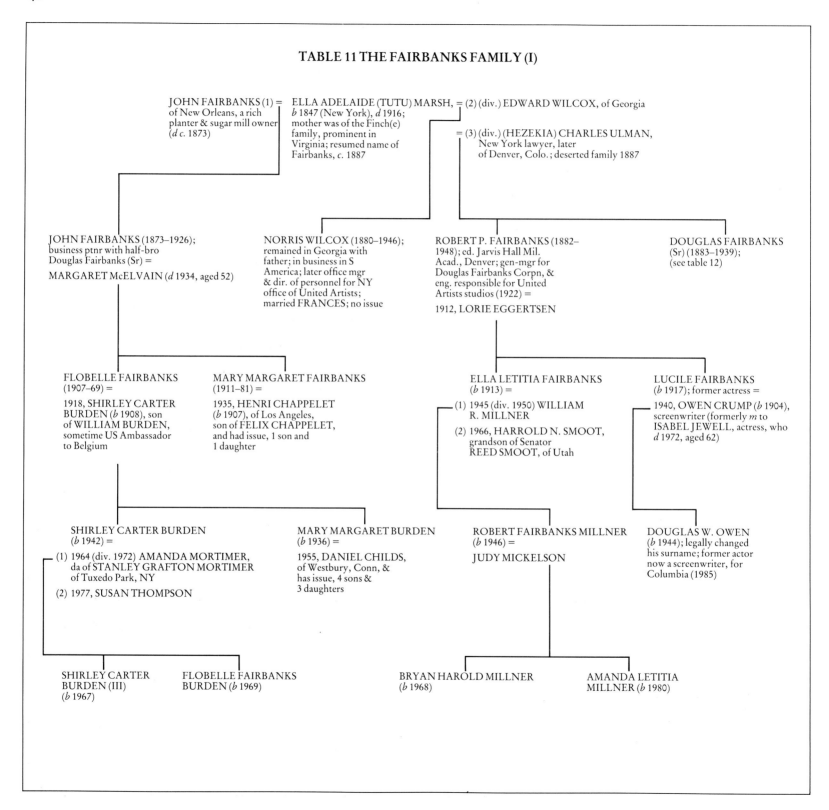

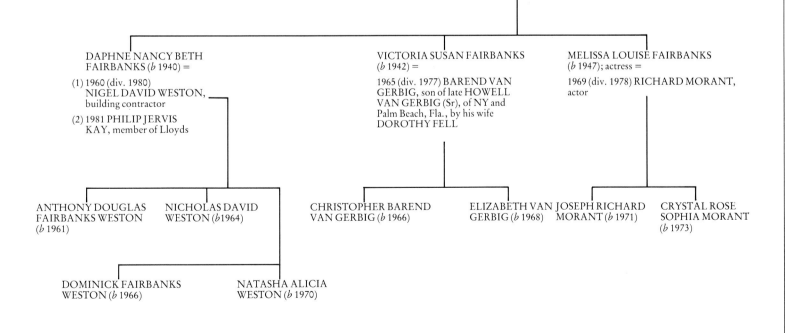

TABLE 12 THE FAIRBANKS FAMILY (II)

DOUGLAS FAIRBANKS (Sr) (1883–1939), son of ELLA ADELAIDE (TUTU) MARSH, by her 3rd husband CHARLES ULMAN; assumed surname of Fairbanks; film & stage actor, formed United Artists with Mary Pickford, Charlie Chaplin & D.W. Griffith (1919) =

= (1) 1902 (div. 1919) ANNA BETH SULLY (1888–1967), da of DANIEL J. SULLY, cotton financier, of Providence, RI, by his wife EMMA FRANCES THOMPSON. She = (2) 1920 (div. 1924) JAMES EVANS, Pittsburgh stockbroker; and (3) 1929, JACK WHITING, musical comedy actor (d 1961)

(2) 1920 (div. 1935) MARY PICKFORD, film actress, da of JOHN CHARLES SMITH of Toronto, and formerly wife of OWEN MOORE, actor (d 1939); she = (3) 1936 CHARLES ('BUDDY') ROGERS, actor, and d 1979, aged 86

(3) 1936 SYLVIA (LADY ASHLEY), ex chorus girl, of London, da of ARTHUR HAWKES, publican, and formerly wife of LORD ASHLEY (son & heir of 9th Earl of Shaftesbury). She = (3) 1944 (div. 1948) 6th BARON STANLEY OF ALDERLEY; (4) 1949 (div. 1951) CLARK GABLE, film actor (d 1960), and (5) 1954, Prince DMITRI DJORDJADZE; she d 1977, aged 73

DOUGLAS FAIRBANKS (Jr), KBE, DSC (b 1909); ed. Knickerbocker Greys Mil. Sch., Collegiate Mil. Sch., NY, and privately tutored in London & Paris; Capt. USNR (ret.); film & stage actor & producer; Vice-Pres. Franco-British War Relief, National Chm. CARE Cttee 1947–51 =

(1) 1929 (div. 1933) JOAN CRAWFORD, film actress (d 1977); she = (2) 1935 (div. 1939) FRANCHOT TONE, film actor (d 1968); (3) 1942 (div. 1946) PHILLIP TERRY, film actor; and (4) 1955 ALFRED STEELE, board chm. Pepsi-Cola (d 1959)

(2) 1939, MARY LEE, yr da of Dr GILES T. EPLING, of Bluefield, W Virginia, and formerly wife of HUNTINGTON HARTFORD, A&P heir

DAPHNE NANCY BETH FAIRBANKS (b 1940) =

(1) 1960 (div. 1980) NIGEL DAVID WESTON, building contractor

(2) 1981 PHILIP JERVIS KAY, member of Lloyds

VICTORIA SUSAN FAIRBANKS (b 1942) =

1965 (div. 1977) BAREND VAN GERBIG, son of late HOWELL VAN GERBIG (Sr), of NY and Palm Beach, Fla., by his wife DOROTHY FELL

MELISSA LOUISE FAIRBANKS (b 1947); actress =

1969 (div. 1978) RICHARD MORANT, actor

ANTHONY DOUGLAS FAIRBANKS WESTON (b 1961)

NICHOLAS DAVID WESTON (b 1964)

CHRISTOPHER BAREND VAN GERBIG (b 1966)

ELIZABETH VAN GERBIG (b 1968)

JOSEPH RICHARD MORANT (b 1971)

CRYSTAL ROSE SOPHIA MORANT (b 1973)

DOMINICK FAIRBANKS WESTON (b 1966)

NATASHA ALICIA WESTON (b 1970)

DOUGLAS FAIRBANKS JR
Only child of Douglas Fairbanks Sr by his first wife Beth Sully

Born on 9 December 1909 in New York City, Douglas Fairbanks Jr was ten years old when his parents divorced, rather plump and shy, and not at all the apple of his athletic father's eye. His mother moved to New York (she was originally from Rhode Island), and married James Evans, a Pittsburgh stockbroker, whom she had known in her youth. The marriage quickly failed, and mother and son divided their time between California and Europe (she divorced Evans in 1924). Unfortunately Beth was also a lot poorer, for her divorce settlement of $500,000 had been spent in unwise speculations. This was the second time she had seen a fortune slip through her fingers, for her wealthy father had also lost a great deal of money through being out-manoeuvred in business.

They returned to Paris and London where young Fairbanks received private tuition in painting, music and sculpture (which he planned to make his career) and where they were to live intermittently for the next three years. Times were very hard for them both, and Beth was reduced to pawning her jewellery. So it must have been a great relief to them when Jesse Lasky Sr, aware of the draw of the Fairbanks name, offered Douglas the title role in a film, *Stephen Steps Out* (1923). He was only thirteen, and had had no training or experience, and his father made some fairly derisory remarks about his performance. But Fairbanks Jr did eventually get a contract (in 1924) with Paramount. In Los Angeles he continued his schooling, studied acting, took fencing classes, and was given small parts. Still supporting his mother, he made some extra money writing the titles for some Ronald Colman–Vilma Banky pictures, and also for his father's film, *The Gaucho* (1927).

Disillusioned with his lack of opportunities, Fairbanks Jr turned to the stage, and was given a good part in John Van Druten's play, 'Young Woodley', which opened at the Majestic Theatre, Los Angeles, on 17 Oct 1927. He was a great success, and even his father was impressed. Fairbanks Sr, Mary Pick-

ford and Gloria Swanson were all at the first night, but what thrilled Fairbanks Jr was that Chaplin, who was also there, came back stage afterwards and stayed up with him until 2 a.m. offering encouragement and advice.

Another in that first-night audience was the recently renamed Joan Crawford. As Lucille Le Sueur she had been working incredibly hard for the last three years for MGM, and was about to make a breakthrough the following year in *Our Dancing Daughters*. She had been brought to the theatre by Paul Bern (who was to commit suicide in 1932, just two months after his marriage to Jean Harlow). Crawford too was impressed by Fairbanks Jr's performance and sent him a note to that effect.

Joan Crawford was a rising star, as Scott Fitzgerald said, 'the best example of the flapper, the girl you see at nightclubs dancing deliciously, laughing a great deal, with wide hurt eyes.' She and Fairbanks became friends, and a romance flourished, to the delight of the fan magazines and the horror of Beth Evans. She didn't like Crawford, and later described her as 'a strange, moody girl, over-flamboyant in her dress, and alternating between gushing enthusiasm and gauche aloofness.' She also believed that she had been born in 1904 (not 1908 as Crawford stated), which made her about five and a half years older than Fairbanks Jr. Mary Pickford was not as openly hostile, but she was acutely aware that an audience which had seen her as *Little Annie Rooney* in 1925 might be shocked to find that she had become a potential step-grandmother in a mere two years. Fairbanks Sr also was of the opinion that it was all too soon.

Ambitious, insecure, and desperately lacking in confidence, Crawford found cold comfort at 'Pickfair'. One thing she undoubtedly did not lack, however, was sex-appeal, and Jesse Lasky Jr who knew her well in those early days, spoke for many men when he commented on 'the tremendous impact of the eyes, and the wonderfully sensual mouth was wonderful to look at.' The late British actress June (later Lady Inverclyde) many years later recalled the 'Pickfair' scene in 1930, 'Mary Pickford, a diminutive figure in white beach pyjamas; her husband

TABLE 13 THE FAIRBANKS' LINKS TO BROOKE SHIELDS AND JULIE ANDREWS

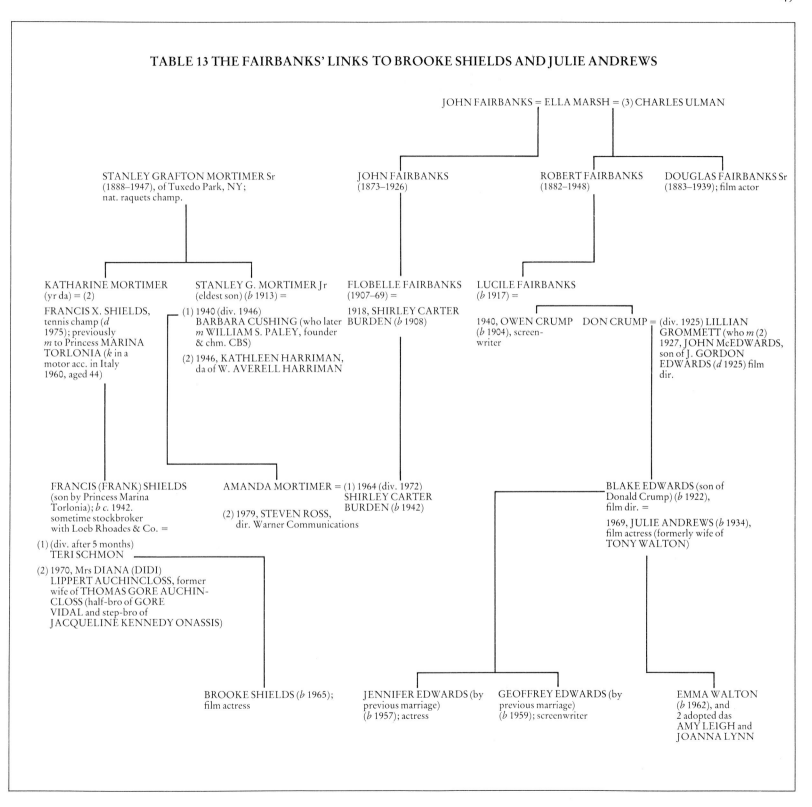

JOHN FAIRBANKS = ELLA MARSH = (3) CHARLES ULMAN

STANLEY GRAFTON MORTIMER Sr (1888–1947), of Tuxedo Park, NY; nat. raquets champ.

JOHN FAIRBANKS (1873–1926)

ROBERT FAIRBANKS (1882–1948)

DOUGLAS FAIRBANKS Sr (1883–1939); film actor

KATHARINE MORTIMER (yr da) = (2) FRANCIS X. SHIELDS, tennis champ (*d* 1975); previously *m* to Princess MARINA TORLONIA (*k* in a motor acc. in Italy 1960, aged 44)

STANLEY G. MORTIMER Jr (eldest son) (*b* 1913) =

(1) 1940 (div. 1946) BARBARA CUSHING (who later *m* WILLIAM S. PALEY, founder & chm. CBS)

(2) 1946, KATHLEEN HARRIMAN, da of W. AVERELL HARRIMAN

FLOBELLE FAIRBANKS (1907–69) = 1918, SHIRLEY CARTER BURDEN (*b* 1908)

LUCILE FAIRBANKS (*b* 1917) =

1940, OWEN CRUMP (*b* 1904), screenwriter

DON CRUMP = (div. 1925) LILLIAN GROMMETT (who *m* (2) 1927, JOHN McEDWARDS, son of J. GORDON EDWARDS (*d* 1925) film dir.

FRANCIS (FRANK) SHIELDS (son by Princess Marina Torlonia); *b c.* 1942. sometime stockbroker with Loeb Rhoades & Co. =

(1) (div. after 5 months) TERI SCHMON

(2) 1970, Mrs DIANA (DIDI) LIPPERT AUCHINCLOSS, former wife of THOMAS GORE AUCHINCLOSS (half-bro of GORE VIDAL and step-bro of JACQUELINE KENNEDY ONASSIS)

AMANDA MORTIMER = (1) 1964 (div. 1972) SHIRLEY CARTER BURDEN (*b* 1942)

(2) 1979, STEVEN ROSS, dir. Warner Communications

BLAKE EDWARDS (son of Donald Crump) (*b* 1922), film dir. =

1969, JULIE ANDREWS (*b* 1934), film actress (formerly wife of TONY WALTON)

BROOKE SHIELDS (*b* 1965); film actress

JENNIFER EDWARDS (by previous marriage) (*b* 1957); actress

GEOFFREY EDWARDS (by previous marriage) (*b* 1959); screenwriter

EMMA WALTON (*b* 1962), and 2 adopted das AMY LEIGH and JOANNA LYNN

Douglas Fairbanks with the torso of a Greek god and the high spirits of a lad; Joan Crawford, their plump young daughter-in-law, with huge hungry eyes and a heavily painted mouth.' Despite the (Fairbanks') parental opposition, they were married on 3 June 1929, in New York.

Although it was clearly a mis-match from the start, the marriage while it lasted was a happy one, and Fairbanks always spoke fondly of Crawford in later years. Certainly his career was stimulated by the Press attention and by Crawford's determination to excel at all she did. MGM starred them together in *Our Modern Maidens* (1929), and then Warners teamed him several times with Loretta Young. With *Little Caesar* (1930), and a good performance as a gigolo, he began to emerge from his father's shadow as an actor in his own right. After two more successes, *Outward Bound* (1930), with Leslie Howard, and *The Dawn Patrol* (1930), with Richard Barthelmess, Warners gave him a starring contract with power of production approval. By mid-1932 he was having business wrangles with Warners and his marriage was under pressure. He and Crawford went on a delayed honeymoon to Europe, Miss Crawford never having been abroad before, but life away from Hollywood served only to emphasize their incompatibility. Fairbanks Jr enjoyed London society, being entertained by Noël Coward and Prince George (created Duke of Kent in 1934), but Crawford found the whole thing a strain, to the point that she declined an invitation to a Buckingham Palace garden party. They were divorced in May 1933.

This was the continuation of a long association for Fairbanks with Britain. His father had already forged links there, and Fairbanks Jr had spent much of his childhood near London. He later worked for Alexander Korda in *Catherine The Great* (1934) as the mad Tsar, and was also in a couple of stage productions, 'The Winding Journey' and 'Moonlight is Silver' both with Gertrude Lawrence, with whom his name was romantically linked. He formed his own production company, the Criterion Films Corporation in 1936, and produced four films before running into financial problems.

He returned to Hollywood, where David Selznick offered him the role of the villain Rupert of Hentzau in *The Prisoner of Zenda* (1937), generally considered his best performance, and following which Selznick signed him for a two-picture deal (the other being *The Young in Heart* (1938)). During these years he travelled constantly between America and Britain as an emissary, for apart from being on friendly terms with the Royal Family, he had also met Winston Churchill and Anthony Eden through his political mentor in the United States, Herbert Bayard Swope.

His time was so divided that Sam Goldwyn was moved to remark, 'He's one of the best leading men in films ... why doesn't he drop all this stuff about politics and come back where he belongs.'

On 22 April 1939 he married Mrs Mary Lee Hartford, formerly wife of George Huntington Hartford, the Atlantic & Pacific Tea Company heir (from whom she is said to have received a $1.5 million settlement), and daughter of Dr Giles Epling, an oral surgeon, of Virginia. This marriage has produced three daughters, and (at the time of writing) eight grandchildren, and is one of the very few Hollywood marriages to remain happy and lasting.

Fairbanks Jr was in a number of pro-British propaganda films, *Gunga Din* (1939), *The Sun Never Sets* (1939), and *Rulers of the Sea* (1939), and was one of the first stars (Constance Bennett was another) to advocate US support for Britain in the Second World War. He served in the US Navy (retired as Lieutenant-Commander), and was the only American officer to command a flotilla of raiding craft for Lord Louis Mountbatten's Commandos (among his many decorations is the DSC, 1944). He was National Vice-Chairman of the Committee to Defend America by Aiding Allies 1940–1, co-organizer of the Franco-British War Relief Association 1939–41, and, probably his most memorable role in post-war politics, Chairman of CARE (Cooperative American Relief Everywhere) 1946–50. In 1949 he was created a KBE by King George VI.

After four years of war service and diplomatic missions his return to Hollywood was rather an anti-climax. 'Darling,' Joan Crawford exclaimed, 'Of course you're so behind the news aren't you? I suppose you haven't even heard I've left MGM. I'm with Warner Bros now.' Fairbanks went on to make the most financially successful film of his career, *Sinbad the Sailor* (1947), for RKO, and he again formed a production company. He returned, with his family, to London, where he bought a magnificent house, 28 The Boltons, where they caused a stir when the Queen and the Duke of Edinburgh came to dine 1952.

He made only one further good film, again in Britain, *State Secret* (1950), a political thriller, but it was poorly distributed in the US. His British production company produced TV films, screened as 'Douglas Fairbanks Presents'. His only involvement in films now is in production, but he has also continued to work in the theatre, including 'My Fair Lady' in the USA and a tour of 'The Pleasure of his Company' in London, Australia, Canada and the USA. His permanent home is in Florida, but he has an office and an apartment in New York and London.

As a successor to his father, Douglas Fairbanks Jr showed himself to be quite as debonair and dexterous, but his acting career was too often at odds with his much wider interests to fully realize its potential.

MARY PICKFORD
Second wife of Douglas Fairbanks Sr. Married 28 March 1920, Hollywood; divorced January 1935

When Mary Pickford died on 29 May 1979, aged eighty-six, *The Times* saluted her as 'the last survivor from amongst the true founders of the American cinema ... through her immense business acumen and understanding she helped to create the American cinema as we know it today, and was a trailblazer on the active involvement of stars in production.' It was the phenomenal popularity of 'America's Sweetheart' that first awakened film producers to the potency of star-appeal, and eventually led to the development of the star system.

It is hard to reconcile such an influential character with the waif-like, child-woman image which Pickford successfully sustained from 1909 to 1927. But Mary Pickford was a tough cookie. Like many other top female stars, her start in life was a rough one. Born on 8 April 1893, as Gladys Mary Smith, she was the eldest of a family of three. Her father, Joseph Smith, whose family originally came from Liverpool, worked as purser on a steamship which ran between Toronto and Lewiston, near Niagara Falls. He died as a result of an accident on board, and his young widow, Charlotte, already the dominant figure of the family, was forced to take in lodgers to make ends meet. It was through one of these lodgers that Gladys, then aged five, was cast in 'The

Douglas Fairbanks Jr, his second wife Mary Lee, and their two elder daughters, Daphne and Victoria, on their way to Buckingham Palace, where he received the insignia of honorary KBE from King George VI in 1949.

Silver King', for a local stock company. There were good parts for juveniles in the melodramas of the day, she was precocious and self-assured and quickly became a popular child actress in her native Canada.

Charlotte Smith saw the possibility of a brighter future in her daughter's blonde ringlets, and took the family off to New York, the nearest theatrical mecca, where Gladys was hired by David Belasco, the famed Broadway producer. She made her début in 'The Warrens of Virginia', as Betty, in December 1907. She was fourteen. While in New York she met another fatherless girl – three years younger – Lillian Gish, who, with her mother and sister Dorothy, became friendly with the Smiths. By this time Mrs Smith and her two younger children, Lottie and Jack, were all performers.

Perhaps sensing where her fortune was to be made, Gladys Smith turned her back on the stage after she had been hired by D. W. Griffith, who was making one-reel film dramas at American Biograph on Long Island. He saw potential in her wistful childishness, gave her a screen test, and offered her $5 a day – she asked for $10 and got it. He changed her name to Mary Pickford and cast her in *The Lonely Villa* (1909), a thriller, and went on to feature her in eighty-five one-reelers over the next three years. He gave her all manner of parts, from infants to grandmothers, and she became an all-purpose utility actress in comedies, thrillers, melodramas, romances and period pieces, but it was Pickford herself who wrote the story of *Lena and the Geese* (1911), the film which first established her in the familiar child-woman image.

On 7 January 1911 she secretly married another Griffith actor, Owen Moore, whom she later described in her autobiography *Sunshine and Shadow* (1956) as '5ft 11in tall, extremely handsome, with a ruddy Irish complexion, perfect teeth, dark blue eyes, and a very musical voice ... the Beau Brummel of the Biograph.' She was afraid to tell her mother until several months later (she never showed any such fear in later life of even the most hardened Hollywood executives), and perhaps she already realized the marriage was a mistake. He was a heavy drinker and resented her financial independence;

nor did he get along with Charlotte, who was much nearer to him in age than was Pickford. They separated before long, although the marriage was not actually terminated until March 1920 (and was dismissed by her as 'a dismal experience').

Known first as 'the Biograph Girl' and then by name, Pickford soon had a huge following. In 1913 she broke with Griffith to go to Adolph Zukor's Famous Players, where her salary eventually rose to $10,000 a week, and where she starred in feature length films with high budgets specifically built to sell her as a star personality. By the age of twenty she had become the American cinema's biggest single asset, and the performer people most wanted to see. She understood that her audience preferred to see her as a mischievous innocent, romantic and funny, and this just what she gave them in: *Caprice* (1913), *Tess of the Storm Country* (1914), *Such A Little Queen* (1914), *Behind the Scenes* (1914), *Cinderella* (1915), *Poor Little Rich Girl* (1916), *Rebecca of Sunnybrook Farm* (1917), etc. Then in 1919 First National made her a spectacular offer – $250,000 each for three films and $50,000 for her mother – which Zukor couldn't or wouldn't match.

Of these three films, *Daddy Long Legs* (1919) was the biggest success, and led her to initiate the formation of an independent company, United Artists, in 1920, the year of her marriage to Fairbanks Sr.

They were the most famous and most publicized couple in the world. They had a month-long honeymoon in Europe and were beseiged by crowds even in such an unlikely spot as the Isle of Wight. Fairbanks had bought 'Pickfair' (so christened by the press), a white-timbered, green-tiled house with twenty acres, in 1919, when the population of Beverly Hills was only 672 and there were still coyotes baying in the woods. Fairbanks loved to entertain, and the table was set for fifteen every night; they were seldom alone, but he had a loathing of restaurants and nightclubs, and they virtually never went out. He was also pathologically jealous and would insist that Pickford always sat next him whether they dined at 'Pickfair' or anywhere else.

The first five years of marriage were the happiest. Pickford had complete control of all her films –

TABLE 14 MARY PICKFORD'S BROTHER AND SISTER

JOHN PICKFORD HENNESSY = CATHERINE FAELY,
of Tralee, Co. Kerry,   a miller's daughter
Ireland

CHARLOTTE HENNESSY (yr da) = (Quebec), JOHN CHARLES SMITH (*d c.* 1898),
d 21 Mar 1928; Catholic   son of JOSEPH SMITH, formerly of Liverpool; Protestant

MARY PICKFORD
b 8 Apr 1893

LOTTIE PICKFORD, *b c.* June 1894;
actress; *d* 9 Dec 1936, Brentwood,
Calif., heart attack =

(1) (div.) ALFRED G. RUPP, car salesman

(2) 1922, (div. 1927) ALLAN FORREST, leading actor
in silent films; *d* 1941

(3) (div. 1933) RUSSELL O. GILLARD, an
undertaker, of Muskogee, Mich.

(4) 1933, JOHN WILLIAM LOCK

JACK PICKFORD, *b* 18 Aug 1896; actor
(including silent versions of *Huckleberry
Finn* and *Tom Sawyer*); served US Navy;
adopted US citizenship 1920; *d* 3 Jan 1933,
American Hospital in Paris, following a
nervous breakdown; bur. Forest Lawn =

(1) 1920, OLIVE THOMAS, a Broadway star, widely known
as 'the world's most beautiful girl'; dark-haired &
violet-eyed beauty, according to Mary Pickford; found
dead in a Paris hotel from an overdose of barbiturates
10 Sep 1920, aged 36. M. Pickford said it was an
accidental overdose

(2) July 1922 (div. 1927), MARILYN MILLER, a Broadway
musical star (described by M. Pickford as 'the most
ambitious human being I have ever met'). In Mar 1930
she announced her engagement to Michael Farmer, but he
married Gloria Swanson the following year. She *d*
7 Apr 1936, New York City, of toxic poisoning, aged 37

(3) 12 Aug 1930 (Del Monte, Calif.), MARY MULHERN, a
Ziegfeld Follies girl

GWYNNE PICKFORD (*b c.* 1918) (legally adopted by her aunt,
Mary Pickford, against her mother's wishes) =

(1) 31 May 1939 (Las Vegas) HUGH (BUD) ERNST,
sometime radio announcer & sec. of Los Angeles
Flying Club. Previously *m* to (1) ALTHEA HENLEY,
a film *ingenue*, & (2) LYDA ROBERTI, film
actress, who *d* 1938, aged 29, of a heart attack
while bending over to tie her shoelace. He later *m* (4)
BETTY FURNESS, sometime TV's highest paid
saleswoman (Westinghouse refrigerators), &
later President Johnson's Special Assist. for
Consumer Affairs

(2) 18 May 1945 ('Pickfair'), GEORGE (BUD) ORNSTEIN,
later of Benalmedena, Spain

MARY CHARLOTTE ORNSTEIN,
b 12 Feb 1946 (Hollywood) =

Nov 1970 ('Pickfair') PETER FULLERTON, of London

A Son, *b* 14 July 1948
(Switzerland)

A Daughter, *b* 15 Sept 1971 (London)

including writers, directors and co-stars – and their distribution. Nearly all of them were standard Pickford vehicles, superbly done, especially *Pollyanna* (1920) and *Little Lord Fauntleroy* (1921). *Dorothy Vernon of Haddon Hall* (1924) was somewhat outside the 'Little Mary' archetype in that she played an eighteen-year-old 'spitfire'. Pickford brought over from Europe the director Ernst Lubitsch to direct this one, though in the end he handled *Rosita* (1923). She would not take his direction, however, and the film was a commercial failure, although it stands up very well today.

By 1925 Fairbanks began to show a restlessness. He took to making extensive tours around Europe, usually not staying more than a night in any one place. Retrospectively, Pickford put this down to 'the change of life', but at that time her own life was also changing pretty drastically. In 1926 she bobbed her hair. Six curls were kept for posterity (two are now in the Museum of San Diego, two at the Los Angeles Museum, and two remained at 'Pickfair'). She made her first modern, completely adult film, *My Best Girl* (1927), co-starring Charles 'Buddy' Rogers, whom she later married. She also won a Best Actress Oscar for her first talkie, *Coquette* (1929), which even required her to have an illegitimate child. Her audience found this grown-up Pickford difficult to accept, and were further disappointed with her choice of subject – *Taming of the Shrew* (1929) – for her only teaming with Fairbanks.

His association with the urbane divorcée Sylvia, Lady Ashley made her unhappiness complete. After two more films Pickford retired (1933), although she retained her interest in United Artists until 1951 and also made an attempt at producing.

She sued for divorce in January 1935. According to her autobiography, Fairbanks made repeated attempts at a reconciliation – and on one occasion sent his first wife, Beth, to intercede for him. When 'Pickfair' was sold, however, her 'Honeymoon Box' was found, containing her wedding dress, a kimono monogrammed 'DF', a teddy bear, a rag doll, and her letters to Fairbanks begging him not to divorce her – if only for the sake of their image as America's 'perfect couple'.

The divorce became absolute in January 1936, and she received 'Pickfair' in settlement. Soon afterwards, Gloria Swanson gave a big party to which she invited Pickford, without previously warning her that Fairbanks and his new wife had also been invited, and the two women met face to face for the first time. Fairbanks refused to introduce Sylvia to his former wife, and it was left to poor Mary Pickford to utter the first few frigid words.

In 1937 Mary married Buddy Rogers and lived in seclusion. They adopted two children, Ronnie and Roxanne, around 1940, but although she provided for them financially she broke off all contact with the foundlings once they had come of age. In 1965, after returning from a retrospective of her films in Paris, she retired to bed and was virtually unseen for her remaining fourteen years (she made a filmed appearance at the 1977 Awards ceremony to receive a special award for her lifetime's participation in the film industry).

After Pickford's death, Buddy Rogers built a $700,000 house on the estate (now reduced to 2.7 acres), and put 'Pickfair' and some of its contents on the market. Mary Pickford's wedding dress was sold for $1,200, Charlene Tilton (the 'Dallas' actress) paid $3,750 for Pickford's fourteen-carat gold six-piece vanity set, and Bette Midler bought an oil painting of the actress for $2,200. The fate of the two remaining curls was not recorded. Perhaps they were not for sale.

SYLVIA, LADY ASHLEY
Third wife of Douglas Fairbanks Sr. Married 7 March 1936, Paris

Born Edith Louise Sylvia Hawkes, *c.* 1904, London. Her birth certificate has yet to be traced, but she was said to be the daughter of Arthur Hawkes, of 18 Carlisle Place, Marylebone, London (in 1927), who is variously described as a footman, publican and Paddington stablehand. At her first marriage she described her father as deceased, but he promptly notified a newspaper that this was not so. She became a well-known figure in *demi-monde* circles, and worked as a mannequin and chorus girl. She married first, 3 February 1927 (divorced 1935), Anthony Ashley-Cooper (Lord Ashley), elder son and heir of the 9th Earl of Shaftesbury. She met him while she was in the 'Midnight Follies' show in London. This Stage-Door Johnny never succeeded to the earldom as he predeceased his father.

She married secondly, 7 March 1936 (Paris), Douglas Fairbanks Sr. As the ultimate cause of the Fairbanks–Pickford divorce, this brought Lady Ashley considerable notoriety. When Fairbanks died, he left the bulk of his estate to Sylvia. She received over $1 million. (Fairbanks Jr was left about $600,000; the four nieces received about $50,000 each, as did his half-brother Norris Wilcox; his full brother Robert Fairbanks received $100,000. Nothing was left either to his first wife, Beth, or to Mary Pickford.)

Fairbanks died on 11 December 1939. Gladys Cooper wrote from California to her daughter in England, ' . . . Doug Fairbanks senior died here very suddenly this week and the papers are full of funeral pictures of Sylvia draped in heavy black, but with her red painted toe-nails sticking through the end of her sandals which rather spoils the effect . . . '

Sylvia's third husband was another English aristocrat: the 6th Baron Stanley of Alderley, whom she married in America on 18 January 1944. He was granted a decree *nisi* in June 1945 on grounds of his wife's desertion, but the divorce was not final until 1948. He was about three years younger than Lady Ashley and came from a highly eccentric family; his great-uncle, the 3rd Baron, was a Muslim.

Her fourth husband was none other than the great Clark Gable (see table 15), generally acknowledged as the 'King of Hollywood'. He was still mourning the death of his wife Carole Lombard (killed in a plane crash in 1942). Gable and Sylvia were utterly unsuited, she being the original hothouse plant, and he being happiest when duck shooting. They were married on 20 December 1949 (Santa Barbara), and divorced in 1951.

Her last husband was Prince Dmitri Djordjadze, known as Mito. He had previously been married to

the heiress Audrey Emery (died 1971). This marriage came apart when he decided to settle in Texas. Sylvia Ashley then lived with her sister, Mrs Vera Bleck, for ten years, in Los Angeles, where she died on 30 June 1977, aged about seventy-three, of cancer. She had no children from her five attempts at matrimony.

JOAN CRAWFORD
First wife of Douglas Fairbanks Jr. Married 3 June 1929, New York; divorced May 1933

'Lucille Le Sueur is dead, long live Joan Crawford.' The outstanding, though dubious, achievement of Joan Crawford's strange life was her ability to create, assume and sustain a phantom identity. This enabled her to develop an intimate and entirely genuine affection for her fans, but prevented her from forming any kind of lasting bond with her husbands, children or friends.

Given the facts of her childhood – sketchy as they are – it is hardly surprising she wanted to kick over the traces. She is said to have met her father for the first time when he turned up unannounced on the set of her film *Chained* (1934), when she was already a well-established star. He stayed around for a few days, and she saw him a couple of times, but of course it was too late for them to remain anything but strangers. When he left town she never saw him again.

Thomas Le Sueur, her father, was from San Antonio, Texas. It seems doubtful whether he ever married her mother, Anna Johnson, although they had three children: Daisy, who died in infancy; Hal, said to have been five years older than Lucille; and Lucille herself, born on 23 March 1904. The year of her birth remains uncertain as births did not have to be registered by law until 1908, the year in which Joan Crawford maintained she was born.

The usual story goes that father left home before Lucille was born, and her mother then formed a liaison with a man named Harry Cassin. The family moved to Kansas in 1915, where they ran a shabby hotel, until Cassin too walked out, when Anna was

TABLE 15 CLARK GABLE

CHARLES GABLE, of Gable Hill, nr Meadville, Penn. = NANCY STAINBROOK (*d* 1927, aged 90)
(*c.* 160 acres) (*d* 1898)

WILLIAM H. GABLE (3rd of 6 sons); farmer & oil = (1) ADELINE (*d* 14 Nov 1901, aged 31), da of JOHN HERSCHELMAN (of
driller; *d* 4 Aug 1948, aged 78, N Hollywood German extraction; *d* 1919), by his wife ROSETTA CLARK (Irish)

= (2) 16 Apr 1903, JEANNIE (*d c.* 1919), da of HENRY DUNLAP, of
Hopedale, Ohio

= (3) 11 Dec 1932, EDNA GABLE (*d* 19 Jun 1948, aged 71, Encino, Calif.)
widow of his brother FRANK GABLE

JOSEPHINE DILLON (*b* 1884; *d* 10 Nov = (1) 18 Dec 1924 (div. 1930) WILLIAM CLARK GABLE = (3) 29 March 1939, CAROLE LOMBARD,
1971, Verdugo City, Calif.), actress & coach, *b* 1 Feb 1901, Cadiz, Ohio; the film star. Darryl Zanuck vivacious & talented Hollywood actress
da of Judge HENRY CLAY DILLON, by lived to regret his early dismissal of Gable ('his ears are (née JANE ALICE PETERS, *b* 6 Oct
his wife FLORENCE HOOD. One of her too big; he looks like an ape'), who, by 1938, was 1908 Fort Wayne, Inc.; *k* in a plane crash
sisters, Florence Dillon changed her name to known as the 'King of Hollywood'; best actor award 16 Jan 1942, when returning from a
Enrica Clay Dillon & became an opera singer for *It Happened One Night* (1934), star of *Gone With* bond-selling tour of Midwest); da of
in Italy (*d* 1946, aged 63) *The Wind* (1939); served in WWII in US Air Force FREDERICK C. PETERS, by his wife
(DFC & Air Medal for flying in bombing missions over ELIZABETH KNIGHT. Miss
Germany); also memorable opposite Marilyn Monroe Lombard was said to have been a 2nd
in *The Misfits* (1961), his last film, in which he insisted cousin of HOWARD HAWKS, the film
on doing all his own stunts; *d* of a heart attack 16 Nov dir. (see table 20) but recent research has
1960 shown this to be unlikely; formerly wife
of WILLIAM POWELL, actor (*d* 1984)

Mrs RIA LANGHAM (née MARIA = (2) 19 June 1931 (div. 1939) = (4) 20 Dec 1949 (div. 1951) SYLVIA, LADY
FRANKLIN, *b* 17 Jan 1884; *d* 24 Sep 1966, ASHLEY (see table 12)
Houston, Texas); wealthy socialite; da of
GEORGE FRANKLIN, of Kentucky; = (5) 11 July 1955, Mrs KAY SPRECKLES
formerly wife of (1) WILLIAM PRENTISS (née WILLIAMS; *d* 25 May 1983, aged
(by whom she had issue one son), (2) 65, Houston, Texas); sometime
ALFRED THOMAS LUCAS, of Houston nightclub entertainer; formerly wife of
(by whom she had further issue, (1) Mr CAPPS, (2) MARTIN DE
GEORGIANNA LUCAS, *b c.* 1913: *m* ALZAGA UNZUE, a restaurateur
1935, Dr THOMAS BURKE, of Houston; known as MACOCO, and (3)
and ALFRED LUCAS Jr, and (3) ADOLPH SPRECKLES, of the wealthy
ANDREW DENZIL LANGHAM, Calif. sugar family (he was jailed for 25
stockbroker days in 1955 for assaulting her with a
jewelled slipper), by him she had issue,
ANTHONY (BUNKER)
SPRECKLES, *b* 15 Aug 1949; *k* in a car
crash 7 Jan 1977, Hawaii, and JOAN
SPRECKLES, *bc.* 1951

(Often said to be Gable's child by
LORETTA YOUNG, actress (*b* 6 Jan 1913))

JUDY YOUNG, *b* 6 Nov 1935 (legally JOHN CLARK GABLE (son by Kay Spreckles),
adopted by Loretta Young) *b* (posthumously) 20 Mar 1961; racing
driver; 3rd in Baja 1,000 (1984); won off-
(Anita Loos in *Kiss Hollywood Goodbye* road racing 'Rookie of the Year' title (1984):
describes her as a Park Avenue matron . . . *m* TRACY —, and has issue, KAYLEY GABLE (*b.*
married to an important young business 1986)
executive)

obliged to find work as a laundress. Without funds to provide her son and daughter with an education, she arranged for Lucille to be educated on a *quid pro quo* basis: Lucille was granted the pearls of wisdom in exchange for waiting at table, washing up, and making beds for the other girls. Children are notoriously quick to despise anyone who may be seen to be at a disadvantage, but Lucille apparently suffered just as much unkindness from the teachers. Even if the stories were exaggerated, she must have had several ghastly years. She changed schools three or more times, ending up at Stephens College, Columbia, Missouri, until the age of sixteen, when she decided she had had enough of school and enough of her mother too.

She had learnt to be tough, was naturally reckless, and had nothing to lose. She hitched a lift to Chicago, where she scraped her way into a dancing job at the Friars Inn for $25 a week, and toured Oklahoma City and Detroit performing eight routines a night with thirty-one other girls. She was plump, freckled and had startling blue eyes. She got a better job and reached Broadway in 'Innocent Eyes', and was then spotted in the chorus of 'The Passing Show of 24' by Howard Dietz, the lyricist. Through him she got a contract with MGM. Once in Hollywood she danced like mad, the Charleston and the Black Bottom, anything modern – and won over a hundred trophies. She gave herself willingly to the MGM publicity men, and was photographed jumping out of crackers and tumbling down chimneys in a Father Christmas outfit. Murky rumours circulated much later that she had also appeared in porno movies, although these allegations were never substantiated. She certainly dieted zealously and probably had her back teeth extracted (like many other female stars) to enhance her bone structure. Much as she liked to appear the sophisticated flapper, she was still very much a child at heart, and many of the non-studio photographs of the time show her surrounded by woolly dolls and clutching little dogs.

Edmund Goulding needed a third girl for his film, *Sally, Irene and Mary* (1925), and chose Lucille for the part. The studio sponsored a contest in *Movie*

Weekly for a new name for a new starlet. 'Joan Arden' was first choice but this was already in use by an extra, and the second choice of Joan Crawford was taken. Her long and ruthless battle to the top thus began.

Landmarks in Crawford's career continued with her role in *Our Dancing Daughters* (1928), her marriage to Hollywood's most eligible bachelor, Douglas Fairbanks Jr (which lasted from 1929 to 1933), and her appearance in *Grand Hotel* (1932) with Greta Garbo, Lionel and John Barrymore, and Wallace Beery. She was also effectively teamed with Clark Gable (with whom she enjoyed a brief but ardent affair) in eight films, and, by the mid-1930s was earning an impressive $300,000 a year. Her standard role as the Depression-wise kid struggling to make good made her the shop-girls' pin-up for a decade. *Dance Fools Dance* (1931), *Laughing Sinner* (1931) and

Joan Crawford as Mildred Pierce *(1945) in one of many tense scenes with Ann Blyth who played her vicious daughter, Veda. Her bravura performance won Crawford her only Oscar, and Blyth was nominated for Best Supporting Actress.*

TABLE 16 JOAN CRAWFORD

THOMAS LeSUEUR =/ ♥ ANNA JOHNSON ♥ HENRY CASSIN
of San Antonio, Texas;   (who d 15 Aug 1958,
a plasterer; d 1 Jan 1938   aged 73, in Hollywood)
(on the eve of his 71st
birthday), Abilene, Texas

DAISY LeSUEUR,
d in infancy

HAL HAYES LeSUEUR
probably b c. 1900; following his
sister's success had a number of
jobs at Metro, first as an actor
& later in make-up dept.; alcoholic;
Douglas Fairbanks Jr suggests he d
of syphilis; when he d 3 May 1963
he was a night clerk & part-time
switchboard operator at Parkway Motel,
Alvarado St, Los Angeles; bur. at
Forest Lawn =

(1) JESSIE (who in 1932 was
reported to be engaged to marry
STANLEY E. LITTLE, cameraman)

(2) (div. 1934) KASHA . . .

JOAN CRAWFORD LeSUEUR,
sometime Broadway dancer

JOAN CRAWFORD
probably b 23 Mar 1904; the film star =

(1) 3 June 1929 (St Malachy's Church, Manhattan)
(div. May 1933) DOUGLAS FAIRBANKS Jr

(2) 12 Oct 1935 (Englewood Cliffe, NJ)
(div. Apr 1939) FRANCHOT TONE (see table 17)

(3) 20 Jul 1942 (Ventura County, Calif.). (div.
1946) PHILLIP TERRY, film actor (né FREDERICK
HENRY KORMANN), b 1909, San Francisco, son of a
research chemist; ed. RADA (London) for 1 year;
toured in rep. (Hull, Manchester, Birmingham,
Croydon, Brighton, etc.) before returning to US;
m (2) 9 Jun 1949, HELEN MYERS

(4) 10 May 1955 (Las Vegas) ALFRED N. STEELE,
chm. Pepsi-Cola; found d in bed April 1959

CHRISTINA CRAWFORD
b 11 Jun 1939; adopted by
Crawford same year; actress;
author of *Mommie Dearest*
(1978) =

(1) 20 May 1966 (New York).
(div.) HARVEY MEDLINSKY,
then a Broadway stage mgr

(2) 14 Feb 1976, DAVID KOONTZ,
former stunt driver

CHRISTOPHER CRAWFORD,
b & adopted 1943; an
electrical company
linesman, Long Island
(1981); married & has
issue

CATHY CRAWFORD,
b & adopted 1947;
a 'twin' =

10 Aug 1968 (New York).
JEROME JON LALONDE,
sportshop mgr, of
Slatington, Penn.

CINDY CRAWFORD
b & adopted 1947
a 'twin' =

(div.) JOHN JORDAN
of Newton, Iowa

CARLA LALONDE
b c. 1970

CASEY LALONDE
b c. 1972

JAN JORDAN
b c. 1969

JOEL JORDAN
b c. 1971

Dancing Lady (1933), all made MGM a fortune, but a change of formula with *The Last of Mrs Cheyney* (1937), and *The Bride Wore Red* (1938), caused a fall from public favour.

Her performances were variable, and in her more dramatic roles, she was criticized for her lack of restraint. At MGM she laboured behind Greta Garbo and Norma Shearer – she cordially disliked the latter. If Fairbanks' opinion that Crawford 'resented those who had become successful without serving the same trying apprenticeship that she herself had experienced' is correct, then Shearer would certainly have been thrust into that category. Worse still, her name appeared on the 'box-office poison' list, placed in *The Hollywood Reporter* by a disgruntled exhibitor in 1938.

On 12 October 1935, at Englewood Cliffe, New Jersey, she married Franchot Tone, another actor from a privileged background (see table 17). By this time her phantom identity had become indelibly fixed, and she dominated their relationship to such an extent that whenever they appeared in public he had to trail behind her carrying the dog and her bag of knitting. As well as having a hygiene complex (stockinged feet only were allowed in the sitting room), she was also a compulsive knitter, and would usually prefer to clack away with her needles than to talk. Tone was not a passive man, and they were divorced in April 1939.

Despite this plunge in her fortunes, Crawford stood firm, and MGM duly renewed her contract – at least for the time being.

The three years between her divorce from Tone and her third marriage to Phillip Terry must have been among the most difficult in her whole screen career. MGM attempted another poor girl – rich man formula picture (Crawford and Spencer Tracy), *Mannequin* (1938), then *The Shining Hour* (1938) and *Ice Follies of 1939* (1939), all of which were dismissed by the critics. Crawford was alone and fighting for survival, when suddenly, in the dark, she saw a little jewelled dagger in the shape of *The Women* (1939), adapted by Anita Loos and Jane Murfin from the Broadway play by Claire Booth Luce. MGM assembled a magnificent cast for this all-female *pièce*

de résistance, starring Norma Shearer, Crawford, Rosalind Russell, Mary Boland, Paulette Goddard and Joan Fontaine.

Joan Crawford no longer disguised her dislike of Norma Shearer, whose own position at MGM had become more tenuous since the death of her husband, Irving Thalberg, MGM's production supervisor, in 1936. With her portrayal of Crystal Allen, the scheming perfume clerk, Crawford was determined to outshine Shearer's wounded society matron. 'I love to play bitches, and she helped me in this part,' said Crawford of her rival.

She gave a viciously spirited performance and the film was a critical and box-office success. MGM showed renewed faith in her by teaming her again (for the last time) with their top male star, Gable, fresh from his triumph in *Gone With the Wind* (1939). This was *Strange Cargo* (1940). Again the critics liked her, and she was given another strong role in *Susan and God* (1940). This was directed by George Cukor, who had also directed her in *The Women*, and went

Joan Crawford looking happy and relaxed surrounded by bewildered children, including her eldest adopted daughter, Christina (at Crawford's right shoulder). This is a gathering of Christina's Brownie chums for a production of Hansel and Gretel, *directed by Crawford.*

TABLE 17 THE FAMILY OF FRANCHOT TONE

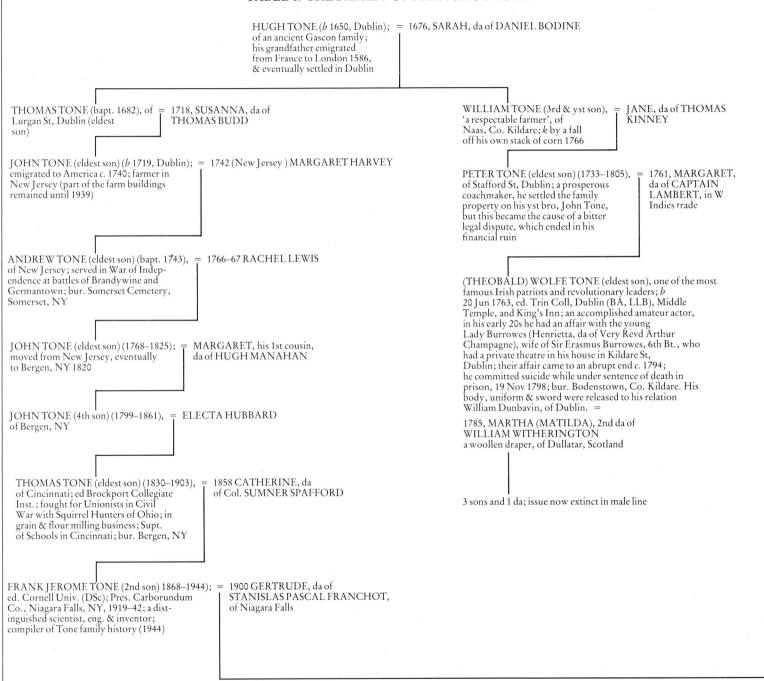

HUGH TONE (*b* 1650, Dublin); = 1676, SARAH, da of DANIEL BODINE
of an ancient Gascon family;
his grandfather emigrated
from France to London 1586,
& eventually settled in Dublin

THOMAS TONE (bapt. 1682), of = 1718, SUSANNA, da of
Lurgan St, Dublin (eldest   THOMAS BUDD
son)

JOHN TONE (eldest son) (*b* 1719, Dublin); = 1742 (New Jersey) MARGARET HARVEY
emigrated to America *c*. 1740; farmer in
New Jersey (part of the farm buildings
remained until 1939)

ANDREW TONE (eldest son) (bapt. 1743), = 1766–67 RACHEL LEWIS
of New Jersey; served in War of Indep-
endence at battles of Brandywine and
Germantown; bur. Somerset Cemetery,
Somerset, NY

JOHN TONE (eldest son) (1768–1825); = MARGARET, his 1st cousin,
moved from New Jersey, eventually   da of HUGH MANAHAN
to Bergen, NY 1820

JOHN TONE (4th son) (1799–1861), = ELECTA HUBBARD
of Bergen, NY

THOMAS TONE (eldest son) (1830–1903), = 1858 CATHERINE, da
of Cincinnati; ed Brockport Collegiate   of Col. SUMNER SPAFFORD
Inst.; fought for Unionists in Civil
War with Squirrel Hunters of Ohio; in
grain & flour milling business; Supt.
of Schools in Cincinnati; bur. Bergen, NY

FRANK JEROME TONE (2nd son) 1868–1944); = 1900 GERTRUDE, da of
ed. Cornell Univ. (DSc); Pres. Carborundum   STANISLAS PASCAL FRANCHOT,
Co., Niagara Falls, NY, 1919–42; a dist-   of Niagara Falls
inguished scientist, eng. & inventor;
compiler of Tone family history (1944)

WILLIAM TONE (3rd & yst son), = JANE, da of THOMAS
'a respectable farmer', of   KINNEY
Naas, Co. Kildare; *k* by a fall
off his own stack of corn 1766

PETER TONE (eldest son) (1733–1805), = 1761, MARGARET,
of Stafford St, Dublin; a prosperous   da of CAPTAIN
coachmaker, he settled the family   LAMBERT, in W
property on his yst bro, John Tone,   Indies trade
but this became the cause of a bitter
legal dispute, which ended in his
financial ruin

(THEOBALD) WOLFE TONE (eldest son), one of the most
famous Irish patriots and revolutionary leaders; *b*
20 Jun 1763, ed. Trin Coll, Dublin (BA, LLB), Middle
Temple, and King's Inn; an accomplished amateur actor,
in his early 20s he had an affair with the young
Lady Burrowes (Henrietta, da of Very Revd Arthur
Champagne), wife of Sir Erasmus Burrowes, 6th Bt., who
had a private theatre in his house in Kildare St,
Dublin; their affair came to an abrupt end *c*. 1794;
he committed suicide while under sentence of death in
prison, 19 Nov 1798; bur. Bodenstown, Co. Kildare. His
body, uniform & sword were released to his relation
William Dunbavin, of Dublin. =

1785, MARTHA (MATILDA), 2nd da of
WILLIAM WITHERINGTON
a woollen draper, of Dullatar, Scotland

3 sons and 1 da; issue now extinct in male line

→

(STANISLAS PASCAL) FRANCHOT TONE (yr son), = (1) 12 Oct 1935 (div. 1939) JOAN CRAWFORD (see table 16)
film & stage actor; *b* 27 Feb 1905
Niagara Falls, NY; ed. The Hill Sch.,
Pottstown, Cornell Univ. (Pres. Drama Soc.)
and Rennes Univ., France; began stage
career with Garry McGarry Stock Co,
Buffalo, NY, 1927, Theatre Guild 1929-31,
Group Theatre 1931-2, etc.; MGM contract
1932, inc. *Mutiny on the Bounty* (best
actor nomination) (1935), *The Lives of a
Bengal Lancer* (1935), and *Three Comrades*
(1938); returned to stage early 1950s;
also directed; *d* 18 Sep 1968 =

(4) 14 May 1956 (div. 1959), DOLORES
DORN-HEFT, actress; she = (2) 6 Aug
1967, BEN PIAZZA, stage dir.

= (2) 18 Oct 1941 (div. 1948) JEAN WALLACE
(née JEAN WALASEK), *b* 12 Oct 1923,
Chicago; blonde leading lady of US
films, da of JOHN T. WALLACE, and
Mrs MARY INGHAM (*k* in a motor acc.
1954, Hollywood)

= (2) 28 Jan 1950 (div. 1950) JIM RANDALL

= (3) 4 Sept 1951 (div. 1985) CORNEL WILDE,
b 13 Oct 1915, New York City; athletic
leading actor of Hungarian-Czech descent;
best actor nomination for *A Song to
Remember* (1945), as Frederic Chopin

= (3) 28 Sept 1951 (div. 1952) BARBARA PAYTON, ♥ TOM NEAL, *b* 28 Jan 1914, Evanston, Ill.,
b 16 Nov 1927, Cloquet, Minn.; leading
lady of Hollywood films in early 1950s;
returned to Neal after div. from Tone,
but lapsed into alcoholism & arrested
on 'morality charges' before her early
death, 8 May 1967; formerly *m* to JOHN
PAYTON (by whom she had a son); she *m*
(3) JESS RAWLEY

son of THOMAS CARROLL NEAL, banker, of
Chicago; leading man of numerous Hollywood 'B' films; ed. Northwestern Univ.; film
career plunged after widely publicized
brawl with Tone over the affections of
Miss Payton; became a landscape gardener
Palm Springs (taught by his own former
gardener); went bankrupt; charged with the
murder of his 3rd wife, GAIL EVATT (former
tennis club hostess) 1965, convicted of
involuntary manslaughter, served 7 yr prison
sentence; *d* 8 Aug 1972

PASCAL FRANCHOT TONE
(son by Jean Wallace), *b* 29 Jul 1943,
Beverly Hills, Calif.; ed. The Hill Sch.,
Univ. of S Carolina (MA), & Columbia
Univ.; MS (Management) Mass. Inst. of
Technology; sometime Pres. Franklin Coll.,
Switzerland (since when a Trustee);
Treas. & Dir. US Equestrian Team since
1981 =

24 Aug 1968, SANDRA PEIRSON COOGAN, da
of HENRY COOGAN, by his wife, ADA SIMPSON

THOMAS JEFFERSON TONE
(son by Jean Wallace), *b* 16 Sep 1945;
ed. The Hill Sch., and George Washington
Univ.; formerly with Drexel Firestone Inc.,
New York, investment bank =

(1) 8 Jul 1972, MALLORY HATHAWAY, da of
PHILLIP HATHAWAY, by his wife KATHERINE
MALLORY

(2) MOIRA LAFRAMBOISE, da of GUY LAFRAMBOISE,
of Luskville, Quebec, by his wife MARY ANNE
COULSON

CORNEL WALLACE WILDE
(son of Jean Wallace & Cornel Wilde),
b 19 Dec 1967

LESLEY COOGAN TONE,
b 1 Aug 1971

PEIRSON FRANCHOT TONE,
b 2 June 1973

THOMAS COULSON TONE,
b 17 Jul 1985

Franchot Tone and Jean Harlow in
Bombshell *(1932). He came from a*
prominent New Jersey family and was a
second cousin five times removed of Wolfe
Tone, the famous Irish patriot. Although
Tone's affray with actor Tom Neal
caused a fall from grace, his two sons have
restored the family name.

on to direct her in her last major film for MGM, *A Woman's Face* (1941). Apart from giving an excellent performance as a woman whose scarred face turns her into a criminal, this picture was significant in that it heralded a new screen role, as a repressed older woman, usually 'suffering in mink' (to use David Shipman's memorable phrase).

Cukor liked Crawford and admired her discipline. He noted the curious trust she had in the artificial eye. 'The closer the camera came the more relaxed she was, the more she showed her seductive side . . . in there she's more melting, more interesting than anything she ever showed in real life.' But despite her renewed credibility with critics and fans, the Second World War brought changes which left Crawford a part of the old regime. Both Shearer and Garbo had retired from the screen, and their places were filled by younger actresses, like Greer Garson and Lana Turner, but Crawford remained in third place in the MGM female hierarchy.

In July 1942 Joan married for the third time,

Phillip Terry, only six weeks after meeting him. Like all her other marriages this was to last a mere four years. He was a supporting actor, best known for his role as Ray Milland's brother in *The Lost Weekend* (1945).

In 1943 a more traumatic event occurred. After seventeen years MGM let her go. Two days later she signed a new deal with Warners, but, with admirable tenacity, she waited for two years before a suitable starring vehicle came along. Then she grabbed it. This was the tale of *Mildred Pierce* (1945), directed by Michael Curtiz, based on the novel by James M. Cain, which was to become one of the finest examples of the *film noir* genre. Broad-shouldered and brooding, Crawford's performance as the scorned mother of a cruel daughter was powerful and yet restrained, and – at last – won her the Best Actress Oscar for 1945.

Sadly, Joan enjoyed no such success in her private life. She divorced Terry in 1946 (later saying 'never marry out of loneliness. I owed him an apology from the first.') Her adopted daughter, Christina, recalled that within twenty-four hours of his departure, Crawford had whipped round the twenty-seven-room mansion and removed all trace of his existence – even tearing him out of photographs.

Crawford had adopted Christina in 1939, in between marriages to Tone and Terry. She was followed by a boy, Christopher, in 1943, and, finally, the so-called 'twins', Cathy and Cindy, in 1948. Undeniably, she was harsh, critical and eventually unloving towards her children. Her fixation on discipline put an intolerable pressure on both her and them; but of the four Christopher and Cathy seemed to get the worst treatment – the former because he was defiant and the latter because she was plain and overweight. This sorry story has, of course, been chronicled by Christina Crawford in her lurid book, *Mommie Dearest*, although it should be noted that the 'twins' did make a rather feeble and little-publicized attempt to clear their mother's name. Also, Crawford was not the only star to suffer estrangement from her adopted children; Mary Pickford, Barbara Stanwyck and Joan Fontaine could all claim similar failures.

In her will, written less than a year before her death, she left $77,500 each to Cathy and Cindy, all personal property to Cathy, small bequests to friends and employees, and the remainder of a $2 million estate to charities. On the last page of the document she said, 'It is my intention to make no provision herein for my son Christopher or my daughter Christina for reasons which are well known to them.'

'Glamour', 'star' and 'perfectionism' are qualities often attributed to Joan Crawford by her contemporaries. Few say they liked her or knew her well. It seems she derived most companionship from a small number of homosexual men, most of whom worked in the film industry, and from her little dogs. But it is engaging to learn that when she took friends to the theatre she would pass small cups of her 100% vodka down the line, and there are glowing references to her generosity – she gave her entire salary for *They All Kissed the Bride* (1942) to the Red Cross, who had discovered the body of her friend Carole Lombard who was killed in a plane crash in 1942.

Her 1955 marriage to Alfred Steele, chairman of Pepsi-Cola, and her promotion of that product as a member of the board, were performed with her customary zeal. Her later film roles showed a toughness, verging on savagery, culminating in that unforgettable celebration of sado-masochism, *Whatever Happened to Baby Jane?* (1962).

Significantly, after Gable, her most effective screen teamings were all with women: Shearer and Russell in *The Women*, Ann Blyth and Eve Arden in *Mildred Pierce*, Mercedes McCambridge in *Johnny Guitar* (1954), and of course Bette Davis in *Whatever Happened to Baby Jane?* Her battles with both McCambridge and Davis are well documented.

After Steele's death in 1959 she shared her time between film making and Pepsi promotion. When Pepsi sacked her, she became increasingly reclusive, her only constant communication being with her loyal fans, to whom she sent signed Christmas cards right up until 1975. She died of cancer on 10 May 1977, alone in New York. One can only wonder whether she ever allowed herself to look back over her famous padded shoulders – which twice named her 'The Most Imitated Woman in the World' – and if so, what she saw.

4 The Norma Shearer Family Circle

When in September 1927, Norma Shearer converted to Judaism and married Irving Thalberg, the brilliant young film producer, she became the uncrowned Queen of MGM. Their wedding was a prestigious affair, with decor by Cedric Gibbons, and Louis B. Mayer's daughters, Edith and Irene, were bridesmaids. Nine years later, in 1936, Thalberg died of pneumonia, aged only thirty-seven, and Miss Shearer made just five more films. She died on 12 June 1983 at the Motion Picture & Television Country Hospital, Los Angeles, the richest screen actress after Mary Pickford.

Unlike many American film stars of British extraction, Miss Shearer's Scottish ancestry can be traced with certainty to her paternal great-grandfather, Traill Shearer, whose family had worked for the Traills of Ratter, near Caithness, for many years. In the custom of the day, the Shearers had incorporated their masters' surname into their own names, and from the surname Shearer it is perfectly feasible to infer that the family were originally sheep farmers and shepherds.

As shown in table 18, Traill Shearer met an unfortunate end when he fell to his death from a farm wagon. Perhaps disillusioned by the lack of opportunity offered to the average tenant farmer by the feudal system, the entire family decided to seek their fortune in the New World. They emigrated to Montreal in 1843, where the elder son, James, founded a prosperous lumber business. His two elder sons went into the family company and all his five daughters made well-heeled marriages.

The second son, Andrew Shearer, a lumber merchant and architect, lost his fortune after the First World War, and his wife took their two daughters, Athole (born 20 November 1900) and Norma (born 10 August 1902) to New York in the hope of establishing them as show girls (the trip was partially financed by them selling the family dog and piano). Mrs Shearer rented a $7.50-a-week room, and Norma found a job seeling sheet-music and played the piano in a small 8th Avenue movie theatre. Norma also earned $5-a-day sitting for artists James Montgomery Flagg and Charles Dana Gibson, and became 'Miss Lotta Miles' for the Kelly-Springfield tyre company's advertising campaign.

Norma worked as an extra in D.W. Griffith's *Way Down East* (1920), and in *The Flapper* (1920), with Olive Thomas. In 1923 her fortunes changed when her agent managed to get her an interview with Irving Thalberg, who spotted her in *The Stealers* (1921), as a clergyman's daughter. Thalberg was then working for Carl Laemmle at Universal; his sickly appearance (his stature was bolstered by padded shoulders) belied his powerful influence in the film industry, and he was soon to become the 'boy-genius' at the Mayer studio. Thalberg gave Shearer a five-year contract at $150 a week, and she arrived in California, with her mother and sister, early in 1923.

Never a great actress, Shearer's natural poise and good looks impressed Thalberg and, despite Louis B. Mayer's opposition, he was determined to star her in their most expensive productions. She was a perfect subject for Thalberg's grooming, and she not only learnt to select her film roles with great care, but also acquired a flair

for knowing exactly what lighting would show her at her best advantage. In Lillian Hellman's opinion, however, Norma had 'a face unclouded by thought'. Between 1927 (the year of her marriage to Thalberg) and 1930 her salary rose from $1,000 a week to $6,000 a week, and in 1932 she took US citizenship.

Norma Shearer's career in silent films was carefully built around 'sophisticated' roles and made her a good second-grade star. Thalberg's implicit trust in the star system inspired him to handle her subsequent career in talkies with such skill it became an object lesson in the triumph of marketing over ability. In her first all-talkie, *The Trial of Mary Dugan* (1929), she was shrewdly cast against type as a brassy showgirl, and her success in the new medium launched her in the 1930s into a series of ultra-stylish dramas and comedies.

Among her most successful films of the 1930s were: *The Divorcée* (1930), for which she won a Best Actress Oscar, *A Free Soul* (1931), *Private Lives* (Noël Coward's classic comedy opposite Robert Montgomery), *Riptide* (1934), *The Barretts of Wimpole Street* (as Elizabeth Barrett, with Fredric March as Browning), and *Romeo and Juliet* (1936). Her son Irving Thalberg Jr was born in 1930, and her daughter Katharine, who was named for Emily Brontë's heroine in 'Wuthering Heights', was born in 1935.

Norma's wedding of 1927 was followed by a remarkable series of family marriages which connected some of the brightest young names of Hollywood's 'Golden Era'. In March 1928 Athole Shearer married Howard Hawks, the film director; earlier that year Kenneth Hawks had married Mary Astor, a wonderfully versatile actress, well remembered as the treacherous Brigid O'Shaughnessy in *The Maltese Falcon* (1941); and the youngest brother William Hawks in 1929 married Bessie Love, another remarkable actress who lived in London for many years, and whose career stretched from the pioneer days of the silent films right up to *Ragtime* (1981).

Norma Shearer's brother, Douglas, who had remained in Canada with his father, came to his sister's wedding to give her away. He subsequently joined the MGM studio and became a renowned sound technician.

TABLE 18 NORMA SHEARER'S ANCESTRY AND FAMILY

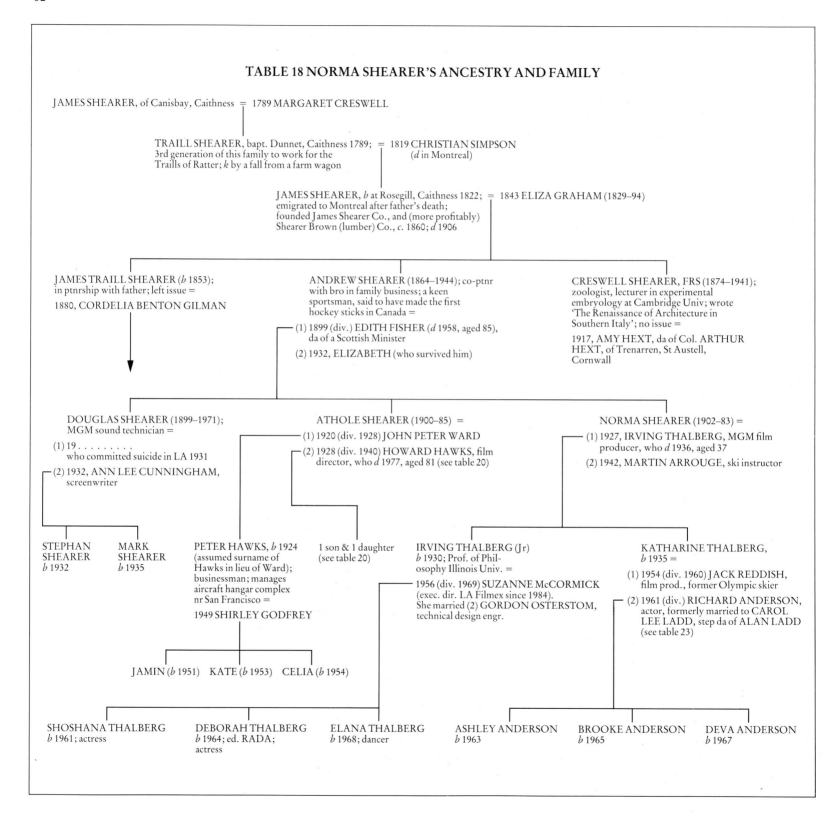

JAMES SHEARER, of Canisbay, Caithness = 1789 MARGARET CRESWELL

TRAILL SHEARER, bapt. Dunnet, Caithness 1789; = 1819 CHRISTIAN SIMPSON
3rd generation of this family to work for the (d in Montreal)
Traills of Ratter; k by a fall from a farm wagon

JAMES SHEARER, b at Rosegill, Caithness 1822; = 1843 ELIZA GRAHAM (1829–94)
emigrated to Montreal after father's death;
founded James Shearer Co., and (more profitably)
Shearer Brown (lumber) Co., c. 1860; d 1906

JAMES TRAILL SHEARER (b 1853);
in ptnrship with father; left issue =

1880, CORDELIA BENTON GILMAN

ANDREW SHEARER (1864–1944); co-ptnr
with bro in family business; a keen
sportsman, said to have made the first
hockey sticks in Canada =

(1) 1899 (div.) EDITH FISHER (d 1958, aged 85),
da of a Scottish Minister

(2) 1932, ELIZABETH (who survived him)

CRESWELL SHEARER, FRS (1874–1941);
zoologist, lecturer in experimental
embryology at Cambridge Univ; wrote
'The Renaissance of Architecture in
Southern Italy'; no issue =

1917, AMY HEXT, da of Col. ARTHUR
HEXT, of Trenarren, St Austell,
Cornwall

DOUGLAS SHEARER (1899–1971);
MGM sound technician =

(1) 19 . . . .
who committed suicide in LA 1931

(2) 1932, ANN LEE CUNNINGHAM,
screenwriter

ATHOLE SHEARER (1900–85) =

(1) 1920 (div. 1928) JOHN PETER WARD

(2) 1928 (div. 1940) HOWARD HAWKS, film
director, who d 1977, aged 81 (see table 20)

NORMA SHEARER (1902–83) =

(1) 1927, IRVING THALBERG, MGM film
producer, who d 1936, aged 37

(2) 1942, MARTIN ARROUGE, ski instructor

STEPHAN
SHEARER
b 1932

MARK
SHEARER
b 1935

PETER HAWKS, b 1924
(assumed surname of
Hawks in lieu of Ward);
businessman; manages
aircraft hangar complex
nr San Francisco =

1949 SHIRLEY GODFREY

1 son & 1 daughter
(see table 20)

IRVING THALBERG (Jr)
b 1930; Prof. of Phil-
osophy Illinois Univ. =

1956 (div. 1969) SUZANNE McCORMICK
(exec. dir. LA Filmex since 1984).
She married (2) GORDON OSTERSTOM,
technical design engr.

KATHARINE THALBERG,
b 1935 =

(1) 1954 (div. 1960) JACK REDDISH,
film prod., former Olympic skier

(2) 1961 (div.) RICHARD ANDERSON,
actor, formerly married to CAROL
LEE LADD, step da of ALAN LADD
(see table 23)

JAMIN (b 1951)   KATE (b 1953)   CELIA (b 1954)

SHOSHANA THALBERG
b 1961; actress

DEBORAH THALBERG
b 1964; ed. RADA;
actress

ELANA THALBERG
b 1968; dancer

ASHLEY ANDERSON
b 1963

BROOKE ANDERSON
b 1965

DEVA ANDERSON
b 1967

Norma Shearer and Clarke Gable in Idiot's Delight *(1939). Shearer's blonde wig was a simple affair in comparison to her head-dress in* Marie Antoinette *(1938), the cast of which film required a staff of 115 hairdressers.*

Thalberg's death left Shearer in a vulnerable position, but she signed a new three-year contract with MGM at $150,000 per film. Of these, *Marie Antoinette* (1938) and Clare Booth Luce's gem *The Women* (1939), were the most notable. In 1942, the year her last film, *Her Cardboard Lover*, was released, she married Martin Arrouge, a ski instructor twenty years her junior. To the surprise of the Hollywood gossip factory the marriage was a success. After Miss Shearer's death, Mr Arrouge married her nurse, a union that had Norma's blessing.

Miss Shearer was survived by both her children, and also six granddaughters, one of whom, Deborah Thalberg, quietly spoken and self-contained, bears a striking physical resemblance to Norma. Deborah was trained at RADA (London), and made her screen début in *Class* (1983), which starred Jacqueline Bisset.

5 Howard Hawks and Mary Astor

HOWARD HAWKS

Born on 30 May 1896, Goschen, Indiana, eldest son of Frank Winchester Hawks, a wealthy lumberman, by his wife Helen, daughter of Charles W. Howard. He had two younger brothers, Kenneth and William Hawks, and two sisters, one of whom died in infancy, and the other, Grace, who died in childhood from eating poisonous berries. Hawks moved with his family to Pasadena, California, *c* 1906; he was educated at the Philips–Exeter Academy, Massachusetts, and Cornell University, where he studied mechanical engineering. He was an enthusiastic car and plane racer from the age of sixteen, and was still tearing about on motor cycles in the desert near his home when in his seventies.

Hawks served in the First World War as a pilot with the Army Air Corps, and after his discharge worked in an aircraft factory designing and flying planes. Going to Hollywood, he served a varied apprenticeship from film cutter to story editor and casting director. In 1925 he sold a story to Fox, *The Road to Glory* (1926), on the condition that he would direct it, and his career as one of Hollywood's most successful and versatile directors began.

His first marriage, 30 March 1928, to Athole Shearer, Norma Shearer's elder sister, brought him into close contact with Irving Thalberg, MGM's head of production. Although exactly three years younger than Hawks, Thalberg did not have his robust health, and he was anxious to make Hawks his chief production aid at MGM. With characteristic independence Hawks declined this offer, being aware of Louis B. Mayer's overpowering influence, and kept his distance.

The career of Howard Hawks stretched from 1925 to 1970 and included first-rate films of every possible genre, all accomplished with equal flair: westerns, gangsters, thrillers, screwball comedy and musicals. He was a classicist, to whom the plot was of first importance, and he eschewed the avant-garde. He is most identified with tough, male-dominated stories: *Scarface* (1932), with George Raft, *Sergeant York* (1941), with Gary Cooper, *To Have and Have Not* (1944) and *The Big Sleep* (1946), both with Humphrey Bogart, *Red River* (1948) and *Rio Bravo* (1959), both with John Wayne. But his comedies were also of exceptional calibre, notably *Bringing Up Baby* (1938), with Cary Grant and Katharine Hepburn, *His Girl Friday* (1940), with Cary Grant and Rosalind Russell, *I Was a Male War Bride* (1949), with Cary Grant and Ann Sheridan, and *Gentlemen Prefer Blondes* (1953), with Marilyn Monroe and Jane Russell.

Although his first wife, Athole, suffered chronic ill-health, they had two children: David Hawks, born in 1929, and Barbara, born on 20 May 1936. In December 1940 Norma Shearer won a divorce for her indisposed sister by proxy (on grounds of Hawks' desertion), and also won for her the custody of the children. Athole Hawks died on 17 March 1985, aged eighty-four. Her son David Hawks is a freelance unit production engineer, and was assistant director on the long running TV series M*A*S*H. Barbara Hawks was credited (as B.H. McCampbell) with the story for *Rio Bravo*.

Ten days after his divorce became absolute, Hawks married secondly, 10 December 1941 (at his parents' house in Pasadena), Nancy Gross, a beautiful twenty-four-year-old screenwriter from California (known as Slim), daughter of Edward B. Gross, of Monterey, California, by his wife, Raye Nell Boyer. Gary Cooper gave the bride away. This marriage lasted until 1948, when they were divorced, and Nancy Hawks married Leland Hayward (see table 6) the following year.

By Nancy, Howard Hawks had a second daughter, Kitty Hawks, born on 11 February 1946. She was only two years old when her parents divorced, and she was raised on the Hayward estate in Manhasset, Long Island, with her step-siblings, Brooke, Bridget and William Hayward. Her father had little contact with her until she was about seventeen.

Kitty Hawks was educated at Westover School, Middlebury, Connecticut, and Smith College (graduated in political science 1967). She went out to California and was engaged to William Friedkin, the director for two years. Breaking with him, she returned to New York, and, in 1972, was named on the International Best Dressed List (taking after her mother). In 1972 she worked for David Susskind as an assistant film producer, and then as an agent for ICM.

In 1976 Kitty Hawks married Ned Tanen, then President of Universal Pictures, where he was responsible for several outstanding films during his ten-year office, including, *American Graffiti* (1974), *Taking Off* (1971), *Missing* (1982), and *ET* (1982). This marriage was dissolved by divorce in 1983.

Early in 1953 Hawks announced his engagement to Marian Marshall, a starlet, but she married Stanley Donen instead (followed ten years later by Robert Wagner), and Hawks married thirdly, 20 February 1953, in Hollywood, Dee Hartford, aged about twenty-six, a very thin New York model, of Mormon stock. By her he had a youngest child, Gregg Hawks, born 1953, who has inherited his father's passion for speed on wheels. This marriage too failed, and Hawks was divorced in 1960. Through Dee Hawks's subsequent marriage to Stu-

art Cramer, further interesting links are forged in the film world, notably to Howard Hughes, whose wife Jean Peters was previously married to Cramer, and also to Grant Cramer, muscular and moody star of an American soap opera, who is Cramer's son by his second wife, Terry Moore (who also claims to have been married to Howard Hughes see table 21).

Howard Hawks discussing the script of Gentlemen Prefer Blondes (1953) with Marilyn Monroe. His elder son works in television and his younger son has inherited Hawks's reputation as a racing driver.

TABLE 19 THE HAWKS DYNASTY (I)

ADAM HAWKS, emigrated from England with his   (said to be brothers, but not proven)   JOHN HAWKS, MA, of Hadley, Mass.,
family to USA 1630 with the Winthrop fleet   & Windsor, Conn.; freeman of General
Court of Massachusetts Bay
Colony 1634; *d* 1662

ELIEZER HAWKS, *b* 20 Dec 1655, of Hadley; fought at Falls in Philip's War   =   JUDITH, da of WILLIAM SNEAD, by his wife
1676; later of Deerfield, Mass., where he was a church warden   ELIZABETH LAWRENCE

ELEAZER HAWKS (eldest son); *b* 26 Dec 1693; settled at Wapping, Deerfield;   =   1714, ABIGAIL, da of EPHRAIM WELLS, by his
later bought 500 acres in Charlemont on both sides of Deerfield river   wife ABIGAIL ALLIS, of New London, Conn.

PAUL HAWKS (younger son); bapt. 7 Nov 1736; remained on father's farm;   =   LOIS, da of MOSES WAIT
his elder brothers settled at Charlemont *c.* 1750, & founded Hawks's Fort;
served in French Wars

CEPHAS HAWKS (3rd son); *b* 1 Nov 1773; moved to Ontario County, New York   =   CHLOE CASE (*d* 25 Dec 1853)
c. 1790, then to Washenau County, Mich., & finally settled at Goschen, Ind.
1838; bought land, founded village of Waterford & established a small
manufacturing community; *d* 18 May 1859

ELEAZER HAWKS (5th son); *b* 24 Dec 1818   =   (3) 1 Oct 1863, JEANNIE GOFF

FRANK WINCHESTER HAWKS (only son); *b* 16 Oct 1864, Goschen, Ind.; in lumber   =   HELEN HOWARD (*d* 27 Aug 1952, aged 81), da of
& paper manufacturing business, Neeh Bay, Wis.; later moved to Pasadena, Calif.   CHARLES W. HOWARD, of Mass.

(see table 20)

TABLE 20 THE HAWKS DYNASTY (II)

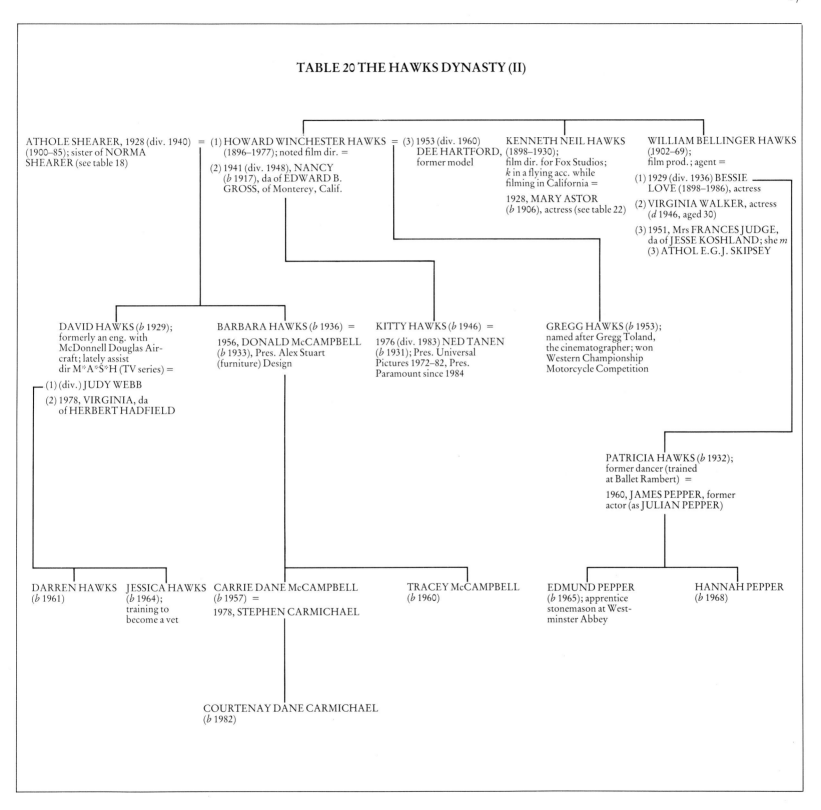

ATHOLE SHEARER, 1928 (div. 1940)
(1900–85); sister of NORMA
SHEARER (see table 18)

= (1) HOWARD WINCHESTER HAWKS
(1896–1977); noted film dir. =

(2) 1941 (div. 1948), NANCY
(b 1917), da of EDWARD B.
GROSS, of Monterey, Calif.

= (3) 1953 (div. 1960)
DEE HARTFORD,
former model

KENNETH NEIL HAWKS
(1898–1930);
film dir. for Fox Studios;
k in a flying acc. while
filming in California =

1928, MARY ASTOR
(b 1906), actress (see table 22)

WILLIAM BELLINGER HAWKS
(1902–69);
film prod.; agent =

(1) 1929 (div. 1936) BESSIE
LOVE (1898–1986), actress

(2) VIRGINIA WALKER, actress
(d 1946, aged 30)

(3) 1951, Mrs FRANCES JUDGE,
da of JESSE KOSHLAND; she m
(3) ATHOL E.G.J. SKIPSEY

DAVID HAWKS (b 1929);
formerly an eng. with
McDonnell Douglas Air-
craft; lately assist
dir M*A*S*H (TV series) =

(1) (div.) JUDY WEBB

(2) 1978, VIRGINIA, da
of HERBERT HADFIELD

BARBARA HAWKS (b 1936) =

1956, DONALD McCAMPBELL
(b 1933), Pres. Alex Stuart
(furniture) Design

KITTY HAWKS (b 1946) =

1976 (div. 1983) NED TANEN
(b 1931); Pres. Universal
Pictures 1972–82, Pres.
Paramount since 1984

GREGG HAWKS (b 1953);
named after Gregg Toland,
the cinematographer; won
Western Championship
Motorcycle Competition

PATRICIA HAWKS (b 1932);
former dancer (trained
at Ballet Rambert) =

1960, JAMES PEPPER, former
actor (as JULIAN PEPPER)

DARREN HAWKS
(b 1961)

JESSICA HAWKS
(b 1964);
training to
become a vet

CARRIE DANE McCAMPBELL
(b 1957) =

1978, STEPHEN CARMICHAEL

TRACEY McCAMPBELL
(b 1960)

EDMUND PEPPER
(b 1965); apprentice
stonemason at West-
minster Abbey

HANNAH PEPPER
(b 1968)

COURTENAY DANE CARMICHAEL
(b 1982)

TABLE 21 THE HOWARD HAWKS MARRIAGE WEB

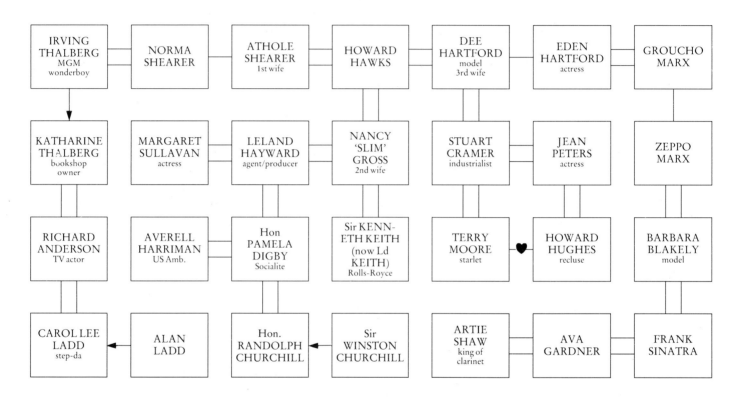

See page 7 for key to symbols.

Howard Hawks was awarded an honorary Oscar for his cumulative work at the Awards ceremony for 1974. He died in December 1977, aged eighty-one.

KENNETH HAWKS
Younger brother of Howard Hawks

Second son of Frank Winchester Hawks, born 12 August 1898, Goschen, Indiana; educated at Cornell University; enlisted in U S Army Air Force February 1918, and was honourably discharged after the Armistice was signed. He then went to Yale, where he was captain of the tennis team, and held the inter-scholastic doubles championship title.

After graduating, Hawks began a career in films as an assistant director at Paramount, then he transferred to Fox; first as a production supervisor, and later as a director. His only complete production was *Big Time* (1929), with Mae Clarke and Stepin Fetchit for when he was filming the retakes for *Such Men Are Dangerous* (1930), his aeroplane collided with another carrying the technical crew. All were killed in the accident, which occurred on 2 January 1930, at Point Vincente, California, over the Pacific Ocean. He had married on 23 February 1928, Mary Astor, and had no children.

WILLIAM HAWKS
Youngest brother of Howard Hawks

Third and youngest son of Frank Winchester Hawks, born 1902, Goschen, Indiana, and educated at Yale. He was an actors' agent before turning to producing at Metro and, later, 20th Century Fox. His films include *The Tall Men* (1955), *Imitation General* (1958), and *The Last Wagon* (1960).

He married first, 27 December 1929 (divorced 1936), Bessie Love, actress, by whom he had a daughter, Patricia; secondly, Virginia Walker, also an actress, who died in 1946; and thirdly, 3 October 1951, Mrs Frances Koshland Judge, daughter of Jesse Koshland.

He died on 10 January 1969, in Santa Monica, following a respiratory illness.

BESSIE LOVE
First wife of William Hawks

Born Juanita Horton on 10 September 1898, in Midland, Texas, the daughter of John Cross Horton and his wife Emma Jane Savage. She was tiny, spirited and very pretty, and showed great promise as Douglas Fairbanks Sr's leading lady in *Reggie Mixes In* (1916), and as the Bride of Cana in the Judean episode of Griffith's *Intolerance* (1916). Sadly, she was frequently miscast in many routine vehicles, which chequered her career in the years of silent films, but she made a sensational sound début in the 1929 musical *The Broadway Melody*, proving herself an excellent singer and dancer, and was nominated for an Oscar.

In 1936, after her divorce from William Hawks, she took her daughter to London, where they stayed ever since. She frequently performed in British plays and films, notably as Aunt Pittypat in the 1972–3 stage version of 'Gone With the Wind'.

She died suddenly in hospital on 26 April 1986, aged eighty-seven.

MARY ASTOR
Wife of Kenneth Hawks

Mary Astor will always be remembered by film historians for three especially fine performances; on screen in *The Maltese Falcon* and *The Great Lie*, and in real life on the witness stand in a Los Angeles courtroom in 1935.

Born on 3 May 1906, Quincy, Illinois, as Lucile Langhanke, she was the daughter of a German immigrant and his American–Portuguese wife. This fairly unusual ancestry contributed to Mary Astor's beautiful appearance, and her dark auburn hair and pale complexion gave her face an ethereal quality seldom seen in the brash days of young Hollywood. But her gentle looks concealed a marked sexual appetite which was eventually to help cause one of the most bitter divorce and child-custody battles ever to come to court.

Her father, Otto Langhanke, a teacher, cherished a desire to see his only child a star in the mould of

Mary Pickford. In her book, *A Life on Film*, Astor describes him as 'ambitious, intense, [with] a great deal of Prussian pompousness, a longing for luxury, a deep appreciation of beauty ... cold in his family relationship.' He encouraged her to enter a beauty contest when she was fourteen, and succeeded in getting her a film role the following year. Her status leapt when she was chosen for her beauty by John Barrymore as his leading lady in *Beau Brummel* (1924). Barrymore, then aged forty-one, was finding his marriage to the eccentric Blanche Oelrichs less than blissful, and he proceded to seduce the eighteen-year-old *ingénue*. Their affair was passionate but brief – like all Barrymore's loves – but it gave Mary Astor her first taste of warmth and affection. She went on to another liaison, this time with John Monk Saunders, a Hollywood scenarist, who later married Fay Wray and unhappily hanged himself in his Florida beach cottage, aged forty-two.

Longing to escape the domination of her parents, Mary Astor married Kenneth Hawks (February 1928), and joined a close circle of family and friends who were to exert considerable influence on Hollywood films over the next decade and beyond. 'My marriage to Ken Hawks had rainbows around it,' she later wrote, 'he had values that have become extinct.' His tragic death in an aeroplane crash, while filming, only two years later must have been hard to bear, particularly as Astor had a pretty low opinion of the vast majority of films that were then being made. She became ill and was without funds, but she was also a realist and knew that work was her only option.

Over the next two years she made approximately fourteen films, notably *Red Dust* (1932), in which she was a well-bred recently married woman, drawn to lustful Clark Gable in the tropics. RKO offered her a starring contract, which she refused, 'because starring was one hell of a gamble ... [whereas] I could go on more or less hiding in feature roles, working consistently, and not being responsible for the product.' Having said that, Mary Astor well knew she was far too subtle and chic ever to be lost among the supporting players.

In 1931 Mary Astor married Dr Franklyn Thorpe, who had attended her during her illness. Their daughter Marylyn was born in Honolulu the following year. In 1933 she gave herself a well-earned break in New York, where she met Bennett Cerf, the publisher (see table 25), and George Kaufman, the playwright. The weeks of freedom and stimulation were a thrilling change from Hollywood, and she enjoyed a 'romantic interlude' with Kaufman. On returning home Mary became dissatisfied with the routine life of film-making, and, unhappy in her marriage (her husband was allegedly spending much of his time with Busby Berkeley girls), continued her affair with Kaufman. Thorpe initiated divorce proceedings in April 1935, which would have gone through the legal sausage factory quite quietly had he not also decided to sue for custody of their daughter.

Mary Astor, of course, initiated a counter suit, and at that point she discovered her diary was missing – and that it was to be used in evidence against her. The newspapers sensed a high-level Hollywood scandal was about to break and printed purple passages which were described as extracts from the diary. According to Mary Astor, she and her lawyer were summoned to a meeting with all the studio heads, Goldwyn, Mayer, Thalberg, Warner and Cohn, who 'had heard of or had seen certain pages in the diary that contained descriptions of sexual acts with almost every well-known actor in the business, with a box score of performance. All I could say was that it just wasn't true, and if there were such pages they had to be a forgery. I was not believed, naturally.'

During the build-up to the trial Mary Astor was filming *Dodsworth* (1936), directed by William Wyler, and starring Walter Huston, Ruth Chatterton and Paul Lukas, in which Astor had a sympathetic role as the widow to whom Huston returns from his impossible wife. In her memoirs, Astor says it was thanks to her work on the composed character of Edith Cortright that she was able to conduct herself so calmly throughout the trial. She must indeed have made a striking figure in the dock, tall for Hollywood female stars at that time (at 5ft 5in), cool, quietly spoken, and immaculate in a

Mary Astor flanked by Philip Dorn and Gloria Grahame in Blonde Fever (*1944*). *Astor's demure image was never quite the same after the alleged 'extracts' from her diary were leaked to the press during her courtroom battle for the custody of her daughter in 1936, which created one of the biggest Hollywood scandals of the decade.*

black, tailored suit. The verdict was that Marylyn should spend six months with each parent; the diary was destroyed.

Fifty years later one can only guess at what the diary contained, but judging from her own writings it would seem probable her relationship with Kaufman was certainly more than a 'romantic interlude' – at least on her side – but equally improbable that a woman of her calibre would spend hours writing up every detail of her extra-marital sex life, or leave the damning document lying about for any member of the household to read. The fact that Thorpe was

prepared to let (or even to suggest) that the diary should be used in evidence does not reflect well on him.

It comes as a pleasant surprise to find that Marylyn Thorpe, despite her parents' bitter combat and her divided childhood, has led an adult life of rare stability. She married in 1950, Frank Roh (to whom she is still married), and has four children and ten grandchildren. She is a certified handwriting expert, a pillar of the Mormon Church, and has made some impressive research into her father's ancestry (see table 22).

TABLE 22 THE ANCESTRY AND DESCENDANTS OF MARY ASTOR, WIFE OF KENNETH HAWKS

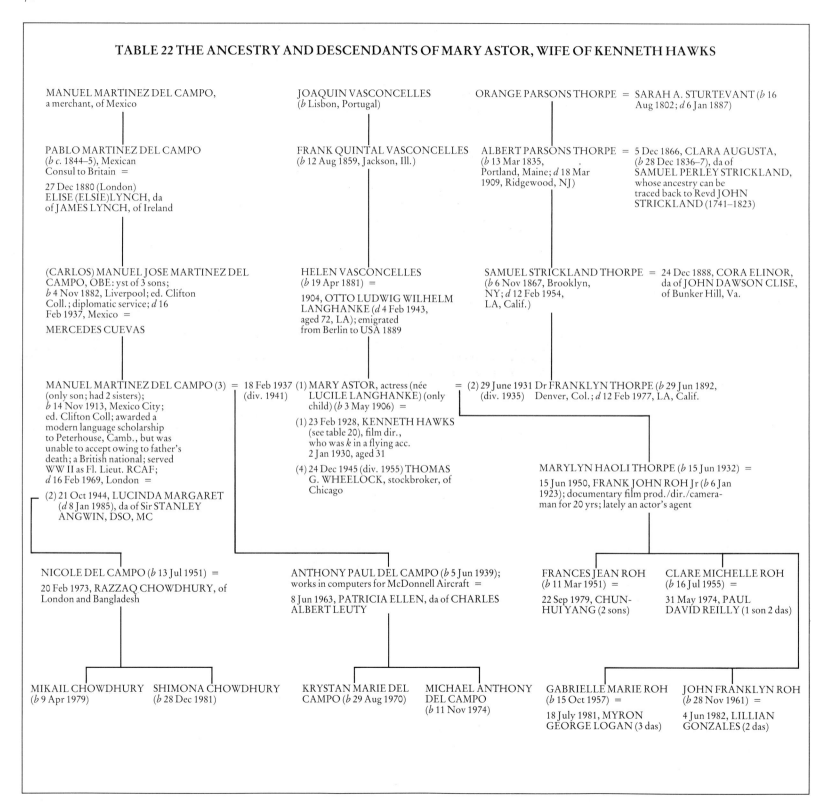

MANUEL MARTINEZ DEL CAMPO,
a merchant, of Mexico

JOAQUIN VASCONCELLES
(*b* Lisbon, Portugal)

ORANGE PARSONS THORPE = SARAH A. STURTEVANT (*b* 16 Aug 1802; *d* 6 Jan 1887)

PABLO MARTINEZ DEL CAMPO
(*b c.* 1844–5), Mexican
Consul to Britain =

27 Dec 1880 (London)
ELISE (ELSIE) LYNCH, da
of JAMES LYNCH, of Ireland

FRANK QUINTAL VASCONCELLES
(*b* 12 Aug 1859, Jackson, Ill.)

ALBERT PARSONS THORPE =
(*b* 13 Mar 1835,
Portland, Maine; *d* 18 Mar
1909, Ridgewood, NJ)

5 Dec 1866, CLARA AUGUSTA,
(*b* 28 Dec 1836–7), da of
SAMUEL PERLEY STRICKLAND,
whose ancestry can be
traced back to Revd JOHN
STRICKLAND (1741–1823)

(CARLOS) MANUEL JOSE MARTINEZ DEL
CAMPO, OBE: yst of 3 sons;
b 4 Nov 1882, Liverpool; ed. Clifton
Coll.; diplomatic service; *d* 16
Feb 1937, Mexico =

MERCEDES CUEVAS

HELEN VASCONCELLES
(*b* 19 Apr 1881) =

1904, OTTO LUDWIG WILHELM
LANGHANKE (*d* 4 Feb 1943,
aged 72, LA); emigrated
from Berlin to USA 1889

SAMUEL STRICKLAND THORPE =
(*b* 6 Nov 1867, Brooklyn,
NY; *d* 12 Feb 1954,
LA, Calif.)

24 Dec 1888, CORA ELINOR,
da of JOHN DAWSON CLISE,
of Bunker Hill, Va.

MANUEL MARTINEZ DEL CAMPO (3) =
(only son; had 2 sisters);
b 14 Nov 1913, Mexico City;
ed. Clifton Coll; awarded a
modern language scholarship
to Peterhouse, Camb., but was
unable to accept owing to father's
death; a British national; served
WW II as Fl. Lieut. RCAF;
d 16 Feb 1969, London =

(2) 21 Oct 1944, LUCINDA MARGARET
(*d* 8 Jan 1985), da of Sir STANLEY
ANGWIN, DSO, MC

18 Feb 1937
(div. 1941)

(1) MARY ASTOR, actress (née
LUCILE LANGHANKE) (only
child) (*b* 3 May 1906) =

(1) 23 Feb 1928, KENNETH HAWKS
(see table 20), film dir.,
who was *k* in a flying acc.
2 Jan 1930, aged 31

(4) 24 Dec 1945 (div. 1955) THOMAS
G. WHEELOCK, stockbroker, of
Chicago

= (2) 29 June 1931
(div. 1935)

Dr FRANKLYN THORPE (*b* 29 Jun 1892,
Denver, Col.; *d* 12 Feb 1977, LA, Calif.

MARYLYN HAOLI THORPE (*b* 15 Jun 1932) =

15 Jun 1950, FRANK JOHN ROH Jr (*b* 6 Jan
1923); documentary film prod./dir./camera-
man for 20 yrs; lately an actor's agent

NICOLE DEL CAMPO (*b* 13 Jul 1951) =

20 Feb 1973, RAZZAQ CHOWDHURY, of
London and Bangladesh

ANTHONY PAUL DEL CAMPO (*b* 5 Jun 1939);
works in computers for McDonnell Aircraft =

8 Jun 1963, PATRICIA ELLEN, da of CHARLES
ALBERT LEUTY

FRANCES JEAN ROH
(*b* 11 Mar 1951) =

22 Sep 1979, CHUN-
HUI YANG (2 sons)

CLARE MICHELLE ROH
(*b* 16 Jul 1955) =

31 May 1974, PAUL
DAVID REILLY (1 son 2 das)

MIKAIL CHOWDHURY
(*b* 9 Apr 1979)

SHIMONA CHOWDHURY
(*b* 28 Dec 1981)

KRYSTAN MARIE DEL
CAMPO (*b* 29 Aug 1970)

MICHAEL ANTHONY
DEL CAMPO
(*b* 11 Nov 1974)

GABRIELLE MARIE ROH
(*b* 15 Oct 1957) =

18 July 1981, MYRON
GEORGE LOGAN (3 das)

JOHN FRANKLYN ROH
(*b* 28 Nov 1961) =

4 Jun 1982, LILLIAN
GONZALES (2 das)

To Mary Astor's lasting credit, the scandal did not diminish her film career in any way (her health took the brunt), and the public at large admired her guts. After a period of recuperation she went into the *Prisoner of Zenda* (1937), with Ronald Colman and Douglas Fairbanks Jr, and then joined Bramwell Fletcher for the Noël Coward cycle of one-act plays, 'Tonight at 8.30', at the Biltmore Theater, Los Angeles. In December 1940 Bette Davis asked for Astor to co-star with her in *The Great Lie* (1941). They got on extremely well, and both women worked hard on the feeble plot and created a character of pure poison for Mary Astor, whose finely judged performance eventually won her a Best Supporting Actress Oscar. From this success she went on to a picture which became a legend, *The Maltese Falcon* (1941), directed by John Huston, starring Humphrey Bogart. Astor was (in the words of David Shipman), 'the lovely, frightened Brigid O'Shaughnessy, the prototype of all frail ladies who turn out to be two-faced and lethal.'

Through her English friend, Auriol Lee, a theatre director, Astor met Manuel del Campo, a cultivated young (seven years her junior) Mexican, who was one of Ruth Chatterton's acolytes with thespian pretensions. He and Astor were married in 1937. As Michael Field he did one or two bits in 'B' films, but soon went to MGM as a film editor. He had many associations with Britain, and when war was declared in 1939 he immediately enlisted with the RCAF, who trained him, and went back to Britain to fight. His wife and their infant son, Anthony, born in 1939, stayed behind. In London he fell in love with another woman, and he and Astor divorced in 1941. He stayed in London, where he worked as a film editor on TV series such as 'The Avengers', and died aged fifty-six, having married thirdly, in 1960, Christine Perry.

Astor accepted a long-term contract with MGM, but although seven years of financial security were more than welcome, the type-casting MGM went in for was not. 'My *femme fatale* image of the Diary days went right down the Culver City drain,' she wrote. She was everyone's mother, most memorably Judy Garland's in *Meet Me in St Louis* (1944), and Elizabeth Taylor, June Allyson, Margaret O'Brien and Janet Leigh's in *Little Women* (1949) (the latter was an experience she found utterly demoralizing).

She married for the fourth and last time in 1945 (divorced 1955), Thomas Wheelock, whose grandfather had held the Chair of Literature at Harvard. In her two autobiographical books *My Story* (1959), and *A Life on Film* (1971) – both as well written and as informed as any film book – she tells candidly of her drinking problems (which started shortly after her diary débâcle), and her attempt at suicide. After a long and painful fight she recovered her self-confidence and continued to turn out more excellent work on stage, TV, and, occasionally, film. She was last seen on film in *Hush Hush . . . Sweet Charlotte* (1964), directed by Robert Aldrich. Astor was the little old murderess, Jewel Mayhew. On the first day of shooting, Bette Davis, with characteristic command said to the director, 'Turn her loose Robert, you might learn something!'

Mary Astor now lives at the Motion Picture Country Home in Calabasas, in poor health as the result of a stroke, but still, according to her daughter, as bright as ever.

6 Alan Ladd and Family

Of all the Hollywood dynasties there is none to equal that of the Ladds for its widespread and continuing influence in the film industry. Although an 'instant' dynasty – they have no theatrical inheritance – their web of blood, marriage and divorce connections bring together some of the most powerful names and studios of the time.

Figuratively speaking we have Alan Ladd, the film star, as the head of the family with his wife Sue Carol, a successful agent. Then his son by a former marriage, Alan Ladd Jr, who has been successively President of 20th Century Fox, his own Ladd Company, and, most recently, MGM/United Artists Entertainment Corporation. He is responsible for *Star Wars* (1977), *Body Heat* (1982), *Julia* (1977), *The Turning Point* (1977), *3 Women* (1977) and many more successful and innovative films.

Alan Ladd's step-daughter, Carol, was married first to Richard Anderson, who subsequently married Irving Thalberg's daughter. Carol's second (and present) husband, John Veitch, was in charge of production at Columbia, and is now an independent producer. The President of Columbia, Guy McElwaine, was formerly married to Leigh Taylor Young, the actress, whose sister, Dey, is now married to David Ladd. David Ladd is the younger son of Alan Ladd, and works for John Veitch.

David Ladd's ex-wife is Cheryl Ladd, the former Charlie's Angel, and Leigh Taylor Young was first married to Ryan O'Neal, father of Tatum, and live-in lover of Farrah Fawcett. This complex web is illustrated on table 23.

The founder of the dynasty was born Alan Walbridge Ladd on 3 September 1913, in Hot Springs, Arkansas. He was the only child of another Alan Ladd, a freelance accountant of American/Scots ancestry, by his wife Ina Raleigh. Ina is said to have been born in Chester, England, according to Ladd's biographer, Beverly Linet, but there is no trace of her birth certificate. It is more likely she was born in West Chester, Pennsylvania.

Alan Ladd senior died when his son was four years old, and Ina married again, to one James Beavers, a house-painter. The family then moved to Oklahoma City, and later to San Fernando Valley, California. Work was hard to find for James Beavers and the family was continually on the breadline. Alan was sent to the North Hollywood High School, where he achieved little in the way of academic honours, but excelled at sport – despite his short stature, 5ft 5in – notably at swimming and diving.

After leaving school, Ladd was accepted by the Universal Studios School – under Carl Laemmle – on a 'provisional trial contract', but he was dropped after four months. He was employed as a grip (handyman) at Warners for $4.50 a week, and at the same time sold advertising space for a newspaper and owned a hot-dog stand (known as 'Tiny's Patio'). He enrolled at the Ben Bard School of Acting. In spite of being twenty-three and virtually destitute, he impetuously married, in October 1936, Midge Harrold, the twenty-one-year-old daughter of an insurance agent. Their son, Alan Ladd Jr, was born in 1937. James Beavers having died in 1933, Ina moved in with her son and his wife which only increased their difficulties. This ended in the tragedy of her suicide by drinking ant poison.

The Ladd family is an example of a Hollywood phenomenon, the 'instant dynasty'. Alan Ladd (pictured) was one of the top stars of the 1940s, and his elder son has been successively president of 20th Century Fox, the Ladd Company and MGM/United Artists Entertainment Corporation.

Alan Ladd's career took off after he was spotted by a former actress-turned-agent, Sue Carol, in 1938. This dynamic woman quickly became the power behind both his personal and professional lives, but it took her four years to make him into a star. In the meantime she got him small parts in a dozen or so films – mainly 'B's – although of passing interest is his appearance at the end of RKO's *Citizen Kane* (1941), as a reporter saying 'Or Rosebud'. RKO gave him his first big chance in *Joan of Paris* (1942), opposite Michèle Morgan, and as a result he was cast as the glacial assassin in *This Gun for Hire* (1942). He divorced Midge in July 1941 and married Sue Carol – as her fourth and final husband – in March 1942, and Paramount signed him up.

His co-star in *This Gun for Hire* (1942) was Veronica Lake, and Paramount – impressed by the success of this teaming – rushed them both into *The Glass Key* (1942). He had a flood of publicity organized by Sue Carol, and was awarded the Women's Press Club's 'Golden Apple' and Picturegoer's annual 'Best Actor's Golden Medal'. The extraordinary acceleration of his popularity allowed him to side-step the customary studio build-up, and in 1947 he was listed as the tenth most popular movie star.

The blond good looks of Alan Ladd were emphasized by a total lack of expression, which suited the menacing roles he played. This was, perhaps, the result of his withdrawn and guarded nature, for he seldom demonstrated any affection for his co-workers or for anyone beyond his immediate family – to whom he was devoted.

From 1942–52 he made twenty-four films for Paramount with fluctuating success. Notable were *The Blue Dahlia* (1946), *The Great Gatsby* (1949), in the title role, and *Shane* (1953), directed by George Stevens, which restored his name to the box-office top ten for 1953–4 and remains the film with which he is chiefly associated. In the latter half of the 1950s his pictures were generally mediocre, although it is interesting to note that he turned down the role that James Dean played in *Giant* (1956) (also directed by Stevens).

Ladd's performance in *The Proud Rebel* (1958) as a drifter was sincere and intelligent and gained further depth from the excellent playing of his real-life son, David, in the part of his mute child. But the film did not receive the success it deserved and his career went into a decline, exacerbated by heavy drinking and occasional rumours of a rift with Sue Carol. In 1962 he was found by his butler with gun-shot wounds, and although these were said to have been the result of an accident, stories of a suicide attempt abounded.

His final appearance, as the ageing cowboy star Nevada Smith, in *The Carpetbaggers* (1964) gave him the best part in the latter stage of his career. His death on 29 January 1964 was caused by a combination of sedatives and alcohol, again said to have been accidental.

By his second wife, Sue Carol, he left further issue, David and Alana Ladd.

MIDGE HARROLD
First wife of Alan Ladd. Married October 1936, divorced July 1941; mother of Alan Ladd Jr

She was born Marjorie Jane Harrold on 25 October 1915, the daughter of Robert Harrold, who was originally from Bloomington, Indiana, and later an insurance agent in Los Angeles. After her divorce from Ladd she married secondly William Farnsworth, an aircraft technician with Lockheed, San Fernando Valley, by whom she had further issue, Cynthia (Cindy) Farnsworth, who died in 1972, aged twenty-five, and a son Derrick Farnsworth, born in 1950 (who suffers from cerebral palsy). Her marriage to William Farnsworth was dissolved by divorce in 1953, and she died on 1 May 1957. Mr Farnsworth, who is no relation to Bette Davis's second husband, Arthur Farnsworth, is now president of Coldwell Baker Residential Estate Services, Fountain Valley, California.

ALAN LADD JR
Only son of Alan Ladd and Midge Harrold

Born on 5 October 1937, he was raised in comparative obscurity by his mother and step-father until the age of fifteen, when he went to live with his father. In the early years of his childhood the majority of Hollywood reporters assumed him to be Ladd's son by Sue Carol, which she did not discourage, but by the time his half-siblings came along he was kept firmly out of the picture as far as the columnists were concerned. As an adult he is commendably philosophical about his unconventional background.

He was educated at the University of Southern California, and later served in the USAAF. Now one of the most successful second generation Hollywood figures, his early ambitions as a film editor and director were thwarted by the major studios and he consequently moved to London. There he produced and/or directed such films as *Villain* (1971), *A Severed Head* (1971), and *Zee & Co* (1972), none of which enjoyed any box-office success.

In 1973 Alan Ladd joined 20th Century Fox. Until his phenomenal success with *Star Wars* (1977), which within months became the highest grossing picture in film history, his only hit was *The Omen* (1976). After *Star Wars* he turned his attention to several excellent films all with strong female roles: *Julia* (1977), *The Turning Point* (1977), *3 Women* (1977), *An Unmarried Woman* (1978), and *Norma Rae* (1979). In May 1976 he was promoted president of Fox.

In the summer of 1979 Ladd resigned and set up a new deal with Warners, whereby they would distribute films produced by his newly formed Ladd Company. His productions there include *Divine Madness* (1981), *Body Heat* (1982), and *Once Upon a Time in America* (1983); he also acquired *Chariots of Fire* (1981), the British made film which had been rejected by every other studio and went on to win the 1981 Best Picture Oscar. His most notable failure was in allowing Lawrence Kasdan's film *The Big Chill* (1984), to slip through his fingers (Kasdan had also made *Body Heat*).

In 1985 he was appointed president and chief executive officer of MGM/United Artists Entertainment Corporation. He married in August 1959, Patricia Beazley, a former dental hygienist, by

whom he has three daughters: Kelly, Tracy and Amanda.

SUE CAROL
Second wife of Alan Ladd. Married 13 March 1942, Tijuana, Mexico; mother of Carol Lee Ladd, David Ladd and Alana Ladd

Born on 30 October 1906, as Evelyn Jean Lederer, to a wealthy Jewish merchant family in Chicago. Her father, S. M. Lederer, died in 1926 in Switzerland. A spirited child, she married in January 1925, when barely nineteen, Allan H. Keefer, a livestock commission man, who was also from an affluent Chicago family. According to a disapproving report in *Variety*, 16 January 1929, she left her husband and went for a vacation to California with her mother in 1927, where she met a handsome film actor, and refused to return home.

Evelyn Lederer divorced Keefer, 'a very quiet and unassuming sort of guy', in January 1929, by which time she had become a jazz-baby starlet under the name of Sue Carol, starring in *Slaves of Beauty* (1927). She married the handsome film actor, Nick Stuart, on 28 July 1929. He had started life as Nicholas Pratza, born in Rumania 10 April 1904, and was briefly an assistant to Howard Hawks at Fox before becoming an actor. By Nick Stuart she had issue, one daughter, Carol Lee Stuart, born on 18 July 1932.

They divorced in 1934; at the hearing Sue Carol complained, among other grievances, that her husband had thrown a crossword-puzzle book at her. He retired from films in the 1930s and became a bandleader. He married secondly, 13 June 1936 (Catalina Island) (divorced May 1937), Ruth Skinner, a nightclub singer, and finally owned a mens' clothing shop in Biloxi, Missouri. In 1952 he married Martha Burnett, and in 1963 he had a cameo role in *It's a Mad Mad Mad Mad World* (1963). He died of cancer on 7 April 1973, at Biloxi.

Sue Carol's third husband is an obscure figure named William Howard Wilson. They were married on 20 November 1936, when he was generally referred to as an actor. Further research reveals he was, in fact, a writer, the author of a novel, *Hollywood Doctor*, which was considered quite *risqué* at the time.

This marriage lasted until 1942, by which time Sue Carol's film career was over. She was gradually demoted to second leads and finally left acting in 1937 in order to start up her own talent agency. She had a good business brain and a fairly wide knowledge of the film industry, and, most importantly, a terrific drive. She first heard Alan Ladd in a radio play, telephoned him to arrange a meeting, and fell headlong in love with him. His subsequent success was almost entirely due to her hard work and determination.

Being seven years older than Ladd and possessed of far greater ambition, their marriage was an interesting reversal of the run-of-the-mill Hollywood mentor/protegée union (Clark Gable was another whose career was advanced by (two) older wives). Alan Ladd was inclined to suffer from deep depressions, perhaps induced by a lonely and insecure childhood, and certainly compounded by his mother's dreadful suicide – when he was only twenty-three. Sue Carol built a protective screen around her husband which not only relieved him of any responsibilities, but also reduced his contact with other people to a minimum. This unnatural inter-dependence came to a head when Ladd struck up a friendship with June Allyson, with whom he co-starred in *The McConnell Story* (1955). Sue became frantically jealous, made a scene, and Ladd packed his bags. The separation lasted less than a week, but his attachment to his children would seem to have been his chief reason for returning to the fold.

Sue Carol's second child, Alana Ladd, was born over ten years after her daughter Carol, and her son, David Ladd, four years later. These children grew up with the children of Henry Fonda, Leland Hayward and Robert Walker – the élite of young Hollywood – but they seem to have had a far less traumatic adolescence than their contemporaries, and speak with an unguarded affection of their parents in Stephen Farber and Marc Green's excellent study, *Hollywood Dynasties*.

Although Ladd was easily Sue Carol's brightest star discovery, she also represented at various times Peter Lawford, Rory Calhoun and Julie London. She survived her husband by eighteen years, and died on 4 February 1982, following a stroke.

DAVID LADD
Only son of Alan Ladd and Sue Carol

Born on 5 February 1947, he became something of a child star, being cast in *The Big Land* (1957), and *The Proud Rebel* (1958), in which he played his real father's mute son. This was produced by Sam Goldwyn Jr, directed by Michael Curtiz and co-starred Olivia de Havilland; it won David Ladd (then eleven years old) rave reviews. He was non-plussed by the sudden star treatment, and was encouraged by both his parents to lead as 'normal' a life as possible. They were naturally protective of their young, and were well aware of the hazards of premature success in films.

Like his father, whom he hero-worshipped, David Ladd excelled at swimming. He was also in *A Dog of Flanders* (1959), and *Misty* (1961). At the age of fourteen he was sent to military school, and later studied at the University of Southern California. In 1970 he attempted to resume his acting career, but the transition to adult roles was not easy and he appeared in various TV commercials and supporting parts, including *The Day of the Locust* (1975). He gave up acting and turned to production, not, as one might expect, with his half-brother, Alan Ladd Jr, but with his half-sister's husband, John Veitch. In 1983 he signed up with Veitch as vice-president for development in his independent production company.

David Ladd married first (divorced) Louise Hendricks, an actress; and secondly May 1974 (divorced 1980), Cheryl Jean Stopplemoor (actress as Cheryl Ladd), whom he had met when they co-starred in *The Treaure of Jamaica Reef* (1973). She was born on 12 July 1951, at Huron, South Dakota, was formerly a model and received much attention when she stepped into Farrah Fawcett's silver slippers for the

TABLE 23 THE LADD FAMILY

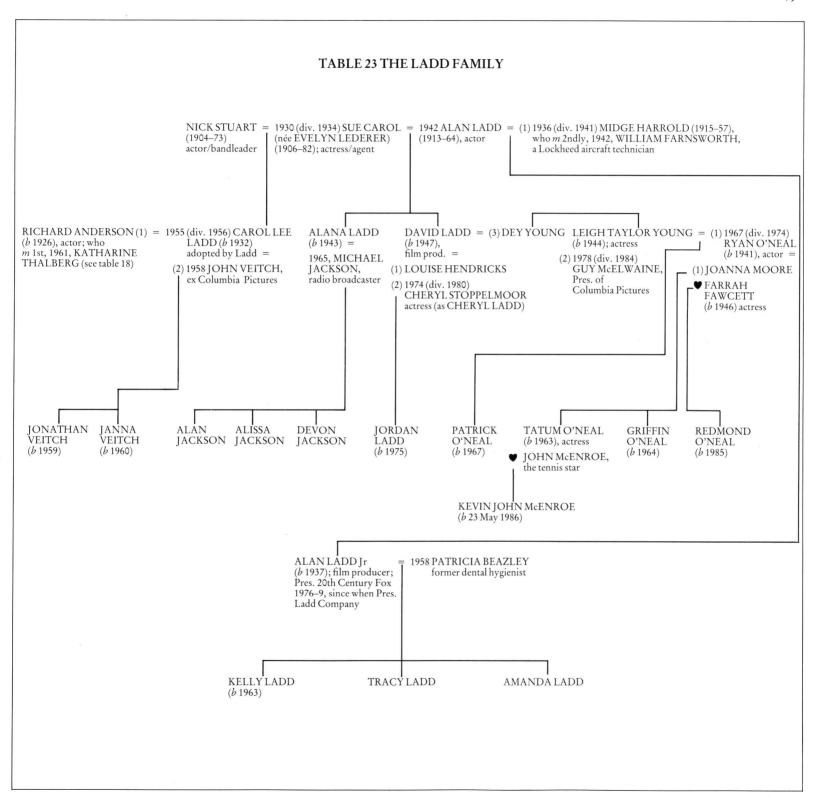

NICK STUART = 1930 (div. 1934) SUE CAROL = 1942 ALAN LADD = (1) 1936 (div. 1941) MIDGE HARROLD (1915–57),
(1904–73)　(née EVELYN LEDERER)　(1913–64), actor　who *m* 2ndly, 1942, WILLIAM FARNSWORTH,
actor/bandleader　(1906–82); actress/agent　a Lockheed aircraft technician

RICHARD ANDERSON (1) = 1955 (div. 1956) CAROL LEE　ALANA LADD　DAVID LADD = (3) DEY YOUNG　LEIGH TAYLOR YOUNG = (1) 1967 (div. 1974)
(*b* 1926), actor; who　LADD (*b* 1932)　(*b* 1943) =　(*b* 1947),　(*b* 1944); actress　RYAN O'NEAL
m 1st, 1961, KATHARINE　adopted by Ladd =　1965, MICHAEL　film prod. =　(2) 1978 (div. 1984)　(*b* 1941), actor =
THALBERG (see table 18)　JACKSON,　(1) LOUISE HENDRICKS　GUY McELWAINE,　(1) JOANNA MOORE
(2) 1958 JOHN VEITCH,　radio broadcaster　(2) 1974 (div. 1980)　Pres. of　♥ FARRAH
ex Columbia Pictures　CHERYL STOPPELMOOR　Columbia Pictures　FAWCETT
actress (as CHERYL LADD)　(*b* 1946) actress

JONATHAN　JANNA　ALAN　ALISSA　DEVON　JORDAN　PATRICK　TATUM O'NEAL　GRIFFIN　REDMOND
VEITCH　VEITCH　JACKSON　JACKSON　JACKSON　LADD　O'NEAL　(*b* 1963), actress　O'NEAL　O'NEAL
(*b* 1959)　(*b* 1960)　(*b* 1975)　(*b* 1967)　(*b* 1964)　(*b* 1985)

♥ JOHN McENROE,
the tennis star

KEVIN JOHN McENROE
(*b* 23 May 1986)

ALAN LADD Jr = 1958 PATRICIA BEAZLEY
(*b* 1937); film producer;　former dental hygienist
Pres. 20th Century Fox
1976–9, since when Pres.
Ladd Company

KELLY LADD　TRACY LADD　AMANDA LADD
(*b* 1963)

TV series 'Charlie's Angels' in 1977. Since then she has tried her hand at marginally more demanding roles, including *Purple Hearts ... A Vietnam Love Story* (1983) (for ex-brother-in-law Alan Ladd Jr), *Once Upon a Time in America* (1983) starring Robert de Niro, *Now and Forever* (1983), and for TV the title role in 'The Grace Kelly Story' (1983), and 'Romance on the Orient Express' (1985).

David and Cheryl Ladd have issue, Jordan Ladd, a daughter, born on 14 January 1975. Following their divorce, Cheryl married, in January 1981, Brian Russell, a Scottish-born songwriter, who co-produces her TV work; and David Ladd married Dey Young, sister of Leigh Taylor Young.

ALANA LADD
Only daughter of Alan Ladd and Sue Carol

Born on 21 April 1943, Alana too had a momentary film career. First with her father in *Guns of the Timberland* (1960), and then in *Young Guns of Texas* (1961). Her last attempt was in *Duel of Champions* (1964), after which she cheerfully threw away her greasepaint and married, in 1965, Michael Jackson, a British born radio broadcaster, by whom she has three children: Alan, Alissa and Devon.

CAROL LEE LADD
Only child of Sue Carol and Nick Stuart; step-daughter of Alan Ladd

Born on 18 July 1932, she was partially named after Dixie Lee (Mrs Bing Crosby). Following the divorce of her parents she was given her step-father's surname, although she was never formally adopted. She was educated at the University of California in Los Angeles. Like her step-brother, Alan Ladd Jr, she was kept in the wings when the Hollywood reporters came to call, and generally assumed to be Ladd's daughter.

She married first, 22 January 1955 (divorced April 1956), Richard Anderson, an MGM contract player, born 1926, who later became quite well known in such TV series as: 'Bionic Woman', 'The Six Million Dollar Man' and 'Cover Up'. There was no issue from this marriage, and he subsequently married Katharine, daughter of Irving Thalberg (see table 18).

Carol Lee married secondly, 9 February 1958, John Veitch (born *c.* 1921), who was then executive vice-president of Columbia Pictures, and later president of production 1979–83. They have two children: Jonathan Veitch, born 1 February 1959, and Janna Veitch (a daughter), born January 1960.

7 The Cansino Dynasty: Rita Hayworth

Through the 1940s Rita Hayworth's star shone as brightly as any other in the Hollywood constellation. Her performance in *Gilda* (1946) fanned the flames of cinema eroticism to new heights, and her 1949 marriage to Aly Khan, prince of playboys, affirmed her desirability in real life. The announcement in June 1981 that she was suffering from rapidly progressive senility – Alzheimer's disease – caused great sorrow to those who remembered her spectacular beauty.

Rita Hayworth was born on 17 October 1918, in Brooklyn, New York, the eldest child and only daughter of Eduardo Cansino by his wife Volga Haworth. Her real name was Margarita Carmen Cansino. Her father was the eldest of six brothers (a seventh died young), all of whom eventually emigrated from Spain to America. Their father, Antonio Cansino, who was born in Seville, was a well-known dancer who formed the style that became the accepted school of Spanish dance. (He is said to have danced at the court of King Alfonso XII of Spain.)

Eduardo Cansino (1895–1968) was initially paired with his younger sister, Elisa, and they toured Europe, England, Canada and Australia, before being brought to the USA in 1913 by the influential Mrs Stuyvesant Fish to entertain her guests. Eduardo stayed in America, and was later hired in the Ziegfeld Follies, where he met Volga, also a dancer, who had run away from her home in Washington, DC, when she was sixteen.

The 'Dancing Cansinos' were successful vaudeville performers, and Margarita was naturally expected to join the act. As soon as she could stand she was taught to dance, and her formative years were spent training and touring. Her brothers Eduardo and Vernon were born in 1920 and 1922 respectively. Her education was neglected, but her father was a strict teacher and she became an accomplished dancer; she also may have developed, at an early age, a need for the approval and guidance of a strong-minded man.

In 1926 her father moved the family to Hollywood, where he opened a dance school, and whenever possible directed dance routines for screen musicals at Fox. When she was thirteen, Margarita was dancing at Agua Caliente, Mexico, with her father, when she was spotted by Winfield Sheehan, the West Coast production head for Fox, and through him she secured a tiny dancing role in *Pampas Moon* (1935), and an acting role in *Dante's Inferno* (1935).

She went on playing bits, usually as a dancer, under her real name, and was beginning to get leads in minor pictures when the Fox–20th Century merger reduced Sheehan's influence and resulted in her dismissal.

In 1937 she married Edward Charles Judson, a wealthy foreign-car-salesman, a little over twice her age. He had seen her in a film, engineered a meeting, and ended up changing her life. He started with her face and figure, masterminded her diet, and got her a seven year contract with crude but shrewd Harry Cohn at $250 a week, rising to $1,750, at Columbia. At his suggestion, Judson abbreviated Margarita's name to Rita, and exchanged Cansino for her mother's surname, slightly modified: thus Rita Hayworth. Columbia's hair stylist Helen Hunt gave

Hayworth's brow a sculptured look by raising her hairline (by painful electrolysis) and changed her hair-colour. As Ephraim Katz says, she was 'transformed from a raven-haired exotic to an auburn-haired sophisticate'. Judson's natural flair for publicity ensured her name was frequently in the papers, and she was seen at all the right premières and parties.

The first promising role she played was for Howard Hawks in *Only Angels Have Wings* (1939), in which she was the second female lead as Richard Barthelmess's faithless wife. Her beauty and glamour were spectacular, but she still lacked confidence and it wasn't until *Blood and Sand* (1941), as another flame-haired temptress (to matador Tyrone Power), that Hollywood realized a new star was born. Ironically, the studio which made that film was 20th Century Fox, who had discarded her six years earlier, and who now paid her five times her normal salary.

Rita Hayworth returned to Columbia for a musical comedy, *You'll Never Get Rich* (1941), with songs by Cole Porter, in which she was Fred Astaire's leading lady. He had reservations about Rita's abilities at first, especially as he'd found her cousin-by-marriage, Ginger Rogers, initially quite heavy going as a dancing partner. Rita, however, being a trained dancer, easily earned Astaire's admiration.

On 11 August 1941 Edward Judson, Rita's husband and manager, reached his publicity zenith with a photograph of Rita in *Life* magazine. She was photographed in a tight-fitting, black diaphanous négligé, kneeling on a satin-sheeted bed, and looking very foxy (Bob Landry, the photographer, said the picture was a fluke; a flash bulb that failed to go off actually accentuated Hayworth's voluptuous figure to good effect). This shot became a cheesecake classic, in such demand as a pin-up by American servicemen overseas it was reproduced in millions (one being stuck to the atom bomb dropped on Bikini). She was again teamed with Astaire in *You Were Never Lovelier* (1942), with songs by Jerome Kern and Johnny Mercer. In September 1943 she filed for divorce from Judson.

Rita had become quite involved with Victor Mature, to whom she announced her engagement, but she dropped him in favour of Orson Welles, whom she met through Joseph Cotten. Welles was then twenty-eight, forceful and charismatic, and at war with RKO over the re-editing of his film *Journey Into Fear* (1942). He completely won her over, and they were married on the day her divorce became absolute, 7 September 1943.

They had one daughter, Rebecca Welles, who was born on 17 December 1944, but it was not long before the marriage showed signs of stress. It was a very uneven mixture of Welles's infatuation for Hayworth, and her reverence for his intellect. Although Rita never aired her views about the failure of her second marriage, she did occasionally allude to Welles's apparent lack of concern for their child.

After making *Cover Girl* (1944), with Gene Kelly, probably her best-remembered musical, the American GIs elected her their 'Number One Back Home Glamour Girl', which was a sharp reminder to Harry Cohn of Hayworth's lust-factor. He promptly put her into *Gilda* (1946), as the ultimate *femme fatale* (she sang 'Put the Blame on Mame, Boys' as she slowly peeled off her long white gloves), directed by Charles Vidor, and co-starring Glenn Ford. This intense, erotic and surprisingly explicit film netted $4 million in domestic distribution, and is certainly the high point of her film career.

When Harry Cohn heard his biggest star's marriage was on the rocks he panicked. He persuaded them to reconcile, and then insisted that Rita should star in Welles's contractual film for Columbia, *The Lady From Shanghai* (1948). Both Cohn and Welles miscalculated over this; Welles attempted to improve on the Gilda-type character, but changed the cut and colour of Hayworth's hair – to white blonde – which helped to make her vicious, but without allure. The film and marriage flopped, and they were divorced in 1948.

Putting Cohn, Welles and Hollywood behind her, Rita took herself on a long tour of Europe, where, in Cannes, she was introduced to Aly Khan by Elsa Maxwell. He was the son of the Aga Khan, spiritual leader and Imam of Ismaili Muslims all

The ravishing Rita Hayworth in Gilda *(1946). Although the Cansinos are best known as dancers, a branch of the family still flourishes in Castilleja de la Cuesta, near Seville, where they have long owned a small factory which makes a traditional Spanish pastry called 'torta'.*

over the world, very attractive, and very, very rich. He had married in 1936 the Hon. Joan Yarde-Buller, formerly wife of Loel Guinness, by whom he had two sons. Rita fell deeply in love with him, and they set off on a romantic progress from the Riviera, to Toledo, Madrid, Lisbon and back to Cannes, followed by the delighted news-hounds who reported the affair in detail while affecting an outraged moral stance. Rita then returned to Hollywood, where she rejected Cohn's latest vehicle, and flew on to Mexico City, where she was joined by her prince. Cohn was incensed and put her on suspension (she lost a yearly salary of $248,000), but Rita, Aly and her daughter Rebecca, merely packed their bags once more and set sail for London on the *Britannia*.

Aly Khan announced their engagement in the spring of 1949. In terms of wealth, glamour and notoriety, their marriage was considered the match of the century, and was only to be surpassed in Hollywood legend by Grace Kelly's marriage to Prince Rainier of Monaco in 1956. Rita's remarks, 'I'm so excited, I can hardly think, I'm sort of lost in a dream world', were obviously said in a trance of happiness, but they were to have a cynical truth barely a year later. The exclusive guest list was the talk of Hollywood – Hedda Hopper went into a state of shock when she learnt her arch-rival Louella Parsons had been invited, and she hadn't!

After the marriage ceremony on 27 May 1949, they were driven to Aly's château, L'Horizon, near Cannes, for a lavish reception by his orange-blossom-scented pool. Each guest was allocated fifteen bottles of champagne, and Aly created a *frisson* among his guests when he kissed Rita's slipper, and presented her with an Alfa-Romeo, four racehorses, assorted diamonds and rubies and a cash dowry. The following day they were married according to Muslim rites.

On 28 December 1949 Rita gave birth to their daughter, Yasmin, in Lausanne. The baby was premature but perfectly healthy, and Rita thankfully retreated into motherhood again. Aly, meanwhile, was irrepressibly sociable, racing and gaming and villa-hopping, with no intention of leading a more mundane life, but with the result that Rita again felt cheated of her domestic pleasures. She was very much a child of the film studios, beautiful, warm and anxious to please, but not really on Aly's frequency at all. She felt uncomfortable with his smart friends, spoke French poorly, and was understandably upset when she realized that Aly was not entirely faithful to her. In an effort to save their marriage they went on a ridiculously extravagent safari to Africa, but this turned into another publicity circus, and ended in Rita flying to Nevada, with her daughters, to apply for a divorce.

There was much talk of reconciliation, but it never happened. In retrospect it seems particularly sad that Rita did not have the strength of character to accept Aly Khan's shortcomings, as she might have found a lasting companion in him. He never married again, but he was seen with many glamorous women, Gene Tierney, Juliette Greco, Kim Novak, and most of all Bettina, a model, who was with him when he was killed in a motor accident in France, on 12 May 1960. Rita collapsed when she heard the news.

Her sad return to Hollywood was notable only for Harry Cohn's reluctance to renew her salary, and she was desperately short of money. The films she made for Columbia during the 1950s were mostly poor things, and her disappointment was apparent in her lack-lustre performances. Her financial situation was worsened by her fourth marriage in September 1953 (only eight months after her divorce was made absolute) to Dick Haymes, whose singing career had taken a nosedive. Not only was he being chased by his second wife's lawyers for unpaid child support, but also by the Internal Revenue Service for alleged back taxes (to the tune of $100,000), and the US Immigration Service were attempting to deport him on grounds of draft-evasion (he pleaded Argentinian citizenship).

While Rita couldn't handle either Welles's brain or Aly Khan's social demands, she stayed remarkably loyal to Haymes during his frequent financial embarrassments, and it was only due to his heavy drinking that the marriage finally broke up in 1955.

TABLE 24 THE CANSINO DYNASTY

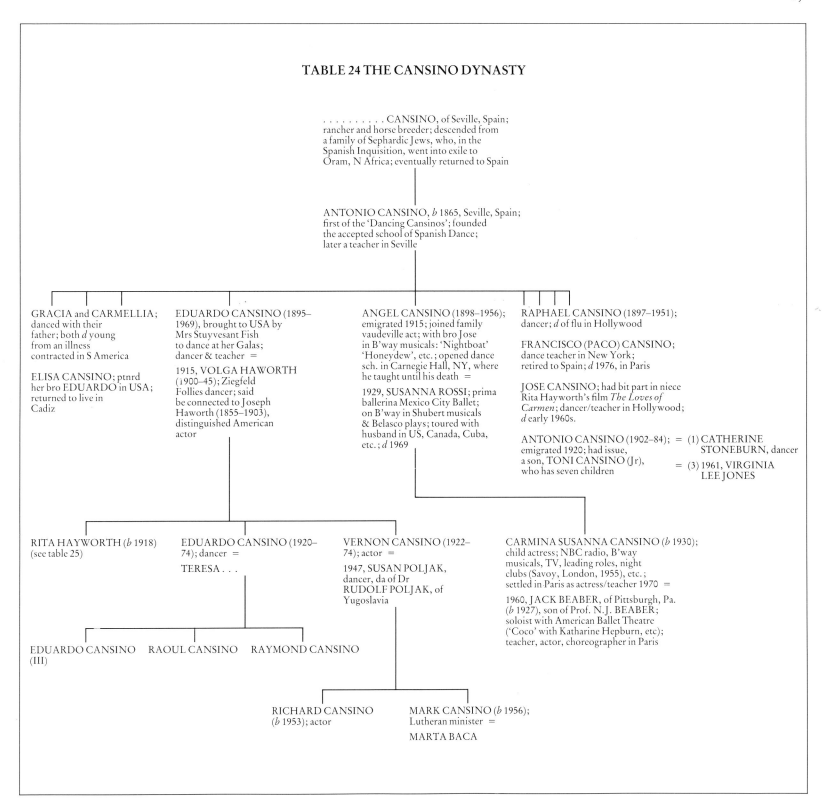

. . . . CANSINO, of Seville, Spain; rancher and horse breeder; descended from a family of Sephardic Jews, who, in the Spanish Inquisition, went into exile to Oram, N Africa; eventually returned to Spain

ANTONIO CANSINO, *b* 1865, Seville, Spain; first of the 'Dancing Cansinos'; founded the accepted school of Spanish Dance; later a teacher in Seville

GRACIA and CARMELLIA; danced with their father; both *d* young from an illness contracted in S America

ELISA CANSINO; ptnrd her bro EDUARDO in USA; returned to live in Cadiz

EDUARDO CANSINO (1895–1969), brought to USA by Mrs Stuyvesant Fish to dance at her Galas; dancer & teacher =

1915, VOLGA HAWORTH (1900–45); Ziegfeld Follies dancer; said be connected to Joseph Haworth (1855–1903), distinguished American actor

ANGEL CANSINO (1898–1956); emigrated 1915; joined family vaudeville act; with bro Jose in B'way musicals: 'Nightboat' 'Honeydew', etc.; opened dance sch. in Carnegie Hall, NY, where he taught until his death =

1929, SUSANNA ROSSI; prima ballerina Mexico City Ballet; on B'way in Shubert musicals & Belasco plays; toured with husband in US, Canada, Cuba, etc.; *d* 1969

RAPHAEL CANSINO (1897–1951); dancer; *d* of flu in Hollywood

FRANCISCO (PACO) CANSINO; dance teacher in New York; retired to Spain; *d* 1976, in Paris

JOSE CANSINO; had bit part in niece Rita Hayworth's film *The Loves of Carmen*; dancer/teacher in Hollywood; *d* early 1960s.

ANTONIO CANSINO (1902–84); = (1) CATHERINE STONEBURN, dancer
emigrated 1920; had issue, a son, TONI CANSINO (Jr), who has seven children

= (3) 1961, VIRGINIA LEE JONES

RITA HAYWORTH (*b* 1918) (see table 25)

EDUARDO CANSINO (1920–74); dancer =

TERESA . . .

VERNON CANSINO (1922–74); actor =

1947, SUSAN POLJAK, dancer, da of Dr RUDOLF POLJAK, of Yugoslavia

CARMINA SUSANNA CANSINO (*b* 1930); child actress; NBC radio, B'way musicals, TV, leading roles, night clubs (Savoy, London, 1955), etc.; settled in Paris as actress/teacher 1970 =

1960, JACK BEABER, of Pittsburgh, Pa. (*b* 1927), son of Prof. N.J. BEABER; soloist with American Ballet Theatre ('Coco' with Katharine Hepburn, etc); teacher, actor, choreographer in Paris

EDUARDO CANSINO (III)

RAOUL CANSINO

RAYMOND CANSINO

RICHARD CANSINO (*b* 1953); actor

MARK CANSINO (*b* 1956); Lutheran minister =

MARTA BACA

She was in only one more really successful film, *Pal Joey* (1957), which made Columbia a fortune. Her co-stars were Frank Sinatra and Kim Novak (Cohn frequently taunted Rita with Novak's name as his new creation). She was also in *Separate Tables* (1958), and still looked very beautiful, but there was no power in her performance.

In 1958, aged thirty-nine, she married James Hill, a producer, aged forty-one. It was her fifth marriage and his first, and was dissolved by divorce in September 1961. She continued to work sporadically throughout the 1960s, occasionally in Europe, but she developed a drinking problem which affected her health and work. She made her last film, *The Wrath of God* in 1972.

In 1977 Rita was reported 'gravely disabled by mental disorder' and a court in Santa Ana, California, was told she was 'unable or unwilling to accept responsibility for her treatment and is a chronic alcoholic'. The shattering truth that she was actually suffering from Alzheimer's disease was not realized until June 1981, and the following month she was put under the care and guardianship of her younger daughter, Princess Yasmin Khan, in New York.

Of her children, Rebecca, her daughter by Welles, studied drama at the University of Puget Sound, Washington, and aged twenty-six, married in a private ceremony in Tacoma, Washington, Perry Moede, a twenty-two year-old sculptor. They separated in 1972 and were finally divorced in 1984. She has no children.

Princess Yasmin, her daughter by Prince Aly Khan, was the subject of much bitterness and custody-wrangling as a child. She was expensively educated at a progressive boarding school in the Adirondack Mountains, New York, and at one time expressed an interest in pursuing a singing career. Her name was linked with a number of well-known men, including Robert Shriver, nephew of the late President Kennedy, Canadian Premier Pierre Trudeau, and restaurateur Peter Kramer. At the age of thirty-five she married, 15 May 1985, in Manhattan, Basil Embiricos, then aged thirty-six, an Old Etonian, the younger son of Nicholas Embiricos, of Lausanne, Switzerland, and a member of the Greek shipping family. They were also married at the Greek Orthodox Cathedral of St Etienne, in Paris, on 23 June 1985. She was attended by Princess Zahra Aga Khan, the daughter of her half-brother, Prince Karim Aga Khan (who succeeded his grandfather as 4th Aga Khan in 1957).

Princess Yasmin gave birth to a son, Andrew, on 11 December 1985, in New York City.

ORSON WELLES
Second husband of Rita Hayworth. Married 7 September 1943, Santa Monica; divorced 1948

Born on 6 May 1915, Kenosha, Wisconsin; director, producer, screenwriter and actor: *Citizen Kane* (1941), directed, produced, co-wrote and starred in title role; *The Magnificent Ambersons* (1942), directed produced, wrote and off-screen narrated; *Jane Eyre* (1944), as Mr Rochester; *The Lady From Shanghai* (1948), directed, wrote, and co-starred (with his estranged wife Rita Hayworth); *Macbeth* (1948), directed, produced, wrote screenplay, acted in title role; *The Third Man* (1949), as racketeer Harry Lime; *Othello* (1952), directed, produced, wrote screenplay, acted in title role; *Touch of Evil* (1958), directed, wrote and acted; *Compulsion* (1959), as the defence attorney, based on the Leopold–Loeb murder trial; *The Trial* (1963), directed, adapted from Kafka novel; *Chimes at Midnight* (1966), a portrait of Shakespeare's Falstaff, directed, wrote and acted; *A Man For All Seasons* (1966), as Cardinal Wolsey; etc; also stage work before going into films: acted at both Gate and Abbey Theatres, Ireland; toured with Katherine Cornell in America; début on New York stage as Tybalt in 'Romeo and Juliet' (1934); became director of the Negro People's Theatre (directed Negro version of Macbeth), 1936; a director of the Federal Theatre Project, New York, 1937; founded Mercury Theatre, 1937 (opened with modern dress version of 'Julius Caesar'). Achieved his radio *tour de force*, 1938, with his production of H. G. Wells's *The War of the Worlds*, which he presented with such realism that half America believed they were being invaded by Martians. He died on 10 October 1985, in Hollywood.

Welles married first, December 1934 (divorced 1940), Virginia Nicolson, a theatre actress (as Anne Stafford), daughter of Leo M. Nicolson, of Wheaton, Illinois. They had one child, a daughter, Christopher Welles, born on 27 March 1938, who is now a text book editor and verse writer. She married first, 1957, Norman R. de Haan, an architect, and secondly, *c.* 1972, Irwin Feder, of New York, and has no children. Virginia Nicolson married secondly, 16 May 1940 (Phoenix, Arizona), Charles D. Lederer (1910–76) (see table 26), nephew of Marion Davies, mistress of William Randolph Hearst, on whom the character of Charles Kane was modelled. Virginia Nicolson married thirdly, 13 April 1948, Major Jack Pringle, MC, and now lives in England.

After his divorce from Rita Hayworth, Welles married thirdly, 8 May 1955, (London), Paola Mori, daughter of Alberto Mori, a lawyer, by whom he had further issue, a daughter, Beatrice, born in November 1955. Although it is tempting to suppose there is a link between Paola Mori and the Mori family connections of Tyrone Power (see table 33), none has so far been established. Paola died in Nevada, 12 August 1986, as the result of a motor accident.

DICK HAYMES

Fourth husband of Rita Hayworth. Married 24 September 1953, Las Vegas; divorced 1955

Born Richard Benjamin Haymes, 13 September 1916, Buenos Aires, son of a Scottish-born cattle rancher by his American wife (a former singer and dancer); raised by his mother after his parents' divorce; educated in Switzerland, and at Loyola University, Montreal. Haymes arrived in the USA in 1936, and began a show business career as a radio announcer, band vocalist and film extra. In the early 1940s he became a highly successful and well-paid recording artist and nightclub crooner; he sang with all the big bands of the decade, Harry James, Benny Goodman and Tommy Dorsey (replacing Frank Sinatra in the latter pair). In 1948 he sold over seven million records and made over $4 million from his singing career, but faced financial ruin through his numerous divorces, alcoholism and legal wrangles. Songs he turned into hits include 'You'll Never Know', 'It's a Grand Night for Singing', 'It Had To Be You', and 'Little White Lies'. His film career was unmemorable, although he made thirty-five pictures in all. He died of lung cancer on 28 March 1980, aged sixty-one, in Los Angeles.

Haymes married first, 1938 (annulled after a few weeks), Edith Harper, a nightclub singer, of Chicago; secondly, 21 June 1941 (divorced 1949), Joanne Dru (born 1923, American film actress), by whom he had issue, Richard Ralph (Skipper) Haymes, born 24 July 1942 (New York), Helen Joanne (Pigeon) Haymes, born 14 May 1944 (Los Angeles), and Barbara Nugent Haymes, born 19 September 1947 (Santa Monica). Haymes married thirdly, 17 July 1949 (divorced 1953), Nora Eddington, former wife of Errol Flynn; fourthly, Rita Hayworth; fifthly, 22 November 1958 (Las Vegas) (divorced 1965), Fran Jefferies (born *c.* 1937–40, American singer), by whom he had further issue, Stephanie Haymes; sixthly, 18 February 1966 (London), Wendy Smith, a fashion model, by whom he had further issue, Sean Haymes, born 19 June 1966 (Dublin), and Samantha Haymes, born 16 March 1969 (London).

8 Ginger Rogers and Husbands

Ginger Rogers's heart surely belonged to Mommie. Not Mommie Dearest, but quite close. Lela Rogers had the most uncanny hold over her daughter's life, both public and private, for about fifty years, and Ginger's devotion to Lela is tediously well documented.

Lela Rogers was born Lela Owens on Christmas Day 1891, in Kansas, eldest of the four daughters of Walter Winfield Owens. She married at eighteen, Eddins McMath, an electrical engineer, and moved to Independence, Missouri, where she worked on a newspaper. Their first child died in infancy, and their second, Virginia Katherine McMath, born on 16 July 1911, became Ginger Rogers. After moving to Ennis, Texas, Lela left her husband and initiated divorce proceedings. The distraught Mr McMath twice kidnapped his daughter and had to be put under legal restraint. This luckless man died eight years later.

Lela returned to Kansas City, where she won a short story competition and was asked to convert her entry into a screenplay. So she went to Hollywood in 1916, leaving Ginger with her parents, and assumed the *nom-de-plume* of Lela Leibrand. The Fox Company sent her to New York, where during the First World War she enlisted in the US Marine corps, writing and editing training films for the forces.

Perhaps worried that she was missing out on her daughter's formative years, Lela returned to Kansas in 1919 and married John Logan Rogers, an insurance man. They moved to Dallas and then to Fort Worth, Texas, where Mr Rogers parted company.

It is said that Lela did not entirely approve of Ginger's stage-struck adolescence, but once she'd been talked round she threw herself into her child's advancement. The rise to power began in 1926, when the fifteen-year-old Ginger won an Interstate Vaudeville Charleston competition. Lela reluctantly took her out of school and Ginger spent the next two years touring in glorified amateur contests. She was gangly, freckled and fairly appealing.

In 1928 Ginger defied her mother for the first time, and married, in New Orleans, Jack Culpepper, whom she had known in Texas, and who was now a vaudeville hoofer as Jack Pepper. They formed a duo, Ginger and Pepper, but the marriage broke up within a year. Following this mini-trauma, Ginger got her best breaks to date, in a solo act with the Eddie Lowry band in Chicago, and the Paul Ash orchestra in New York. She was still relying on the Charleston and her mother's baby-talk monologues, but she also began to develop a certain panache, which was noticed by Walter Wanger, the film producer, who signed her up for *Young Man of Manhattan* (1930).

The Rogers went to Hollywood in 1931, where they were later joined by Ginger's cousin, Phyllis Fraser (née Helen Maurine Brown), whose mother, Virginia Owens, was Lela's younger sister. The youngest Owens sister, Jean, an actress, is the aunt of Rita Hayworth (see table 25).

Ginger's high spirits caught the attention of up-and-coming director Mervyn LeRoy (see table 28), and it was he who first sensed that Lela's influence over her daughter was not entirely admirable. Lela was a rather pretentious woman who cultivated a superior manner and encouraged Ginger to do the same. Her high-handed attitude towards the lower echelons in show-business became an unattractive characteristic of Ginger's in later life.

LeRoy urged her to accept a role in *42nd Street* (1933), in which she posed as a be-monocled Brit and sang 'Shuffle Off to Buffalo'. He also paid court to Ginger, and although their romance was short-lived he cast her in *Gold Diggers of 1933*, in which her song 'We're in the Money' became a classic. In January 1934 LeRoy married Doris, daughter of Harry Warner (see table 28), and Ginger signed a long-term contract with RKO.

It was for RKO that Ginger, at the last minute, was assigned a part in *Flying Down to Rio* (1933), in which she was first teamed with Fred Astaire, and began a partnership as magical as any to grace the silver screen. Astaire's skilful elegance was well matched by Ginger's athleticism, and although he was exasperated by her inclination to have weights sewn into her sleeves, and decorate her dresses with feathered baubles, one feels his understated tribute to her as 'the hardest working gal I ever knew' is entirely sincere. He certainly turned her into a polished dancer. They were in ten pictures together (after *Rio*)· *The Gay Divorcee* (1934), *Roberta* (1935), *Top Hat* (1935), *Follow the Fleet* (1936), *Swing Time* (1936), *Shall We Dance?* (1937), *Carefree* (1938), *The Story of Vernon and Irene Castle* (1939), and *The Barkleys of Broadway* (1949). Katharine Hepburn's analysis of the Astaire–Rogers chemistry, 'She gave him sex, he gave her class', is pretty near the truth.

In November 1934, after a courtship of over three years, Ginger Rogers married again. Her second husband was Lew Ayres, a young actor as sensitive as Ginger was brash. Her biographer, George Eells

Ginger in Follow the Fleet *(1936), her fifth teaming with Astaire; during the 'Let's Face the Music and Dance' number, one of her heavy-beaded sleeves slashed Astaire's face – partially stunning him. They spent the rest of the day repeating the routine only to find that the first take had actually been all right.*

notes in *Ginger, Loretta and Irene Who?* that Ginger's Christmas present of an electric train set to her new husband perhaps indicated a lack of insight – but then Ayres may have been a train enthusiast – at all events they had separated by 1936, and were divorced in 1941.

In 1941 Ginger won an Oscar for *Kitty Foyle* (1940), but her subsequent films were mainly unremarkable. Three that should be mentioned, however, are *Roxie Hart* (1942), which contained a scintillating comic performance by Ginger, *The Major and the Minor* (1942), which was Billy Wilder's directing début, and *The Barkleys of Broadway* (1949), in which she eagerly replaced the ailing Judy Garland. This was her last teaming with Fred Astaire, and, not having worked with him for around ten years, it was noted that her dancing had more push than polish.

Lela's influence over Ginger remained undiminished. She was appalled when she heard of her alleged affair with George Stevens, the distinguished (and married) director ('this man is destroying my daughter'), and she damaged her daughter's image quite seriously with her ill-considered and dangerous statements about Communist propaganda she had found hidden in some of the scripts offered to RKO.

Ginger was the industry's highest paid star in 1943. This same year she married Jack Calvin Briggs II, a twenty-two-year-old Marine and former bit player at RKO. He had had a small part in *Tom, Dick and Harry* (1941) (in which Ginger demonstrated a deft comic touch), but she hardly knew him. However, it was during their six-year marriage that Ginger had her first opportunity to put her private life before her career. They shared their time between their ranch in Oregon and her Beverly Hills house, and were divorced in 1949.

Her next husband, Jacques Bergerac, was even younger. He was twenty-four and Ginger forty-two. He was French, handsome, played a good game of tennis and said all the right things. Ginger was transported and hoped they might form a husband and wife acting partnership, but sadly this was not to be. MGM dropped his option. It also seems

that Ginger's endless enthusiasm, which had been such an attractive quality in her youth, had begun to lose its charm. They were divorced in 1957 after four years.

Ginger's fifth husband (1961–71) was William Marshall, an American actor. Their partnership was as much business as pleasure, and they attempted to set up a deal with the Jamaican government in 1963 to produce films in Kingston, but this was not a success.

Hugely successful – at least with her faithful army of fans – was her comeback on Broadway, when she took over the lead in the musical 'Hello Dolly' from Carol Channing, and in 1969 she scored a personal hit as the star of the London production of 'Mame'.

Ginger's cousinship with Rita Hayworth is something which neither actress has ever publicly alluded to. There is no actual blood link, and, as has already been emphasized, Ginger's family devotion was centred entirely on her mother. Apart from both women being celebrated performers, and both having been married and divorced five times, perhaps the only thing they have in common is their mutual first cousin, Vinton Hayworth, an actor and writer, born in 1935.

LEW AYRES
Second husband of Ginger Rogers. Married 14 November 1934; divorced 1941

Born on 28 December 1908, in Minneapolis; educated at the University of Arizona (studied medicine). He achieved international recognition for his portrayal of the disillusioned young German soldier in Louis Milestone's pacifist classic, *All Quiet on the Western Front* (1930), and he gave a sensitive performance as the doctor caring for Jane Wyman in *Johnny Belinda* (1948) (one of the most sympathetic and understated pieces of screen acting in the immediate post-war years), but he was not given enough substantial roles. He acquired a large following in the title role in the *Doctor Kildare* film series, in which he appeared between 1939 and 1942, but lost favour with both studios and fans in 1941

TABLE 25 GINGER ROGERS AND RITA HAYWORTH – COUSINS BY MARRIAGE

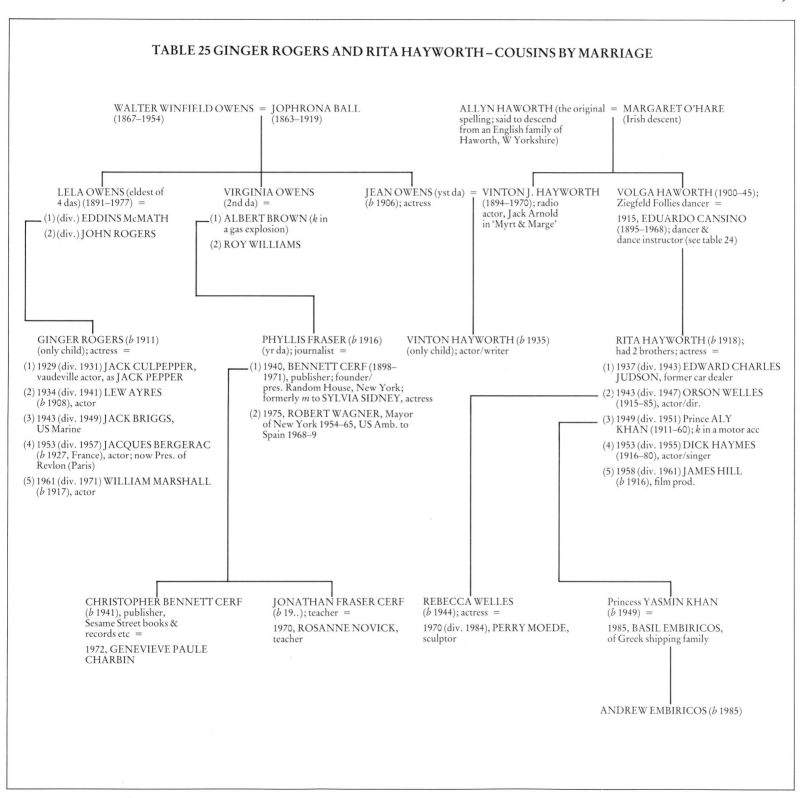

WALTER WINFIELD OWENS = JOPHRONA BALL
(1867–1954)   (1863–1919)

ALLYN HAWORTH (the original = MARGARET O'HARE
spelling; said to descend   (Irish descent)
from an English family of
Haworth, W Yorkshire)

LELA OWENS (eldest of
4 das) (1891–1977) =

(1) (div.) EDDINS McMATH

(2) (div.) JOHN ROGERS

VIRGINIA OWENS
(2nd da) =

(1) ALBERT BROWN (k in
a gas explosion)

(2) ROY WILLIAMS

JEAN OWENS (yst da) = VINTON J. HAYWORTH
(b 1906); actress   (1894–1970); radio
actor, Jack Arnold
in 'Myrt & Marge'

VOLGA HAWORTH (1900–45);
Ziegfeld Follies dancer =

1915, EDUARDO CANSINO
(1895–1968); dancer &
dance instructor (see table 24)

GINGER ROGERS (b 1911)
(only child); actress =

(1) 1929 (div. 1931) JACK CULPEPPER,
vaudeville actor, as JACK PEPPER

(2) 1934 (div. 1941) LEW AYRES
(b 1908), actor

(3) 1943 (div. 1949) JACK BRIGGS,
US Marine

(4) 1953 (div. 1957) JACQUES BERGERAC
(b 1927, France), actor; now Pres. of
Revlon (Paris)

(5) 1961 (div. 1971) WILLIAM MARSHALL
(b 1917), actor

PHYLLIS FRASER (b 1916)
(yr da); journalist =

(1) 1940, BENNETT CERF (1898–
1971), publisher; founder/
pres. Random House, New York;
formerly m to SYLVIA SIDNEY, actress

(2) 1975, ROBERT WAGNER, Mayor
of New York 1954–65, US Amb. to
Spain 1968–9

VINTON HAYWORTH (b 1935)
(only child); actor/writer

RITA HAYWORTH (b 1918);
had 2 brothers; actress =

(1) 1937 (div. 1943) EDWARD CHARLES
JUDSON, former car dealer

(2) 1943 (div. 1947) ORSON WELLES
(1915–85), actor/dir.

(3) 1949 (div. 1951) Prince ALY
KHAN (1911–60); k in a motor acc

(4) 1953 (div. 1955) DICK HAYMES
(1916–80), actor/singer

(5) 1958 (div. 1961) JAMES HILL
(b 1916), film prod.

CHRISTOPHER BENNETT CERF
(b 1941), publisher,
Sesame Street books &
records etc =

1972, GENEVIEVE PAULE
CHARBIN

JONATHAN FRASER CERF
(b 19..); teacher =

1970, ROSANNE NOVICK,
teacher

REBECCA WELLES
(b 1944); actress =

1970 (div. 1984), PERRY MOEDE,
sculptor

Princess YASMIN KHAN
(b 1949) =

1985, BASIL EMBIRICOS,
of Greek shipping family

ANDREW EMBIRICOS (b 1985)

when he declared himself a conscientious objector and refused to fight in the Second World War (he volunteered for non-combatant medical service and distinguished himself under fire). He wrote, produced and narrated the documentary, 'Altars of the East' (1955), a study in comparative religion.

Lew Ayres married first, 15 September 1931 (Las Vegas) (divorced 1933), Lola Lane (1909–81), actress; secondly, Ginger Rogers; thirdly, 7 February 1964, Diana Hall, a former airline stewardess, by whom he has issue his only child, Justin Ayres, born 26 December 1968.

JACQUES BERGERAC
Fourth husband of Ginger Rogers. Married 7 February 1953, Palm Springs; divorced 1957

Born on 26 May 1927, Biarritz, France; trained as a lawyer, but went on the stage. Jacques came to Hollywood in 1953, and found film work as the smooth Continental lover (notably in *Gigi*, 1958). Ginger Rogers was his first wife; after their divorce he married secondly, 27 June 1959 (Hong Kong) (divorced 1964), Dorothy Malone (born 1925, American actress, who won a Best Supporting Actress Oscar in 1956 for her role as a frustrated nymphomaniac in *Written on the Wind*), by whom

he has two daughters, Mimi Bergerac, born *c.* 1961, and Diane Bergerac, born *c.* 1963. He married thirdly, 1975, Edith Brennan, and, having retired from films, is president of Revlon, in Paris.

WILLIAM MARSHALL
Fifth husband of Ginger Rogers. Married 16 March 1961, Hollywood; divorced 1971

Born on 2 October 1917, Chicago. Said to be descended from Oliver Cromwell (died 1658), Lord Protector. Started his career as a singer and bandleader, and went into films in 1940. He was blond, good-looking but dull, and never had much of a following; he also tried directing, again without success. He married first, 16 September 1942 (Santa Barbara) (divorced), Michèle Morgan (born 1920, exotic French actress with haunting eyes), by whom he has issue, Michael Marshall, born 12 September 1944 (Hollywood), a bit-part actor, mainly in American films, has been married twice and has one daughter, Samantha; he lives in Paris. William Marshall married secondly, 8 September 1949 (divorced), Micheline Presle (born 1922, French actress), by whom he has further issue, a daughter, Toni Marshall, born 29 November 1951, an actress.

9 Marion Davies and Sisters

There were four Davies sisters: Reine, Ethel, Rose and Marion. Marion was the youngest, not the most beautiful, but, by virtue of her long association with William Randolph Hearst, easily the most famous.

She was born Marion Cecilia Douras, on 3 January 1897, in Brooklyn. Her original surname was Douras, being the daughter of Judge Bernard Douras, of Irish descent, who died at the respectable age of eighty-two.

Reine Davies was the eldest and prettiest sister. She sang in vaudeville and musicals, and married George Lederer, who became one of the most successful theatrical producers of his day. He ran the Casino theatre in New York 1893–1903, where he put on such shows as 'The Passing Show', and 'The Belle of New York' – the first American musical to enjoy major international success. George Lederer directed his young sister-in-law in her first film, *Runaway Romany* (1917). She had already made her stage début in a Broadway chorus line in 'Chin-Chin' aged sixteen and straight from her convent school.

Marion's first meeting with William Randolph Hearst, the famous Press baron, is not documented, but by early 1918 (when he was fifty-five and she twenty-one) he had set the wheels of her stardom in motion. He also arranged for her to star in her first big picture: *Cecilia of the Pink Roses* (1918). At his express order the Hearst columnists praised her beauty and presence to the heavens, especially his arch-creature, Louella Parsons, whose line, 'And Marion never looked lovelier', became a standing joke. Hearst commanded that Marion's name be mentioned at least once in every single Hearst newspaper.

In 1919 Hearst signed a deal with Adolph Zukor to release Marion's films through Paramount, thus forming a new company, Cosmopolitan, which ran until 1923. Nearly all of the eleven films that were made there lost money, primarily because Hearst insisted on the most expensive production techniques for his protegée. *When Knighthood Was in Flower* (1922), in which Marion played Henry VIII's skittish sister Mary, cost an astonishing $1.5 million. Hearst is said to have lost as much as $7 million on his Cosmopolitan ventures alone.

Marion Davies had a quite large following but she was so entirely restricted by Hearst's image of her as a pink-and-white milk-maid heroine, she bored herself and her fans to distraction. Her natural flair was for light comedy – she had a bawdy sense of humour, and more than liked a drink – but Hearst continued to dress her up in tizzy organdie dresses and puff sleeves, even when she was far too old for this style. He also strongly disapproved of hard liquor, and Marion was obliged to hide her gin in her bedroom.

When Hearst broke with Zukor he made a new deal with Sam Goldwyn, who then joined up with Louis B. Mayer to form MGM. This arrangement was financially very flattering to both Marion and Hearst, and at last she was given the chance to do some comedy. Two of her funniest films were *The Patsy* (1928), which contains some wicked Davies mimicry of Pola Negri, Mae Murray and Lillian Gish, and *Show People* (1928) – a marvellous film and a burlesque of Gloria Swanson's career.

Her stammer was quite noticeable on the transfer to sound, and her dialogue was consequently

Marion Davies with her lover and mentor, W. Randolph Hearst. Their relationship was one of Hollywood's best known 'secrets', and provided Orson Welles with much material for his Citizen Kane *(1941).*

limited. More troublesome, however, was a new bride at MGM – Norma Shearer – whose influential husband, Irving Thalberg, snatched all the peach roles from under Marion's nose. Thus she lost Elizabeth Barrett Browning in *The Barretts of Wimpole Street* (1934), and *Marie Antoinette* (1938) to her rival Shearer. After the inevitable break with MGM, Hearst banned all mention of Norma in his Press.

Now with Warner Bros, Marion made *Page Miss Glory* (1935), about a chambermaid who becomes a beauty queen, *Heart Divided* (1936), a Napoleonic love story, *Cain and Mabel* (1936), with Clark Gable, and *Ever Since Eve* (1937), with Robert Montgomery. With these films (she made forty-five in all) her film career came to an end. Hearst had sunk millions of dollars into her career but never made her into a box-office draw. When he finally relinquished control of his publications he was found to be $126 million in debt, and Marion did at least return some of the money he had squandered on her.

Marion and Hearst were the film colony's most inveterate party-givers. Extravagant costume balls were the entertainments most favoured by hosts and guests alike, and each one had to have its own theme. These varied from homely Tyrolean and high camp Spanish fiesta to 'come as your first ambition'. At one such event Norma Shearer deliberately snubbed Marion and ignored the 'all-American' theme. She arrived in a hugely elaborate and voluminous Marie-Antoinette costume, but the affront backfired somewhat as Shearer not only had to have the seats removed from her car in order to accommodate her skirts, but she was even too wide to effect an entrance through the main door. In the end the ballroom doors had to be specially opened up. Once inside, one could scarcely imagine a more incongruous scene than that of the French Queen surrounded by a sea of blue jeans and plaid shirts.

Although her hospitality was legendary, Marion was oddly neglectful of her niece, Pepi Lederer, who at one time showed some acting ability, and who needed a guiding hand. In fact, Marion had an ambivalent attitude to all her family. Her eldest sister Reine would drink too much and then start railing at Marion accusing her of taking her son and

daughter (Charles and Pepi Lederer) away from her, yet she continued to accept Marion's generosity and lived at her expense in the large Beverly Hills house she provided for the whole Davies family. The two middle sisters, Ethel and Rose, also lived there, but Rose set herself up as the mistress to another wealthy (and married) publisher, Edward B. McLean, who owned the *Washington Post*, and she annoyed Marion by making an exhibition of herself.

Charles Lederer was the only one of the second generation of the Davies dynasty to make a successful mark. He began as a journalist, then went to Hollywood in 1931 as a screenwriter, where he became a collaborator and close friend of Ben Hecht. He was highly respected for his ready wit and good humour, which may be seen in his work on *The Front Page* (1931), *His Girl Friday* (1940), *I Was a Male War Bride* (1949), and *Gentlemen Prefer Blondes* (1953). His first wife, socialite actress Virginia Nicolson, was formerly married to Orson Welles (thus creating an interesting link between Welles and his model for *Citizen Kane*), and his second wife, film actress Anne Shirley, is the mother-in-law of Robert Towne, himself a successful Hollywood director and writer.

Lederer's sister, Pepi, was a sad figure. She was born Josephine Rose Lederer on 18 March 1910, and nicknamed Peppy for her high spirits. She legally assumed this name (adapting the spelling to Pepi) in 1928. Her parents were divorced, and Marion, who never had any children of her own, exerted considerable influence over her adolescence. She was observant, creative and undisciplined. She ruined her delicate looks through gluttony, drink and drugs, and was all too easy prey for the freeloaders.

Perhaps the best thing that ever happened to Pepi was meeting Louise Brooks, the late actress, who wrote an affectionate memoir to her friend in *Lulu in Hollywood*. She describes how Pepi, unashamedly bi-sexual, gave a wild party in the Beverly Hills house while her aunt Marion and the others were away. King Vidor was finishing his all-Negro version of *Hallelujah!* (1929), and Pepi went to watch the final shooting; on the last day she asked her

Marion Davies's love of dressing up was notable both on and off the set. For Hearst's seventy-fourth birthday in 1937, Marion staged a circus party, for which she borrowed a carousel from Warner Bros. back lot, even though it meant tearing down one wall of her palatial Santa Monica beach house in order to install it.

friend, Nina Mae McKinney, and other members of the cast to come to a party. The revels were a great success and lasted three days. On the third day an anxious neighbour telephoned Marion who instantly told her sister Ethel to go round and investigate. Said Pepi, 'I'll never forget the expression on aunt Ethel's face when she opened my door and saw me in bed with Nina Mae.'

Sadly, the party was over all too soon for Pepi. In an attempt to establish some sort of independence she went to London for five years, but she couldn't escape her addictions and was summoned back by Marion, who had her committed to the Good Samaritan Hospital, Los Angeles. On the 12 June 1935 she leapt to her death from the 6th floor of the psychiatric wing. She was only twenty-five years old.

Louise Brooks was also an occasional visitor to 'San Simeon', the gloomy castle Welles re-named Xanadu in *Citizen Kane*. This was built on the site of a cattle ranch owned by Hearst's mother's family. In 1919 Hearst commissioned his mother's architect, Julia Morgan, to draw up plans for a new house, and over the next thirty years there were between a hundred and three hundred workmen permanently on the site. Hearst had married in 1903 Millicent Willson, by whom he had five sons. Although the marriage was only a façade by the time he met Marion Davies a divorce was out of the question.

Marion Davies once described to Louise Brooks, in a moment of rare intimacy, an accidental meeting she had with Mrs Hearst at a railway station. Marion was, of course, with Mr Hearst. 'We all stared at each other for a second, and W. R. went over to talk to her, leaving me standing there alone, and she gave me a look of such contempt – I could have killed her.' Marion was not only jealous of his wife, but she was constantly watchful of any other young actress who might catch Hearst's eye. It seems that Hearst was, if anything, a rather prudish man who much preferred to look than to touch.

Marion was probably extremely jealous of Miss Brooks, whose dazzling looks and clever tongue were much admired by Pepi and the younger generation. However, she was never banned from 'the ranch' – as 'San Simeon' was known to the chosen few – and she recalled its splendour over fifty years later: 'To me the most wondrously magnificent room in the castle was the great dining hall. I never entered it without a little shiver of delight. High above our heads, just beneath the ceiling, floated two rows of many-coloured Sienese racing banners dating from the thirteenth century. In the huge Gothic fireplace between the two entrance doors, a black stone satyr grinned wickedly through the flames rising from logs propped against his chest. The refectory table sat forty. Marion and Mr Hearst sat facing each other in the middle of the table with their important guests seated at either side.'

'San Simeon', like all the best fantasies, was never completed. Its rear façade and wings are still of rough-cast concrete, unfaced, but for Hearst it was a symbol of power. As far back as 1898 and the Spanish–American war over Cuba, Hearst displayed his belief that wealth equalled power, to which end he ran his newspaper empire. He commissioned Frederick Remington to be the official Hearst war artist in Cuba, and sent him out there. Before the fighting began, Remington complained he had nothing to do and was anxious to return home. Hearst's cabled reply was a classic: 'Please remain. You furnish the pictures, and I'll furnish the war.'

Hearst was a tired old man of seventy-eight when Welles completed his masterpiece *Citizen Kane*, a portrait of an ailing millionaire and his ageing actress-mistress doing jigsaw puzzles in an empty castle. He failed to have the film suppressed, and died ten years later on 14 August 1951.

Some ten weeks after Hearst's death, Marion married on 31 October 1951 (for the first and last time), Captain Horace Brown, a sometime skipper of an ocean-going tanker and former policeman, who bore an uncanny resemblance to her late lover. The similarity was purely physical, however, for his sense of humour was tiresomely juvenile. He pushed Marion into their swimming pool, his monkey bit her, and he had a habit of letting the air out of the tyres of her friends' cars.

Marion had lost her pretty blonde looks long before the time she died on 22 September 1961.

TABLE 26 THE DAVIES DYNASTY

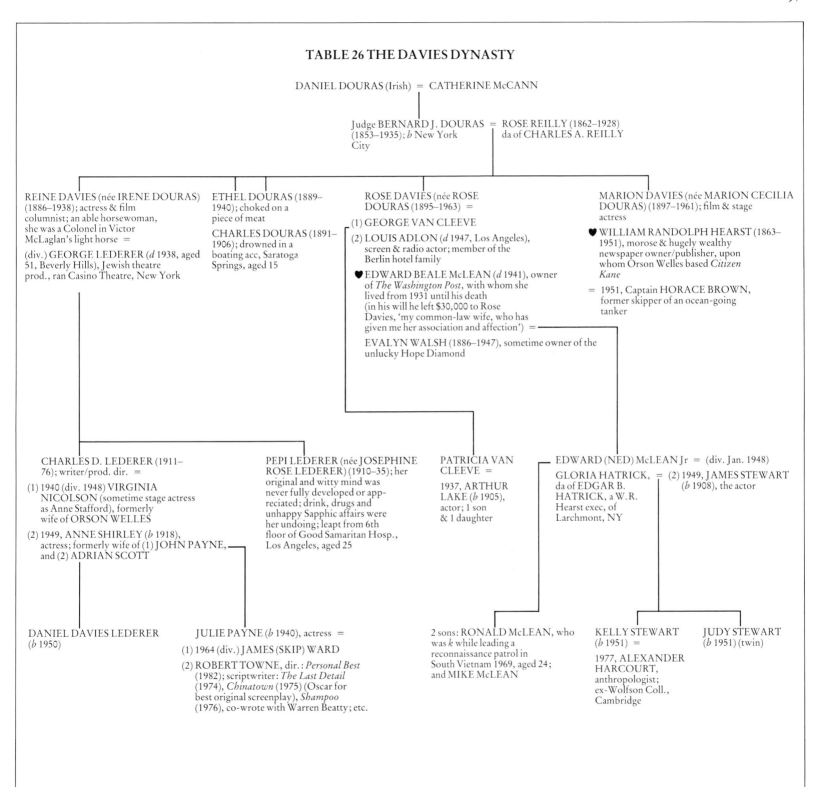

DANIEL DOURAS (Irish) = CATHERINE McCANN

Judge BERNARD J. DOURAS = ROSE REILLY (1862–1928)
(1853–1935); *b* New York   da of CHARLES A. REILLY
City

REINE DAVIES (née IRENE DOURAS) (1886–1938); actress & film columnist; an able horsewoman, she was a Colonel in Victor McLaglan's light horse =

(div.) GEORGE LEDERER (*d* 1938, aged 51, Beverly Hills), Jewish theatre prod., ran Casino Theatre, New York

ETHEL DOURAS (1889–1940); choked on a piece of meat

CHARLES DOURAS (1891–1906); drowned in a boating acc, Saratoga Springs, aged 15

ROSE DAVIES (née ROSE DOURAS (1895–1963) =

(1) GEORGE VAN CLEEVE

(2) LOUIS ADLON (*d* 1947, Los Angeles), screen & radio actor; member of the Berlin hotel family

♥ EDWARD BEALE McLEAN (*d* 1941), owner of *The Washington Post*, with whom she lived from 1931 until his death (in his will he left $30,000 to Rose Davies, 'my common-law wife, who has given me her association and affection') =

EVALYN WALSH (1886–1947), sometime owner of the unlucky Hope Diamond

MARION DAVIES (née MARION CECILIA DOURAS) (1897–1961); film & stage actress

♥ WILLIAM RANDOLPH HEARST (1863–1951), morose & hugely wealthy newspaper owner/publisher, upon whom Orson Welles based *Citizen Kane*

= 1951, Captain HORACE BROWN, former skipper of an ocean-going tanker

CHARLES D. LEDERER (1911–76); writer/prod. dir. =

(1) 1940 (div. 1948) VIRGINIA NICOLSON (sometime stage actress as Anne Stafford), formerly wife of ORSON WELLES

(2) 1949, ANNE SHIRLEY (*b* 1918), actress; formerly wife of (1) JOHN PAYNE, and (2) ADRIAN SCOTT

PEPI LEDERER (née JOSEPHINE ROSE LEDERER) (1910–35); her original and witty mind was never fully developed or appreciated; drink, drugs and unhappy Sapphic affairs were her undoing; leapt from 6th floor of Good Samaritan Hosp., Los Angeles, aged 25

PATRICIA VAN CLEEVE =

1937, ARTHUR LAKE (*b* 1905), actor; 1 son & 1 daughter

EDWARD (NED) McLEAN Jr = (div. Jan. 1948)

GLORIA HATRICK, = (2) 1949, JAMES STEWART
da of EDGAR B.   (*b* 1908), the actor
HATRICK, a W.R.
Hearst exec, of
Larchmont, NY

DANIEL DAVIES LEDERER (*b* 1950)

JULIE PAYNE (*b* 1940), actress =

(1) 1964 (div.) JAMES (SKIP) WARD

(2) ROBERT TOWNE, dir.: *Personal Best* (1982); scriptwriter: *The Last Detail* (1974), *Chinatown* (1975) (Oscar for best original screenplay), *Shampoo* (1976), co-wrote with Warren Beatty; etc.

2 sons: RONALD McLEAN, who was *k* while leading a reconnaissance patrol in South Vietnam 1969, aged 24; and MIKE McLEAN

KELLY STEWART (*b* 1951) =

1977, ALEXANDER HARCOURT, anthropologist; ex-Wolfson Coll., Cambridge

JUDY STEWART (*b* 1951) (twin)

10 The Lasky, Goldwyn and Warner Dynasties

Through various family ramifications it is possible to link three of the major Hollywood studios: Paramount, Goldwyn and Warner. The three tables, 27, 28 and 29, show how it's done.

The main characters of this studio network are Jesse Lasky, Sam Goldwyn and Jack Warner. They were all powerful, distinguished and colourful figures with a distinct tendency to overshadow their heirs.

JESSE LASKY

Jesse Lasky was the most tractable of the three. He was born in San Francisco in 1880, where he worked briefly as a reporter. After an uncharacteristic attempt at gold speculating in Alaska, he turned to his musical talents and played in a cornet duo act in vaudeville with his sister Blanche. From performing, he gradually moved into the business side of vaudeville as a promoter and impresario. In 1910 Blanche married Sam Goldfish, an ambitious young glove cutter, who urged Lasky to set up a film studio, and in 1913 Lasky and Goldfish and their friend Cecil B. De Mille formed the Jesse L. Lasky Feature Play Company.

They scored an immediate success with their maiden venture, *The Squaw Man* (1914), the first large-scale Western, which became a milestone in film history and helped put Hollywood on the map. In 1916 they merged with Adolph Zukor's Famous Players to form Famous Players – Lasky Corporation, of which Zukor was president and Lasky vice-president. Through a series of mini-mergers this company was eventually renamed Paramount. In the early 1930s it suffered from the Depression and Lasky was ousted. His quiet integrity was unsuited to the devious ploys practised by the new men in the changing Hollywood scene, and Lasky became an independent producer at Fox, Warners and RKO. Among other films he made were *The Power and the Glory* (1933), with Spencer Tracy, and the splendid *Sergeant York* (1941), starring Gary Cooper. Although the latter made a handsome profit, Lasky was unwisely advised to register the earnings as a capital gain, which provoked the Internal Revenue and eventually lead to his financial ruin.

Lasky's wife, Bessie Ginzberg, was an accomplished concert pianist, who won the gold medal of the Boston Conservatory of Music. She was the daughter of Bernard Himmelhoff, originally from Russia, who assumed the surname of Ginzburg *c.* 1870, by his Australian-born wife Ray Harris. She was also a painter and writer, and published an autobiography, *Candle in the Sun*.

All three of their children are/were writers. The eldest, Jesse Lasky Jr graduated from Princeton in 1932 and wrote, or co-wrote, several films for his father's former partner, Cecil B. De Mille, including *Union Pacific* (1939), *Reap the Wild Wind* (1942), and *Unconquered* (1947); also two of his biblical epics, *Samson and Delilah* (1949) and *The Ten Commandments* (1956). He later moved to London, where he wrote episodes for the TV series 'The Avengers' and 'The Saint', but he turned increasingly to other forms of writing, generally with his third wife, former actress Barbara Hayden, and has published a book about

TABLE 27 THE GOLDWYN DYNASTY

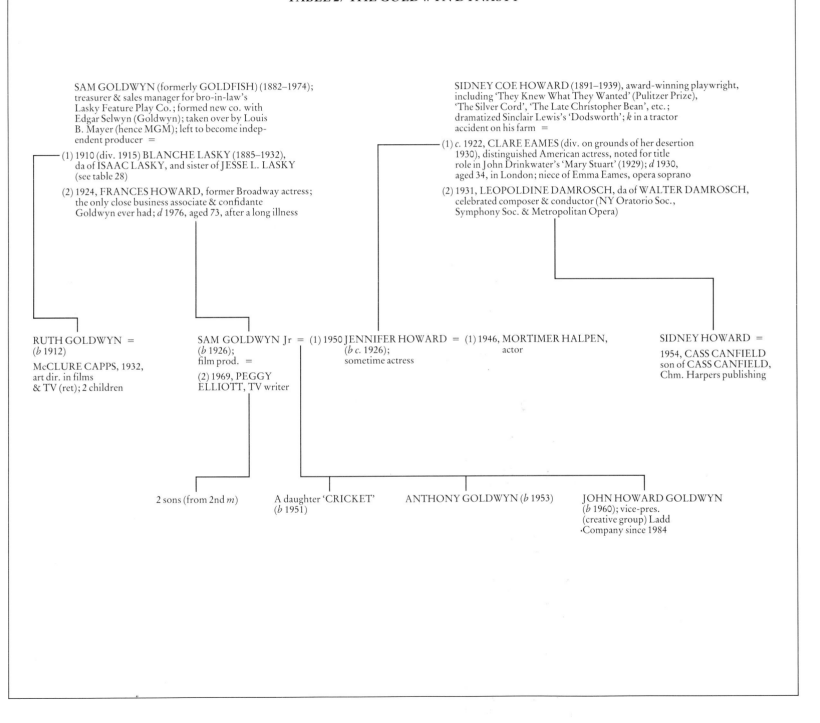

SAM GOLDWYN (formerly GOLDFISH) (1882–1974);
treasurer & sales manager for bro-in-law's
Lasky Feature Play Co.; formed new co. with
Edgar Selwyn (Goldwyn); taken over by Louis
B. Mayer (hence MGM); left to become indep-
endent producer =

(1) 1910 (div. 1915) BLANCHE LASKY (1885–1932),
da of ISAAC LASKY, and sister of JESSE L. LASKY
(see table 28)

(2) 1924, FRANCES HOWARD, former Broadway actress;
the only close business associate & confidante
Goldwyn ever had; d 1976, aged 73, after a long illness

SIDNEY COE HOWARD (1891–1939), award-winning playwright,
including 'They Knew What They Wanted' (Pulitzer Prize),
'The Silver Cord', 'The Late Christopher Bean', etc.;
dramatized Sinclair Lewis's 'Dodsworth'; k in a tractor
accident on his farm =

(1) c. 1922, CLARE EAMES (div. on grounds of her desertion
1930), distinguished American actress, noted for title
role in John Drinkwater's 'Mary Stuart' (1929); d 1930,
aged 34, in London; niece of Emma Eames, opera soprano

(2) 1931, LEOPOLDINE DAMROSCH, da of WALTER DAMROSCH,
celebrated composer & conductor (NY Oratorio Soc.,
Symphony Soc. & Metropolitan Opera)

RUTH GOLDWYN =
(b 1912)

McCLURE CAPPS, 1932,
art dir. in films
& TV (ret); 2 children

SAM GOLDWYN Jr = (1) 1950 JENNIFER HOWARD = (1) 1946, MORTIMER HALPEN,
(b 1926);   (b c. 1926);   actor
film prod. =   sometime actress

(2) 1969, PEGGY
ELLIOTT, TV writer

SIDNEY HOWARD =

1954, CASS CANFIELD
son of CASS CANFIELD,
Chm. Harpers publishing

2 sons (from 2nd m)

A daughter 'CRICKET'
(b 1951)

ANTHONY GOLDWYN (b 1953)

JOHN HOWARD GOLDWYN
(b 1960); vice-pres.
(creative group) Ladd
·Company since 1984

Laurence Olivier and Vivien Leigh, and a memoir rhetorically entitled *Whatever Happened to Hollywood?* He is a short, quietly-spoken man with a diffident and scholarly manner, in striking contrast to his former uncle-by-marriage, Sam Goldwyn.

The younger Lasky son, animal-lover William Raymond Lasky, served as assistant director to his father on *Sergeant York* (and married its director Howard Hawks's personal assistant, Margery Lowe). Then he wrote, directed and filmed *The Boy and the Eagle* (1940), a touching story of a crippled boy who nurses a wounded eagle back to health and in doing so is inspired to walk again. It was nominated for an Oscar as the best short film for 1941, when he was still only twenty years old, and it was to be the highlight of his career.

Unfortunately William never lived up to his early promise. His marriage failed and he had difficulty in holding down any job. Although he preferred working with animals to humans he was sacked from his post in the reptile house at the Griffith Park Zoo, and he was finally reduced to selling his prize collection of humming-birds in order to eat. He turned to religion, first to Buddhism and then he became a Born-Again Christian. He recounted his unhappy career in a quasi-religious tract *Tell It on the Mountain* (1976), and died in 1984, survived by a son.

Jesse Lasky's only daughter, Betty Lasky, youngest of the three children, is a film historian, and wrote *RKO; The Biggest Little Major of them All* (1985).

SAM GOLDWYN

Lasky's temperamental brother-in-law, Sam Goldfish, had a remarkable history. He was born in Warsaw in 1882, and at eleven years old made his way, alone, to England where he stayed with relations and worked for a blacksmith. Two years later he arrived in the USA, destitute and friendless. He found work as an apprentice glove-maker, which paid for his classes at night school, and then became a travelling glove salesman. He was still a

glove-man when he met and married Blanche Lasky, who, ironically, sought wedded bliss as a means of escape from the vaudeville life her brother had chosen for her.

The glove industry took a tumble in 1912, at which point Goldfish persuaded his brother-in-law to leave vaudeville and break into films. Sam became their sales manager and treasurer. After an adventurous and lucrative three years with Lasky and De Mille, Goldfish agreed to be bought out for $900,000, and, in 1916, formed a new partnership with Edgar Selwyn. This led to the birth of Goldwyn – the celebrated merger of their two surnames (Goldwyn as opposed to Selfish) – which Sam legally assumed in 1918 in lieu of Goldfish.

In spite of Goldwyn's high-flown intentions to produce films of 'intelligence and refinement', and a fair number of successful movies, the company was forced to accept Louis B. Mayer's take-over bid (which thus formed Metro–Goldwyn–Mayer). A dispossessed and disillusioned Sam swore he would never take another business partner – a vow he kept, excepting his second wife, Frances, who became his unofficial production assistant. In 1924 he formed Sam Goldwyn productions, with total independence, and he invested every single cent in recruiting the best writers, directors and actors available. As Katz summarizes, 'Goldwyn had the rare knack of consistently being able to put the right team together and inspire it with his intuitive artistry.'

Probably his most rewarding artistic association was with William Wyler, who directed some of his best films for the Goldwyn Company, among others: *These Three* (1936), *Come and Get It* (1936; co-directed), *Dodsworth* (1936), *Stella Dallas* (1937), *Wuthering Heights* (1939), *The Little Foxes* (1941), and *The Best Years of Our Lives* (1946), the last of which won Goldwyn the Irving Thalberg Memorial Award in the 1946 Oscar ceremony. He was also responsible for giving a large number of stars their first starring roles: Ronald Colman, Gary Cooper, Danny Kaye, David Niven, Will Rogers, Susan Hayward, Merle Oberon and Vera-Ellen, etc.

By his first wife, whom he divorced in 1915, he had issue one daughter, Ruth Goldwyn, whom he

Jesse Lasky shakes hands with Cecil B. DeMille, flanked by Sam Goldwyn (left) and Adolph Zukor, at the designation in 1956 of the barn on Jacob Stern's farm in Hollywood village as an historical landmark. It was here that DeMille directed The Squaw Man *(1914), produced by Lasky, which became a milestone in film history. The barn was moved to Paramount's lot in 1927.*

seldom mentioned in later life. She married McClure Capps, a designer and assistant director, by whom she has issue, Blanche, now Mrs Stern, born 1933, and Alan Henshaw Capps, born 1939, who had been a motion picture and still cameraman. Sam's second marriage in 1924, to former Broadway actress Frances Howard, some twenty-one years his junior, was a success, and lasted until his death in 1974. She died two years later.

Goldwyn's legacy also included some very funny malapropisms: for example, 'Include me out,' 'A verbal contract isn't worth the paper it's written

on,' and, on being told Lasky's younger son was to be called William, 'Why would you name him Bill? Every Tom, Dick and Harry is named Bill.'

His only child by Frances was a son, Sam Jr, born in 1926. After graduating from the University of Virginia, he joined his father's company. While acknowledging his father's achievements, many of Goldwyn Jr's productions have dealt indirectly with the subject of father-and-son conflict and the escape from paternal influence, for example *Huckleberry Finn* (1960), and *The Proud Rebel* (1958) which had the interesting father–son casting of Alan and

David Ladd.

Sam Jr's first wife, Jennifer Howard, was the daughter of Sidney Howard, an eminent American playwright, by whom he has three children. His younger son, John Goldwyn, has followed his father into film production and, in 1984, was appointed a vice-president of the Ladd Company.

MERVYN LEROY

Returning to Jesse Lasky, the precise link between him and director Mervyn LeRoy has not been established. LeRoy is variously described as a nephew and cousin of Lasky Sr, but neither side of the family seems to have ascertained what the exact relationship was. It is certain, however, that LeRoy arrived in Hollywood in 1919, where his first job in the wardrobe department at Famous Players–Lasky may be attributed to his family connection.

Mervyn LeRoy became a first-rate all-genre film director. He established his reputation at Warner Bros. with *Little Caesar* (1931), which launched Edward G. Robinson's career and Warner's cycle of gangster pictures, and *I am a Fugitive From a Chain Gang* (1932), which starred Paul Muni. He successfully turned to musicals and comedy with *Gold Diggers of 1933*, also at Warners, *Tugboat Annie* (1933), and *Sweet Adeline* (1935). He moved to MGM in 1939 where his output included *Waterloo Bridge* (1940) and *Random Harvest* (1942), both romantic tear-jerkers, *Unholy Partners* (1941), crime melodrama, *Johnny Eager* (1942), gangster melodrama, *Madame Curie* (1943), stodgy biopic in which Greer Garson discovers radium, *Thirty Seconds Over Tokyo* (1944), war picture, *Without Reservations* (1946), romantic comedy, *Little Women* (1949), syrupy adaptation, *Any Number Can Play* (1949), and *East Side West Side* (1950), both melodramas. He returned to musicals with *Million Dollar Mermaid* (1952), starring Esther Williams, and *Lovely to Look At* (1952), with Kathryn Grayson and Howard Keel. As a producer his outstanding achievement was *The Wizard of Oz* (1939).

Dynastically speaking his second (of three) marriages is the most interesting. This was in 1934 – in the midst of his work for Warners – to Doris Warner, daughter of Harry Warner the company president. Doris became an influential figure in her own right, first as a theatre backer, and then as a governing trustee of the American Ballet Theatre and a director of the American National Theatre and Academy. Her marriage to LeRoy was dissolved by divorce in 1944, and her subsequent marriages to Charles Vidor and Billy Rose continued her involvement in show business.

JACK WARNER

The central figure of the Warner family was Jack Warner, the youngest of twelve children of Polish immigrants. Four of the brothers, Harry, Albert, Sam and Jack established the Warner Bros. company in 1923, with Jack as the production chief. They made screen history in 1927 with the first ever talkie feature, *The Jazz Singer*, in which Al Jolson uttered the immortal words, 'You ain't heard nothin' yet.'

Tactless and tight-fisted, Jack Warner frequently clashed with some of his biggest stars, notably Humphrey Bogart, James Cagney, Bette Davis and Olivia de Havilland (the latter won an important legal battle against Warners which resulted in seven years being the absolute limit, including suspensions, of any studio–player contract). Others in the Warners' stable were Errol Flynn, Joan Blondell and Lauren Bacall.

Jack felt most at home with his gangster pictures, and it was only at the insistence of his elder brother, Harry, that Max Reinhardt, the Austrian stage director, was asked by Warners to co-direct (with William Dieterle) his only US production, *A Midsummer Night's Dream* (1935). Warners also brought out a number of biographical pictures, two of which starred Paul Muni in the title role: *The Story of Louis Pasteur* (1936), and *The Life of Emile Zola* (1937), but the most memorable of all were the tense romantic

TABLE 28 THE LASKY AND LEROY DYNASTIES

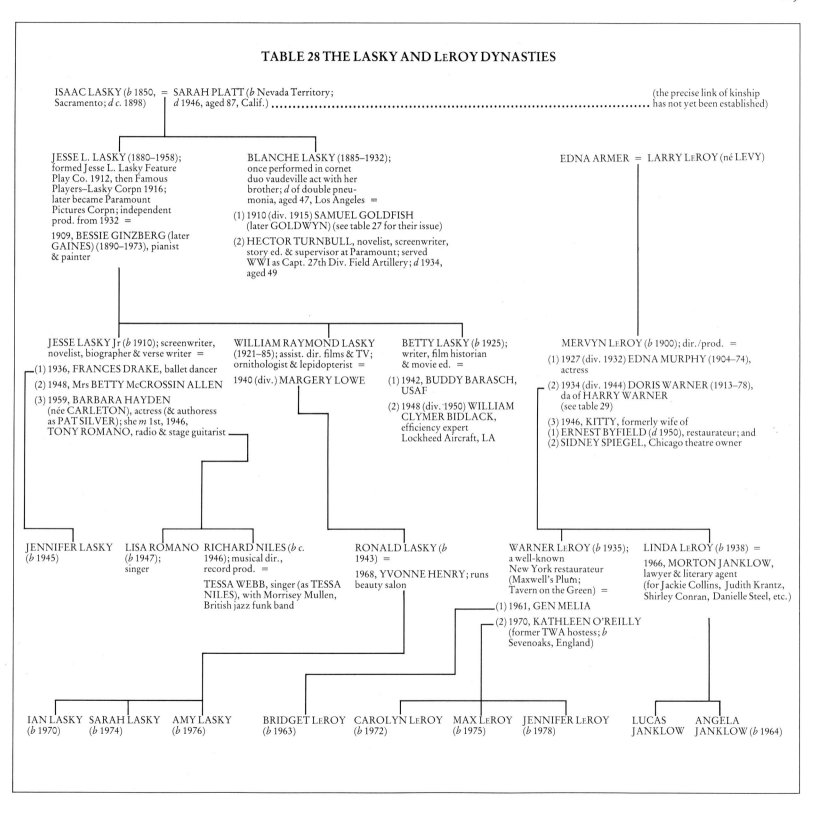

ISAAC LASKY (*b* 1850, = SARAH PLATT (*b* Nevada Territory; Sacramento; *d c.* 1898) *d* 1946, aged 87, Calif.) .... (the precise link of kinship has not yet been established)

JESSE L. LASKY (1880–1958); formed Jesse L. Lasky Feature Play Co. 1912, then Famous Players–Lasky Corpn 1916; later became Paramount Pictures Corpn; independent prod. from 1932 =

1909, BESSIE GINZBERG (later GAINES) (1890–1973), pianist & painter

BLANCHE LASKY (1885–1932); once performed in cornet duo vaudeville act with her brother; *d* of double pneumonia, aged 47, Los Angeles =

(1) 1910 (div. 1915) SAMUEL GOLDFISH (later GOLDWYN) (see table 27 for their issue)

(2) HECTOR TURNBULL, novelist, screenwriter, story ed. & supervisor at Paramount; served WWI as Capt. 27th Div. Field Artillery; *d* 1934, aged 49

EDNA ARMER = LARRY LeROY (né LEVY)

JESSE LASKY Jr (*b* 1910); screenwriter, novelist, biographer & verse writer =

(1) 1936, FRANCES DRAKE, ballet dancer

(2) 1948, Mrs BETTY McCROSSIN ALLEN

(3) 1959, BARBARA HAYDEN (née CARLETON), actress (& authoress as PAT SILVER); she *m* 1st, 1946, TONY ROMANO, radio & stage guitarist

WILLIAM RAYMOND LASKY (1921–85); assist. dir. films & TV; ornithologist & lepidopterist =

1940 (div.) MARGERY LOWE

BETTY LASKY (*b* 1925); writer, film historian & movie ed. =

(1) 1942, BUDDY BARASCH, USAF

(2) 1948 (div. 1950) WILLIAM CLYMER BIDLACK, efficiency expert Lockheed Aircraft, LA

MERVYN LeROY (*b* 1900); dir./prod. =

(1) 1927 (div. 1932) EDNA MURPHY (1904–74), actress

(2) 1934 (div. 1944) DORIS WARNER (1913–78), da of HARRY WARNER (see table 29)

(3) 1946, KITTY, formerly wife of (1) ERNEST BYFIELD (*d* 1950), restaurateur; and (2) SIDNEY SPIEGEL, Chicago theatre owner

JENNIFER LASKY (*b* 1945)

LISA ROMANO (*b* 1947); singer

RICHARD NILES (*b c.* 1946); musical dir., record prod. =

TESSA WEBB, singer (as TESSA NILES), with Morrisey Mullen, British jazz funk band

RONALD LASKY (*b* 1943) =

1968, YVONNE HENRY; runs beauty salon

WARNER LeROY (*b* 1935); a well-known New York restaurateur (Maxwell's Plum; Tavern on the Green) =

(1) 1961, GEN MELIA

(2) 1970, KATHLEEN O'REILLY (former TWA hostess; *b* Sevenoaks, England)

LINDA LeROY (*b* 1938) =

1966, MORTON JANKLOW, lawyer & literary agent (for Jackie Collins, Judith Krantz, Shirley Conran, Danielle Steel, etc.)

IAN LASKY (*b* 1970)

SARAH LASKY (*b* 1974)

AMY LASKY (*b* 1976)

BRIDGET LeROY (*b* 1963)

CAROLYN LeROY (*b* 1972)

MAX LeROY (*b* 1975)

JENNIFER LeROY (*b* 1978)

LUCAS JANKLOW

ANGELA JANKLOW (*b* 1964)

Max Reinhardt (centre) with Jack L. Warner (left), who produced his only US production, A Midsummer Night's Dream *(1935) for Warner Bros. and W. Randolph Hearst, whose Cosmopolitan Films moved from MGM to Warners in 1934.*

melodramas of the 1940s: *The Letter, High Sierra, The Maltese Falcon, Casablanca,* and *Mildred Pierce.*

The antipathy between Jack and Harry worsened considerably when Jack divorced his wife of twenty-one years in order to marry a young Gentile actress. To Harry this was quite unacceptable. He was also bitterly upset by the premature death of his only son, Lewis Warner, whom he had hoped would succeed him in the business side of the company. Lewis had been educated at Worcester Academy, Massachusetts, and Columbia University, and met his end when, having had a tooth out, he ignored medical advice and insisted on going to Havana for a holiday. While there blood poisoning set in, and although he was immediately flown to New York, he died within a matter of weeks. Harry Warner donated $250,000 to Worcester Academy to build a theatre as a memorial to his son.

Jack's divorce also alienated his only son, Jack Jr. He was eighteen at that time and had always been close to his mother. Although he was temperamentally unsuited to the scheming world of the film industry, Jack nevertheless corralled him into the business. Jack Sr had never spent a great deal of time with his son, and when his new wife provided him with a child, a daughter Barbara, he concentrated all his attention on her and his new step-daughter Joy.

Complete estrangement of father and son occurred in 1958 when Jack Sr was involved in a serious motor accident in France. Jack Jr's statement to the Press was so muddled by the journalists that it sounded as though Jack Sr had been killed. Jack Jr was banned from the Warner lot and consequently went into independent production, but without success. He derived much of his plot for his book *Bijou Dream* (1982) from the conflicts within his own family.

TABLE 29 THE WARNER BROS. DYNASTY

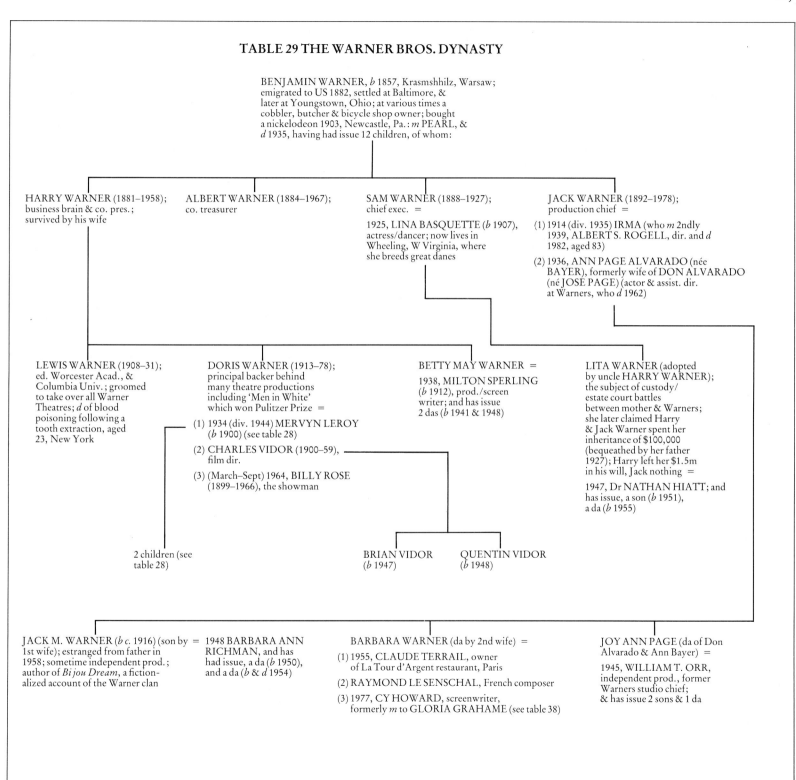

BENJAMIN WARNER, *b* 1857, Krasmshhilz, Warsaw;
emigrated to US 1882, settled at Baltimore, &
later at Youngstown, Ohio; at various times a
cobbler, butcher & bicycle shop owner; bought
a nickelodeon 1903, Newcastle, Pa.: *m* PEARL, &
d 1935, having had issue 12 children, of whom:

HARRY WARNER (1881–1958);
business brain & co. pres.;
survived by his wife

ALBERT WARNER (1884–1967);
co. treasurer

SAM WARNER (1888–1927);
chief exec. =

1925, LINA BASQUETTE (*b* 1907),
actress/dancer; now lives in
Wheeling, W Virginia, where
she breeds great danes

JACK WARNER (1892–1978);
production chief =

(1) 1914 (div. 1935) IRMA (who *m* 2ndly
1939, ALBERT S. ROGELL, dir. and *d*
1982, aged 83)

(2) 1936, ANN PAGE ALVARADO (née
BAYER), formerly wife of DON ALVARADO
(né JOSE PAGE) (actor & assist. dir.
at Warners, who *d* 1962)

LEWIS WARNER (1908–31);
ed. Worcester Acad., &
Columbia Univ.; groomed
to take over all Warner
Theatres; *d* of blood
poisoning following a
tooth extraction, aged
23, New York

DORIS WARNER (1913–78);
principal backer behind
many theatre productions
including 'Men in White'
which won Pulitzer Prize =

(1) 1934 (div. 1944) MERVYN LEROY
(*b* 1900) (see table 28)

(2) CHARLES VIDOR (1900–59),
film dir.

(3) (March–Sept) 1964, BILLY ROSE
(1899–1966), the showman

BETTY MAY WARNER =

1938, MILTON SPERLING
(*b* 1912), prod./screen
writer; and has issue
2 das (*b* 1941 & 1948)

LITA WARNER (adopted
by uncle HARRY WARNER);
the subject of custody/
estate court battles
between mother & Warners;
she later claimed Harry
& Jack Warner spent her
inheritance of $100,000
(bequeathed by her father
1927); Harry left her $1.5m
in his will, Jack nothing =

1947, Dr NATHAN HIATT; and
has issue, a son (*b* 1951),
a da (*b* 1955)

2 children (see
table 28)

BRIAN VIDOR
(*b* 1947)

QUENTIN VIDOR
(*b* 1948)

JACK M. WARNER (*b c.* 1916) (son by =
1st wife); estranged from father in
1958; sometime independent prod.;
author of *Bijou Dream*, a fiction-
alized account of the Warner clan

1948 BARBARA ANN
RICHMAN, and has
had issue, a da (*b* 1950),
and a da (*b* & *d* 1954)

BARBARA WARNER (da by 2nd wife) =

(1) 1955, CLAUDE TERRAIL, owner
of La Tour d'Argent restaurant, Paris

(2) RAYMOND LE SENSCHAL, French composer

(3) 1977, CY HOWARD, screenwriter,
formerly *m* to GLORIA GRAHAME (see table 38)

JOY ANN PAGE (da of Don
Alvarado & Ann Bayer) =

1945, WILLIAM T. ORR,
independent prod., former
Warners studio chief;
& has issue 2 sons & 1 da

11 Tyrone Power: Ancestry and Family

The Powers are a family of theatrical and musical achievement. Irish in origin, they flourished in London in the nineteenth century as soldiers, engineers and actors, but world recognition was attained in the present century, first with Sir Tyrone Guthrie, the leading Shakespearean director of his day, and later with Tyrone Power, the film star. Through various connections by marriage it is possible to draw Evelyn Waugh and Lord Olivier into the family web.

The first Tyrone Power was 'handsome and well made'. According to the *Dictionary of National Biography* he was 'about five feet eight inches . . . light and agile . . . with a very animated and expressive face, light complexion, blue eyes and brown hair.' He was best in representations of blustering, good-natured and eccentric Irish characters, and his spontaneous good humour shone through even the most indifferent comedies.

His father came from a well-off Waterford family and died when Tyrone was still very young. His mother, Maria Maxwell (who once told her son, 'You're a proud man Tyrone, but if you knew who your father really was you'd be even prouder'), was the daughter of either a Colonel Maxwell who fell in the American War of Independence, or perhaps an officer in the Waterford Militia. She was personally acquainted with Grattan and Curran and other patriots of the 1798 Rebellion.

Following her husband's death, Mrs Power left Ireland and rented a small cottage near Cardiff, in Wales, from a Mr Bird, bookseller, printer and keeper of the post office, whose wife was a distant relation of the Powers. He was also the printer to the Cardiff Playhouse, and it is through him that Tyrone, then aged fourteen, met and joined a company of travelling players. In 1815 he visited the Isle of Wight where he met his future wife, Anne Gilbert. They were married in 1817. She had a little money of her own, and, discouraged by his lack of theatrical success, Tyrone temporarily abandoned the stage and entered a speculation for the settlement of Algoe Bay in the Cape Territory of South Africa. He went to live there in January 1820, but his health suffered and he returned to England in June 1821. On the passage home he sailed close by St Helena, where he saw an eagle rise high into the sky above the island; later he learnt it was on that very day Napoleon had died in exile there.

Power returned to the stage. While working in various small parts at Covent Garden in 1826 (aged twenty-nine), a heaven-sent opportunity arrived. Charles Connor, the leading Irish comedian of the London stage, suddenly dropped dead in St James's Park, and Power was engaged to replace him. His parts were as Serjeant Milligan in 'Return Killed', and O'Shaughnessy in 'One Hundred Pound Note'. An overnight success, he went on to enjoy long runs for high fees in London's leading theatres, Haymarket, Adelphi and Covent Garden.

He also made annual appearances at the Theatre Royal, Dublin, where he received a spirited welcome. Between 1833 and 1840 he made four tours of America. On his second tour in 1837 he had a bad riding accident in Virginia; he was riding through the night to catch his boat home, his horse fell and he had to ride a further twenty miles to Richmond with a broken collar bone. His third

American tour consisted of sixty-eight performances from which he made $17,500. He bought 25,000 acres in Texas and a plot of land in New York (where Madison Square Gardens now stands); he also invested in a bank which subsequently got into financial difficulties.

Returning from his fourth American tour he bought a ticket from his friend Joe Wood (who had decided not to travel) for his passage home on the steam-ship *President*. This was the largest steamer afloat, not yet six months old, with a cargo of cotton bales and 123 passengers, including his young friend, Lord FitzRoy Lennox, second son of the 5th Duke of Richmond. According to *The Times*, Power was returning with $30,000 in cash, having sold his American lands, and was due to open the Haymarket season in London on Easter Monday, 12 April 1841, in his own farce ironically entitled 'Born to Good Luck, or the Irishman's Fortune'. The ship set sail from New York on 11 March 1841, but the following night a great storm arose and it is thought that she may have struck an iceberg. Before daybreak of Sunday, 14 March the *President* had disappeared forever. All passengers and crew perished, and no trace of the wreck was ever found. Power was aged forty-four.

His widow was left with seven children to raise. Briefly, her four sons were as follows: (1) Sir William Power, a soldier, who fought in the Crimea, was acting Governor General for New Zealand, and knighted by Queen Victoria; his grandson was the stage director Sir Tyrone Guthrie. (2) Maurice Power, who acted 'with small success' at the Park Theatre, New York, 1848, but who died in poverty aged twenty-eight. (3) Frederick Power, who became a civil engineer and immensely rich. He bought Frank's Hall, Kent, an imposing Elizabethan manor house, built in 1549, part brick, part stone, which is still standing. When he died the *Dartford Chronicle* reported that 'although he owned the most beautiful mansion in the neighbourhood, he resided there only for short periods, and was known to only a limited circle.' (4) Harold Power, the youngest son, whose line we follow.

Of Harold Power only odd scraps of his life are known. Unlike his three elder brothers he was not educated at Tonbridge School. As he was only eight when his father was drowned, he probably had not started his education, and there may not have been enough money to send him to a private school. He got a job in a post office, and, after his marriage to Eliza Lavenu, had a stab at acting (under the name Harold Page). He is thought to have been the original Cox of Sir Arthur Sullivan's opera 'Box and Cox', which was first produced as a benefit performance by the staff of *Punch* at the Adelphi Theatre in 1867. He is also said to have toured with his wife in a comedy turn, 'An Entertainment' by W. S. Gilbert, but on his marriage certificate he was clearly described as a wine merchant. He inherited a quarter share of his brother Frank's fortune and died in 1901 leaving over £37,000.

Harold Power's wife, Eliza (known as Ethel) Lavenu came from a family of musicians. Her grandfather, Lewis Lavenu, founded a musical publishing business, and by 1808 had obtained the patronage of the Prince Regent. Eliza's father, also named Lewis Lavenu, was a 'cellist and composer before becoming director of music at the Sydney Theatre, Australia.

From Eliza Lavenu's grandmother's second marriage to Nicholas Mori (see table 33), there are further musical associations. Mori himself was a brilliant violinist, and at the age of nineteen was appointed leader of the Philharmonic orchestra. He was also a member of the first board of professors of the Academy of Music (now the Royal Academy) in 1823. An aggressive and competitive character, he eventually became mentally deranged – a condition to which syphilis had probably contributed – and immediately before his death, aged forty-two, he announced a concert, the programmes for which were headed by the macabre device of a skull over the legend, *Memento Mori*. The *Gentleman's Magazine* obituary for Nicholas Mori said, 'His attitude had the grace of manly confidence; his bow-arm was bold, free and commanding; and he produced an eminently firm, full and impressive tone.'

Of the four Power brothers, only Harold has

Tyrone Power with his mother, Patia. She survived him by one year and died at the age of seventy-seven – a far greater age than all the theatrical Powers.

surviving male descendants. His son, Tyrone Power (II), was removed from his school at the age of fourteen and sent to Florida to learn to grow citrus fruit. He tolerated his oranges and lemons for three years, but after his crop failed he ran away from the farm and joined a touring company of actors. Through Ellen Terry he obtained a letter of introduction to Augustin Daly, for whom he worked for ten years. His earliest American success was as Lord Steyne in Mrs Fiske's production of 'Becky Sharp', in which he gave a performance of 'grizly eccentric force' (according to William Winter). He followed this with a memorable Judas in 'Mary of Magdala' (1902).

His subsequent roles in poetic dramas and romantic tragedies resulted in him being identified as the classical 'heroic' figure of the rhetorical school – then popular with the public. He was successful too in Charles Rann Kennedy's 'The Servant in the House' (New York, 1908), and as Brutus in 'Julius Caesar' (1912). The great social changes brought in by the First World War made Power's melodramatic style of bearing and speech seem hopelessly 'ham'

and antique, and he fell from favour. He was a powerfully built man with a deep voice and handsome features, but he lacked the humour of his comedian grandfather and was altogether too conscious of his 'establishment' image. He went to Hollywood where he appeared in a number of silent pictures, ranging from leading roles to character parts; he was in one 'talkie', *The Big Trail* (1930), and he died in Los Angeles, on 30 December 1931, aged sixty-two.

He married three times. First to Edith Crane, by whom he had no children and from whom he separated. She died in 1912. His second wife was Patia Reaume (née Helen Emma Reaume), of Cincinatti (her mother's sister was Helen Schuster, who founded the Schuster Martin drama school in Cincinnati). They had two children, Tyrone Power (III), the film star, and Ann Power, and they were divorced after about four years. His third and last wife was a well-connected young actress, Bertha Knight (he was fifty-seven, she thirty-four); she was the daughter of William Henry Knight, scientific writer and lecturer, and sometime editorial writer on the *Los Angeles Times*. She died seven years later. There was no issue from this marriage.

TYRONE POWER (III)
Only son of Tyrone Power (II) and Patia Reaume

This handsome leading man was born on 5 May 1913, in Cincinnati. Following his parents' divorce, when he was about three years old, he was raised by his mother. She married again, to one Clarence T. Arper, of California, but she again divorced in 1922. She worked for an electrotherapy doctor in Hollywood and outlived her son by one year, dying in 1959, aged seventy-seven.

At sixteen Tyrone Power joined his father in New York, where he was starring in 'The Merchant of Venice', and young Tyrone got a walk-on part. Two years later, in 1931, Power took his son to Hollywood, where he was to start rehearsals for the title role in *The Miracle Man* (1932) for Paramount. After four days Tyrone Sr died from a heart attack.

Tyrone decided to stay in Hollywood and was signed up by Darryl Zanuck at 20th Century Fox. His splendid looks were perfect for the screen, and his films of the 1930s won him tremendous popularity: *Lloyds of London* (1936), *In Old Chicago* (1937), *Alexander's Ragtime Band* (1937). Norma Shearer particularly asked for him to play her lover, Count Fersen, in *Marie Antoinette* (1938). By 1939 he had overtaken both Gable and Tracy at the box-office, and he was second only to Mickey Rooney.

Fox rushed him into another costume drama, *Suez* (1938), with the French actress, Annabella (five years his senior), whom he married in 1939. He was her third husband; they were married at her home on St Pierre Road, Bel Air, Los Angeles; Don Ameche was best man, and Pat Paterson (Mrs Charles Boyer) was matron of honour.

Power continued to make a fortune for Fox. Three of his most popular films were *Jesse James* (1939), with Henry Fonda; *The Rains Came* (1939), as a selfless Indian doctor pursued by British colonial Myrna Loy (the *New York Times* described him as 'young, impetuous and charming, with all the depth of a skin dye'); and *The Mark of Zorro* (1940), the remake of the classic Fairbanks silent, one of his own favourites, in which he was an effete fop by day and a dashing bandit by night.

He served in the Marines in the Second World War, and returned to the screen in a prestigious but rather leaden production of Somerset Maugham's *The Razor's Edge* (1946) with Gene Tierney and Anne Baxter (the Power–Tierney drawing-room kiss took three days to shoot, ran for 4 minutes 25 seconds, and cost $70,714). This was followed by *Nightmare Alley* (1947), co-starring Joan Blondell, in which he played an unscrupulous fairground trickster who climbs to the top only to end up an alcoholic in a freak show. His more mature performance in an unattractive role was commended by James Agate, who noted that Power specifically asked for the part, and 'steps into a new class as an actor'.

His marriage to Annabella, having survived his unhappy affair with Judy Garland, finally came to grief over his more serious relationship with Lana

Turner. They were divorced in January 1948, she received their house, 139 Saltair, Brentwood – for which she had paid half – plus an annual settlement of $50,000. Tiring of Lana's demanding temperament, however, Power married an MGM starlet, Linda Christian.

Demoralized by the lack of good film offers, Power tried his hand again at stage work, and got the lead in Joshua Logan's production of 'Mister Roberts' (1951) in London. Sadly, he did not enjoy the same success as Henry Fonda had in the US version, and he returned to Hollywood and mediocre movies.

By Linda Christian he had two daughters, Romina and Taryn. Miss Christian was named as co-respondent in the Edmund Purdom divorce of 1956. They lived together for about seven years and were briefly married after her divorce from Power. In 1952 Power's contract with Fox expired. After a number of indifferent films he had a winner with *The Eddie Duchin Story* (1956), for Columbia, which was one of the year's box-office top ten.

Having often said he would not marry again, Power took a third wife, Deborah Minardos, in 1958. He was forty-four, she twenty-six. Their time together proved brief, for he died of a heart attack in Madrid while filming *Solomon and Sheba*, on 15

Tyrone Power and his first wife, Annabella, at their home at Bel Air, California. He represented the fourth generation of a remarkable dynasty of actors and musicians, and was a second cousin of the celebrated Shakespearean director, Sir Tyrone Guthrie.

November 1958. His only son, Tyrone (IV), was born four months later.

Tyrone Power was only forty-five when he died – a year younger than his great grandfather, the founder of the dynasty, who was drowned in 1841. Although a Catholic, he was denied Catholic funeral rites at his burial in the Hollywood Memorial Park owing to his two divorces.

ANNABELLA
First wife of Tyrone Power. Married 23 April 1939; divorced 1948

Born on 14 July (Bastille Day) 1908, at La Varenne-St Hilaire, near Paris, Annabella's real name is Suzanne Georgette Charpentier. Her father, Paul Charpentier, publisher of *Le Journal des Voyages*, was acquainted with the young Baden-Powell, through whose influence he introduced the Boy Scout movement to France. Her first husband was Albert Sorre, a French writer, by whom she has her only child, Anne Power; she married secondly, 4 October 1934 (divorced), Jean Murat (1888–1968), French actor and First World War correspondent.

She made her film début in Abel Gance's silent classic, *Napoleon* (1926), as Violine, and she later worked with René Clair in *Le Million* (1931), and *Quatorze Juillet* (1933).

She next went to London, to the then prosperous Gaumont-British studios, for *Wings of the Morning* (1937), filmed in Ireland, which brought her to the attention of Fox Studios who imported her to Hollywood. Once there, they were unable to find any material to suit her elfin charm, and ended up casting her in the leaden costume drama, *Suez* (1938), and then as the villainess in *13 Rue Madeleine* (1946). More noteworthy was her role in Jean-Paul Sartre's 'No Exit', on Broadway, also in 1946, when Brooks Anderson commended her in the *New York Times*, 'as the homosexual, Annabella is giving a bold and calculated performance that packs one corner of Hell with horror.'

Following her divorce from Power (they remained on excellent terms), she returned to France, where she now has a house near Paris and another in the Pyrenees. She has not married again.

ANNE POWER
Daughter of Annabella, and adopted daughter of Tyrone Power

Born *c.* 1930–32, she is the only daughter of Annabella by her first husband, Albert Sorre. She was adopted by Power, and given his surname in 1943. In 1954 she married Oskar Werner, the Austrian actor (see table 31), whom she met on the set of *Decision Before Dawn* (1951), when she was in charge of the horses; they divorced in 1968, and he died in 1984. They had no children and she has not married again. She is a teacher of deaf children in North Hampton, Long Island, New York.

LINDA CHRISTIAN
Second wife of Tyrone Power. Married 27 June 1949, Rome; divorced 1955

Born Blanca Rosa Welter, 13 November 1923, in Tampico, Mexico; the daughter of Gerard Welter, a Dutch petroleum engineer, by his wife, Blanca Alvarez. Before arriving in Hollywood she worked at the office of the British censor in Palestine. Despite her considerable beauty, she never broke through the starlet ranks, and is better known for her energetic social life than her films.

Linda married secondly, 24 March 1962 (Mexico City) (divorced 1963), her lover Edmund Purdom, a considerably paler version of Tyrone Power, who appeared in several lavish MGM costume pictures. As an actor he was talent-free, and he is now more rewardingly engaged as chief recording engineer and editor for EMI, and others, and has recorded the complete symphonies of Schubert, and much Mozart and Haydn. He lives in Rome.

Probably the most celebrated of Miss Christian's lovers was Alfonso de Portago, Grandee of Spain, a racing driver who was killed in the Mille Miglia, near Milan, on 12 May 1957, aged twenty-nine. At his funeral it was noted that Miss Christian effortlessly upstaged the Grandee's widow.

DEBORAH MINARDOS
Third wife of Tyrone Power. Married 7 May 1958, Tunica, Mississippi

Born Deborah Jean Smith, *c.* 1932, she is the daughter of Jefferson Cooper Smith, of Jackson, Mississippi, by his wife Freddie Mae Montgomery (who subsequently married Rice Hungerford of Tunica). She married first (divorced) Nico Minardos, a Greek actor, who in 1952 enjoyed a brief affair with Marilyn Monroe; and secondly, Tyrone Power, who died six months later, by whom she has issue his only son, Tyrone Power (IV). She married thirdly, 26 October 1959 (Las Vegas) (divorced 1962), Arthur Marcus Loew, by whom she has further issue, Gerald Zukor Loew, born 11 May 1960.

ROMINA POWER
Elder daughter of Tyrone Power and Linda Christian

Born on 2 October 1951, in Rome, her full names are Romina Francesca Power. She was educated at Cobham Hall, Kent, and in Rome. She made her screen début aged thirteen in Italy, and has continued to appear in films and on Italian TV. She married, 26 July 1970 (Cellino San Marco), Albano Carrisi (born 1943), a singer and songwriter. As a singing duo they have achieved great success in Europe ('Aria Pura' sold over 500,000 copies and won them a platinum disc; 'Ci Sara' won the 34th San Remo Festival, 1984). They have three children: Ylenia (a daughter), born 29 November 1970; Yari (a son), born 21 April 1973; and Cristel (a daughter), born 25 December 1985.

TARYN POWER
Younger daughter of Tyrone Power and Linda Christian

Born on 13 September 1953, in Hollywood, her full names are Taryn Stephanie Power. Like her sister she was educated at Cobham Hall, and raised mainly by her mother in Italy. Now an actress in America, her credits include (TV), *The Count of Monte Cristo*

(1974), with Tony Curtis, Louis Jourdan, and Richard Chamberlain (with whom her name was playfully linked), and *Tracks* (1976), with Dennis Hopper. Her most recent film to date is *Sea Serpent*, with Timothy Bottoms.

Taryn Power married Norman Seeff, a former *Time–Life* photographer, from whom she is divorced (he also photographed the cover of Joni Mitchell's 1985 album, 'Dog Eats Dog'), and has issue, Tai Seeff (a daughter). She now lives with Tony Sales, a rock musician (once with Chequered Past), son of Soupy Sales, the American comedian, by whom she has further issue, Tony Tyrone Sales, and Valentina Sales.

TYRONE POWER (IV)
Son of Tyrone Power and Deborah Minardos

Born (posthumously) on 22 January 1959, in Hollywood, his full names are Tyrone William Power. He represents the fifth generation of this dynasty to go on to the stage. His stage works includes 'Another Country', the British public school drama (1983), and he made his screen début in *Cocoon* (1985).

Tyrone Power and his second wife, Linda Christian, at the Danieli Hotel, Venice, shortly before their marriage in 1949. Their elder daughter, Romina Power, is now working on a definitive biography of her father who died when she was seven.

TABLE 30 THE POWER DYNASTY (I)

TYRONE POWER = *c.* 1789, MARIA MAXWELL, said to be the orphaned
d 1796–98 in USA   da of Col. MAXWELL (*k* during American
War of Independence); she had a small
property nr Dublin; following the death
of her husband she settled at Cardiff

(WILLIAM HENRY GRATTAN) TYRONE POWER (I), = 1817, ANNE GILBERT (1794–1876), 3rd
b 1795, Kilmacthomas, Co. Waterford; actor/playwright;   da of W. JOHN GILBERT (see
drowned in the steamship *President* on return voyage from   table 32), attorney, of New-
USA 1841. Residence: Oxford Sq, Hyde Park   port, Isle of Wight. She is
bur. Horton Kirby, Dartford, Kent

Sir WILLIAM POWER, KCB (1819–1911); ed. Tonbridge Sch. & College Bourbon, Paris; Commissary-Gen. British Army; author of travel books; bur. Aghabog, Co. Monaghan. Residences: Annaghmakerrig, Newbliss, Co. Monaghan; 25 Holland Park =

1859, MARTHA MOORHEAD (*d* 1859), da of Dr JOHN MOORHEAD, of Annaghmakerrig, & formerly of Leesborough, Co. Monaghan, by his wife SUSAN ALIBONE, of Cincinnati, USA

MAURICE POWER, *b* 1821; ed. Tonbridge Sch.; barrister-at-law (Lincoln's Inn 1840), forsook law for the stage; *d* of cholera in Bath 1848; left £10

FREDERICK POWER, *b* 1824; ed. Tonbridge Sch.; civil eng., involved in construction of Trans-Caucasian Railway; *d* 1896, left a fortune of £197,000; bur. Horton Kirby, Kent. Residences: Frank's Hall, Farningham, Kent; 11 Hyde Park Gdns =

1858 (Kensington), ANNIE SOMERS (*d* of pneumonia in Monte Carlo 1881), da of CHARLES SOMERS, of Addison Rd, Kensington

HAROLD LITTLEDALE POWER, *b* 1833; actor (as Harold Page); worked for post office, a wine merchant, & finally a civil eng.; *d* 1901; bur. Horton Kirby, Kent. Residences: 24 Fitzroy St, & later 24 Portland Place =

1866 (Marylebone), ELIZA (ETHEL), LAVENU, yr da of LEWIS LAVENU (see table 33), composer & music seller, of London

4 daughters (1 *d* in infancy)

JOHN MOORHEAD POWER (1862–1937); ed. Wellington Coll., & Trin. Coll., Cambridge; *d* Palma de Mallorca, without issue =

1887, SUSAN OWEN DENNIS, da of HENRY DENNIS

1 son & 2 das

NORAH EMILY GORMAN POWER (2nd da) (1867–1955) =

1899, THOMAS CLEMENT GUTHRIE, BSc (Edin.), MD, who *d* 1929. Inherited Annaghmakerrig

(see table 31)

(FREDERICK) TYRONE EDMOND POWER (II) *b* 1869, London; ed. Dover Coll. (for 1 year 1883); sent to Florida to learn to farm citrus fruit, when 1st crop failed he decided to become an actor, worked with Augustin Daly's company, toured with Beerbohm Tree, etc.; a highly acclaimed & popular stage actor; *d* Los Angeles 1931

= (1) (div.) EDITH CRANE, actress, who *d* 1912, aged 40

= (2) (div.) PATIA REAUME, actress/coach, who *d* 1959, aged 77

= (3) 1920, BERTHA KNIGHT, actress

(see table 31)

TABLE 31 THE POWER DYNASTY (II)

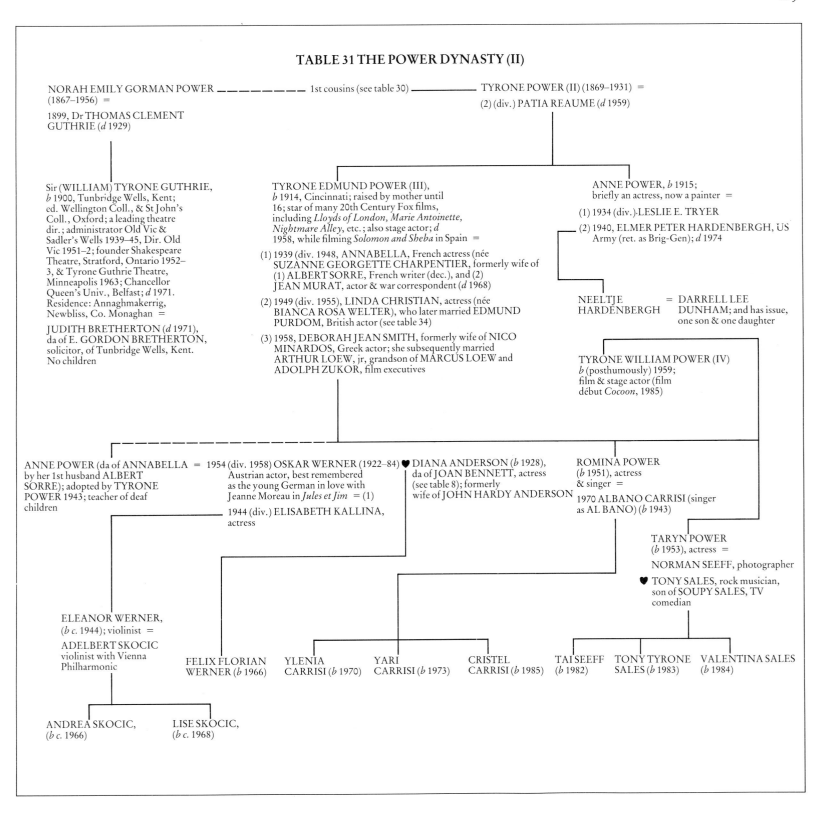

NORAH EMILY GORMAN POWER ———————— 1st cousins (see table 30) ———————— TYRONE POWER (II) (1869–1931) =
(1867–1956) =

1899, Dr THOMAS CLEMENT
GUTHRIE (d 1929)

(2) (div.) PATIA REAUME (d 1959)

Sir (WILLIAM) TYRONE GUTHRIE,
b 1900, Tunbridge Wells, Kent;
ed. Wellington Coll., & St John's
Coll., Oxford; a leading theatre
dir.; administrator Old Vic &
Sadler's Wells 1939–45, Dir. Old
Vic 1951–2; founder Shakespeare
Theatre, Stratford, Ontario 1952–
3, & Tyrone Guthrie Theatre,
Minneapolis 1963; Chancellor
Queen's Univ., Belfast; d 1971.
Residence: Annaghmakerrig,
Newbliss, Co. Monaghan =

JUDITH BRETHERTON (d 1971),
da of E. GORDON BRETHERTON,
solicitor, of Tunbridge Wells, Kent.
No children

TYRONE EDMUND POWER (III),
b 1914, Cincinnati; raised by mother until
16; star of many 20th Century Fox films,
including *Lloyds of London, Marie Antoinette,
Nightmare Alley*, etc.; also stage actor; d
1958, while filming *Solomon and Sheba* in Spain =

(1) 1939 (div. 1948, ANNABELLA, French actress (née
SUZANNE GEORGETTE CHARPENTIER, formerly wife of
(1) ALBERT SORRE, French writer (dec.), and (2)
JEAN MURAT, actor & war correspondent (d 1968)

(2) 1949 (div. 1955), LINDA CHRISTIAN, actress (née
BIANCA ROSA WELTER), who later married EDMUND
PURDOM, British actor (see table 34)

(3) 1958, DEBORAH JEAN SMITH, formerly wife of NICO
MINARDOS, Greek actor; she subsequently married
ARTHUR LOEW, jr, grandson of MARCUS LOEW and
ADOLPH ZUKOR, film executives

ANNE POWER, b 1915;
briefly an actress, now a painter =

(1) 1934 (div.) LESLIE E. TRYER

(2) 1940, ELMER PETER HARDENBERGH, US
Army (ret. as Brig-Gen); d 1974

NEELTJE   = DARRELL LEE
HARDENBERGH   DUNHAM; and has issue,
                  one son & one daughter

TYRONE WILLIAM POWER (IV)
b (posthumously) 1959;
film & stage actor (film
début *Cocoon*, 1985)

ANNE POWER (da of ANNABELLA   = 1954 (div. 1958) OSKAR WERNER (1922–84)   DIANA ANDERSON (b 1928),   ROMINA POWER
by her 1st husband ALBERT   Austrian actor, best remembered   da of JOAN BENNETT, actress   (b 1951), actress
SORRE); adopted by TYRONE   as the young German in love with   (see table 8); formerly   & singer =
POWER 1943; teacher of deaf   Jeanne Moreau in *Jules et Jim* = (1) wife of JOHN HARDY ANDERSON
children   1970 ALBANO CARRISI (singer
                                  1944 (div.) ELISABETH KALLINA,   as AL BANO) (b 1943)
                                  actress

TARYN POWER
(b 1953), actress =

NORMAN SEEFF, photographer

TONY SALES, rock musician,
son of SOUPY SALES, TV
comedian

ELEANOR WERNER,
(b c. 1944); violinist =

ADELBERT SKOCIC
violinist with Vienna
Philharmonic

FELIX FLORIAN
WERNER (b 1966)

YLENIA
CARRISI (b 1970)

YARI
CARRISI (b 1973)

CRISTEL
CARRISI (b 1985)

TAI SEEFF
(b 1982)

TONY TYRONE
SALES (b 1983)

VALENTINA SALES
(b 1984)

ANDREA SKOCIC,
(b c. 1966)

LISE SKOCIC,
(b c. 1968)

TABLE 32 ANCESTRY OF ANNE GILBERT, GREAT GRANDMOTHER OF TYRONE POWER (FILM ACTOR), AND THE LINK TO LAURENCE OLIVIER

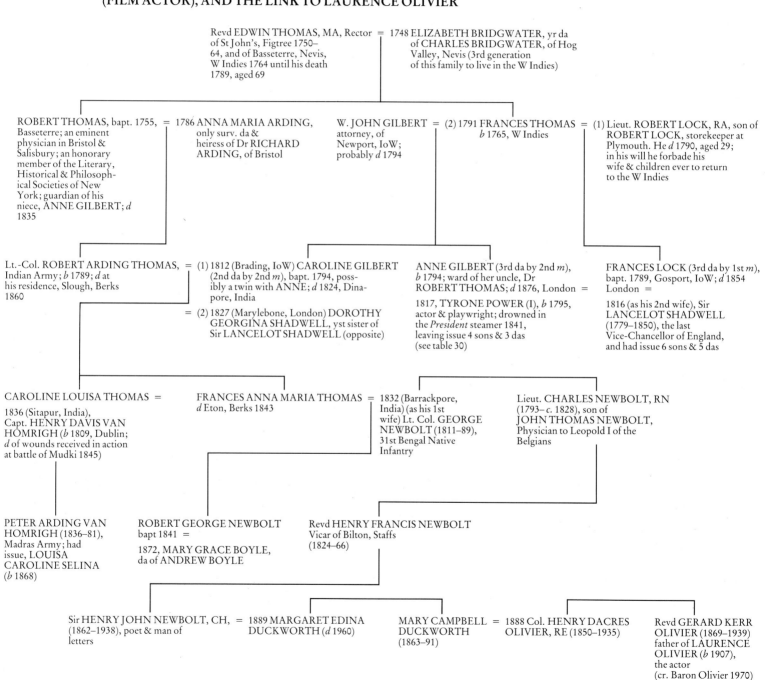

Revd EDWIN THOMAS, MA, Rector = 1748 ELIZABETH BRIDGWATER, yr da
of St John's, Figtree 1750–64, and of Basseterre, Nevis, W Indies 1764 until his death 1789, aged 69

of CHARLES BRIDGWATER, of Hog Valley, Nevis (3rd generation of this family to live in the W Indies)

ROBERT THOMAS, bapt. 1755, = 1786 ANNA MARIA ARDING, Basseterre; an eminent physician in Bristol & Salisbury; an honorary member of the Literary, Historical & Philosophical Societies of New York; guardian of his niece, ANNE GILBERT; d 1835

only surv. da & heiress of Dr RICHARD ARDING, of Bristol

W. JOHN GILBERT = (2) 1791 FRANCES THOMAS = attorney, of Newport, IoW; probably d 1794

b 1765, W Indies

(1) Lieut. ROBERT LOCK, RA, son of ROBERT LOCK, storekeeper at Plymouth. He d 1790, aged 29; in his will he forbade his wife & children ever to return to the W Indies

Lt.-Col. ROBERT ARDING THOMAS, = (1) 1812 (Brading, IoW) CAROLINE GILBERT Indian Army; b 1789; d at his residence, Slough, Berks 1860

(2nd da by 2nd m), bapt. 1794, possibly a twin with ANNE; d 1824, Dinapore, India

= (2) 1827 (Marylebone, London) DOROTHY GEORGINA SHADWELL, yst sister of Sir LANCELOT SHADWELL (opposite)

ANNE GILBERT (3rd da by 2nd m), b 1794; ward of her uncle, Dr ROBERT THOMAS; d 1876, London =

1817, TYRONE POWER (I), b 1795, actor & playwright; drowned in the *President* steamer 1841, leaving issue 4 sons & 3 das (see table 30)

FRANCES LOCK (3rd da by 1st m), bapt. 1789, Gosport, IoW; d 1854 London =

1816 (as his 2nd wife), Sir LANCELOT SHADWELL (1779–1850), the last Vice-Chancellor of England, and had issue 6 sons & 5 das

CAROLINE LOUISA THOMAS = 1836 (Sitapur, India), Capt. HENRY DAVIS VAN HOMRIGH (b 1809, Dublin; d of wounds received in action at battle of Mudki 1845)

FRANCES ANNA MARIA THOMAS = d Eton, Berks 1843

1832 (Barrackpore, India) (as his 1st wife) Lt. Col. GEORGE NEWBOLT (1811–89), 31st Bengal Native Infantry

Lieut. CHARLES NEWBOLT, RN (1793– c. 1828), son of JOHN THOMAS NEWBOLT, Physician to Leopold I of the Belgians

PETER ARDING VAN HOMRIGH (1836–81), Madras Army; had issue, LOUISA CAROLINE SELINA (b 1868)

ROBERT GEORGE NEWBOLT bapt 1841 =

1872, MARY GRACE BOYLE, da of ANDREW BOYLE

Revd HENRY FRANCIS NEWBOLT Vicar of Bilton, Staffs (1824–66)

Sir HENRY JOHN NEWBOLT, CH, = 1889 MARGARET EDINA (1862–1938), poet & man of letters

DUCKWORTH (d 1960)

MARY CAMPBELL = 1888 Col. HENRY DACRES DUCKWORTH OLIVIER, RE (1850–1935) (1863–91)

Revd GERARD KERR OLIVIER (1869–1939) father of LAURENCE OLIVIER (b 1907), the actor (cr. Baron Olivier 1970)

TABLE 33 ANCESTRY OF ELIZA LAVENU, GRANDMOTHER OF TYRONE POWER (FILM ACTOR), AND THE LINK TO EVELYN WAUGH

LEWIS LAVENU, probably of (1) = ELIZABETH (ELIZA), continued = (2) 1826, NICHOLAS MORI, violinist; son of
French Huguenot descent; music publishing business an Italian wig-maker; a child prodigy,
flautist; music seller to after 1st husband's death; on at the age of 8 he gave a public per-
the Prince Regent; *d* 1818 2nd *m* the company became Mori formance of a Barthélemon concerto; ran
& Lavenu, 28 New Bond St; *d* Lavenu music publishing business with
1838 (bur. Kensal Green) stepson, producing among others *The
Musical Gem*; *d* 1839 (bur. Kensal Green)

THOMAS WAUGH,   Revd JAMES HAY WAUGH
of Grove End,   Rector of Corsley,
Camberwell   Wilts

LEWIS HENRY LAVENU, *b* 1818,   FRANCISCO (FRANK) MORI,   NICHOLAS MORI, *b* 1822,   ELIZABETH MARIA MORI   ALEXANDER WAUGH, of
London; cellist of Westmin-   *b* 1820, London; Prof of Singing   London; composed music for   (2nd of 3 das; the   Midsomer Norton,
ster Abbey Festival 1834;   at Crystal Palace, Sydenham;   W.S. Gilbert's faery comedy   only one to leave issue)   Bath: *d* 1905 =
ptnr in family co.; composed   composer: 'The River Sprite' (at   'The Wicked World', etc. =   (*d* 1859) =
'Loretta, a Tale of Seville',   Covent Gdn 1865), etc.; *d* 1873,   EPHEGE ADELAIDE (*b c.* 1826,   1846 FRANCIS WAUGH   ANNE MORGAN
successfully prod. at Drury   Chaumont, France =   Paris); Prof. of French; had   Lieut. Indian Army;
Lane 1846; emigrated to   issue 4 das, 3 of whom were   *d* 1848, Madras,
Australia, where became dir.   MARIE SOPHIE FONTAINE,   aged 25
of music at Sydney Theatre;   who survived him
d 1859 =

1841, JULIA, da of Maj. JOHN
BLOSSETT, Indian Army

EPHEGE MORI =   BESSIE MARIAN WAUGH   ARTHUR WAUGH (elder son)
                 (only child); *d* 1919 =   (1866–1943); author; Chm.
1870 (London) ADOLF   Capt. EDWARD HENRY HODGES,   Chapman & Hall Ltd =
THEODOR ERICH BOCKING,   RN (1843–1920), of Hart-   1893, CATHERINE RABAN
DPhil, of Kansas, USA   land, Devon

ELIZA (ETHEL) LAVENU =

1866, HAROLD LITTLEDALE POWER
(see table 30); wine merchant
& former actor (*d* 1901)

ELISA MORI =   ESTELLE MORI =

1873 (Kansas) HERMANN   1879 (Paris) FELIX
MUNTEFERING, of Cotton   DELACQUIS, of Paris
Wood Farm, Chase Co., Kansas

FRANK AIMABLE MORI,   ARTHUR LAWRENCE MORI   ALFRED BENVENUTO SALVATORI   EDWARD HENRY HODGES   EVELYN WAUGH (yr son)
of London & Paris; *b* 1842 =   (1849–1901), of East   MORI (1858–1914); ed. St   (1877–1938); served   (1903–66); the celebrated
                Dereham, Norfolk; a   Paul's Sch.; wine merchant   S African War; mgr   author of *Decline and
1866, LEONORA MARY,   dental surgeon; *m* twice   in Bordeaux =   Boots, Brighton, for   Fall, Vile Bodies, Brides-
da of SAMUEL JACOB   & had issue   13 years =   head Revisited*, etc.; left
SIMMONDS, of Trinidad   CHARLOTTE MORRIS (1857–   issue 3 sons & 3 das
& London; and had   1910); probably left issue   1907, MAUD WILKINSON
issue 1 son & 1 da

TYRONE POWER II (1869–1931) = (2) (div.) PATIA REAUME (*d* 1959)   EDWARD FREDERICK HODGES
                                           (*b* 1908), of Haywards
                                           Heath, Sussex.

TYRONE POWER (1914–53)
the film actor

TABLE 34 FAMILY OF EDMUND PURDOM, SECOND HUSBAND OF LINDA CHRISTIAN

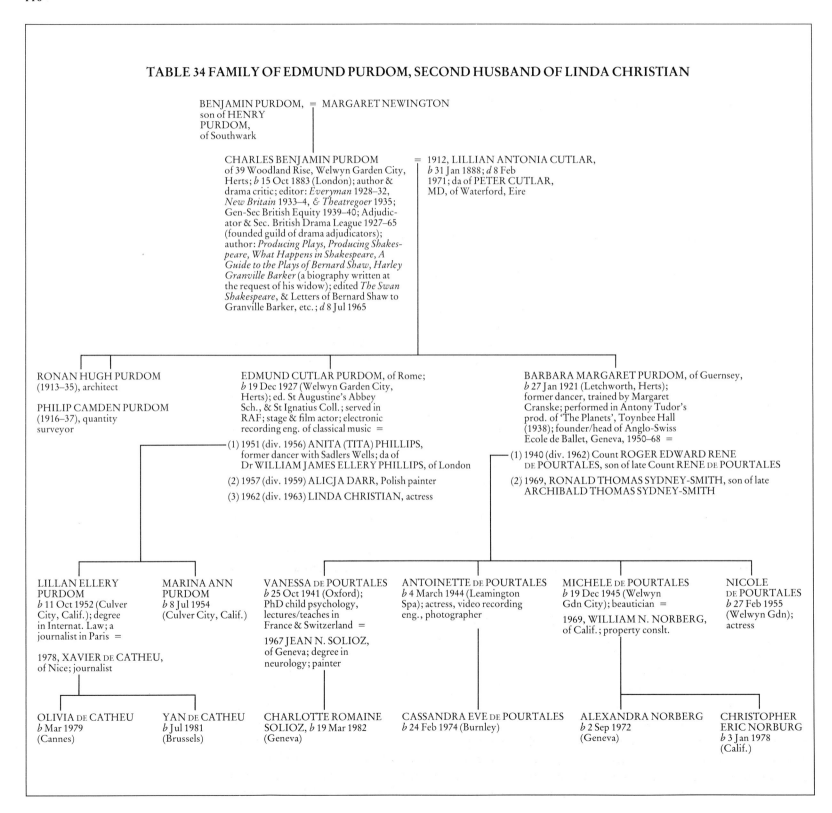

BENJAMIN PURDOM, = MARGARET NEWINGTON
son of HENRY
PURDOM,
of Southwark

CHARLES BENJAMIN PURDOM = 1912, LILLIAN ANTONIA CUTLAR,
of 39 Woodland Rise, Welwyn Garden City, *b* 31 Jan 1888; *d* 8 Feb
Herts; *b* 15 Oct 1883 (London); author & 1971; da of PETER CUTLAR,
drama critic; editor: *Everyman* 1928–32, MD, of Waterford, Eire
New Britain 1933–4, & *Theatregoer* 1935;
Gen-Sec British Equity 1939–40; Adjudic-
ator & Sec. British Drama League 1927–65
(founded guild of drama adjudicators);
author: *Producing Plays, Producing Shakespeare, What Happens in Shakespeare, A
Guide to the Plays of Bernard Shaw, Harley
Granville Barker* (a biography written at
the request of his widow); edited *The Swan
Shakespeare,* & Letters of Bernard Shaw to
Granville Barker, etc.; *d* 8 Jul 1965

RONAN HUGH PURDOM
(1913–35), architect

PHILIP CAMDEN PURDOM
(1916–37), quantity
surveyor

EDMUND CUTLAR PURDOM, of Rome;
b 19 Dec 1927 (Welwyn Garden City,
Herts); ed. St Augustine's Abbey
Sch., & St Ignatius Coll.; served in
RAF; stage & film actor; electronic
recording eng. of classical music =

(1) 1951 (div. 1956) ANITA (TITA) PHILLIPS,
former dancer with Sadlers Wells; da of
Dr WILLIAM JAMES ELLERY PHILLIPS, of London

(2) 1957 (div. 1959) ALICJA DARR, Polish painter

(3) 1962 (div. 1963) LINDA CHRISTIAN, actress

BARBARA MARGARET PURDOM, of Guernsey,
b 27 Jan 1921 (Letchworth, Herts);
former dancer, trained by Margaret
Cranske; performed in Antony Tudor's
prod. of 'The Planets', Toynbee Hall
(1938); founder/head of Anglo-Swiss
Ecole de Ballet, Geneva, 1950–68 =

(1) 1940 (div. 1962) Count ROGER EDWARD RENE
DE POURTALES, son of late Count RENE DE POURTALES

(2) 1969, RONALD THOMAS SYDNEY-SMITH, son of late
ARCHIBALD THOMAS SYDNEY-SMITH

LILLAN ELLERY
PURDOM
b 11 Oct 1952 (Culver
City, Calif.); degree
in Internat. Law; a
journalist in Paris =

1978, XAVIER DE CATHEU,
of Nice; journalist

MARINA ANN
PURDOM
b 8 Jul 1954
(Culver City, Calif.)

VANESSA DE POURTALES
b 25 Oct 1941 (Oxford);
PhD child psychology,
lectures/teaches in
France & Switzerland =

1967 JEAN N. SOLIOZ,
of Geneva; degree in
neurology; painter

ANTOINETTE DE POURTALES
b 4 March 1944 (Leamington
Spa); actress, video recording
eng., photographer

MICHELE DE POURTALES
b 19 Dec 1945 (Welwyn
Gdn City); beautician =

1969, WILLIAM N. NORBERG,
of Calif.; property conslt.

NICOLE
DE POURTALES
b 27 Feb 1955
(Welwyn Gdn);
actress

OLIVIA DE CATHEU
b Mar 1979
(Cannes)

YAN DE CATHEU
b Jul 1981
(Brussels)

CHARLOTTE ROMAINE
SOLIOZ, *b* 19 Mar 1982
(Geneva)

CASSANDRA EVE DE POURTALES
b 24 Feb 1974 (Burnley)

ALEXANDRA NORBERG
b 2 Sep 1972
(Geneva)

CHRISTOPHER
ERIC NORBURG
b 3 Jan 1978
(Calif.)

12 Humphrey Bogart and Lauren Bacall

Humphrey Bogart was not descended from actors, nor have his son or daughter gone into the business, but there is a genealogical curiosity in his lineage that gives it a theatrical twist.

The American genealogist Gary Boyd Roberts has worked extensively on the American ancestry of Diana, Princess of Wales, and has found she descends from Joseph Strong, a Philadelphia doctor. This good man was something of a xenophobe, and was once driven to exclaim that 'the curse of this country is the foreign marriages made by our girls – if I had my way I'd make it a hanging matter.' It was just as well that he didn't get his way, for his great granddaughter married an Irish aristocrat, the 3rd Baron Fermoy, and was the great grandmother of the Princess.

Table 35 shows how Humphrey Bogart's ancestors came from the same stock as Doctor Strong (Bogart's mother was in fact an eighth cousin of the American Lady Fermoy), and it also illustrates how Bogart himself was a ninth cousin of Blanche Oelrichs, who became John Barrymore's second wife. A further dynastic link was forged on Christmas Eve 1985, when Blanche's great nephew, Peter Duchin, married Brooke Hayward, daughter of the late Leland Hayward and Margaret Sullavan.

As all this would imply, Humphrey Bogart came from a distinguished background – quite unlike most of the characters he played on the screen. He was born on 23 January 1899, in New York City, the only son of Belmont de Forest Bogart, a noted Manhattan surgeon, by his wife Maude Humphrey. Although Bogart had to wait fifty-three years before he won his Oscar, he achieved unsolicited fame in infancy through his magazine illustrator mother, who, in an idle moment, sketched her child playing in his pram, and sold the drawing to Mellins Baby Feed Company, who used it for their label all over the country.

His father was a well-educated, old fashioned and strictly undemonstrative character, very representative of his class and generation. He seemed to lose his vocation early in his married life, and much preferred to spend his time at his country retreat on Canandaigua Lake than at his practice. A pompous man by all accounts, he is said to have handed his young son a copy of *Who's Who in New York* suggesting he 'look through this for a familiar name'.

Bogart and his two younger sisters, Frances (known as Pat), and Catherine (Kay), were raised in the manner to which their parents had been accustomed. He was sent to Trinity School, New York, at the age of fourteen, where his smart school uniform – blue serge suit, white shirt and overcoat with a black velvet collar – may have given him an early distaste for 'dressing-up', for, in later life, he was loath to wear anything other than a track suit and a battered old yachting cap.

Even as a schoolboy he exhibited a rebellious and eccentric streak, and insisted on sporting a black derby during all his lessons. When he was seventeen he was sent to his father's Alma Mater, Phillips Academy, Andover, Massachusetts, where he was unhappy, sullen and uncooperative. He repeatedly failed his exams and was eventually asked to leave. His father was greatly upset by this as he had hoped that Humphrey would later go to Yale. His mother was outspoken in her condemnation of her son's refusal to conform.

Bogart enlisted in the US Navy in July 1918, aged nineteen, where he served on a troop transporter, *Leviathan*. While serving there he was hit in the mouth by a manacled prisoner, which resulted in the characteristic set of his jaw and his lisp. Warner Bros. later adjusted his biography and said the scar was the result of an attack on the *Leviathan* by a U-boat. They also sanctified his hoodlum screen-image by altering his birthday to Christmas Day. He was honourably discharged from the Navy after two years.

Foot-loose and fancy-free once more, Bogart approached a family friend, William Brady, the Broadway producer, who employed him as a stage manager. Although there was a basic fondness between the two, they were continually at odds, and their association was not improved by Bogart's decision to become an actor. Bogart was not to be dissuaded, and the theatre then being in its prime (on average there were about fifty-one productions being played at any given time in New York), work was plentiful. He was usually cast in callow, romantic roles. After a dithering four-year courtship with actress Helen Menken, they were married on 20 May 1926. They lived together for only a few months during their one and a half years of marriage, and these were poisoned by their recriminations of career versus marriage.

Almost a year to the day after his divorce from Miss Menken, Bogart married Mary Philips, another actress, with whom he had worked in one of his more successful stage plays, 'What Price Glory'. Many years later she recalled him as a 'strangely puritanical man with very old-fashioned virtues; he had class as well as charm.' She was also courted by Kenneth McKenna, actor and director, whom she married after her divorce from Bogart, and she later became a story editor at MGM.

Through his brother-in-law Stuart Rose (married to his sister Pat), a story editor at Fox, Bogart obtained a screen test for *The Man Who Came Back* (1930). He didn't get the part, but he stayed on and eventually was cast in a series of colourless second-

feature leads for Fox, Universal and Columbia. In 1935 he finally got a real break when he was cast entirely against type in the Broadway production of 'The Petrified Forest', starring Leslie Howard. Bogart's role as Duke Mantee, the stony-hearted gangster, won him his first good reviews, and Leslie Howard promised that in the event of the play being filmed he would insist on Bogart being retained in his part. Warners bought it but intended to replace him with Edward G. Robinson. In an act of generosity rare in fickle Hollywood, Howard was as good as his word, and, although Bogart was made to audition fifteen times, he got the part.

Stagy and dreadful though the film now seems, with Bogart's performance verging on the embarrassing, it was a great success at the time. Warners, however, carried on casting him in supporting roles – but now as a villain. His wife, Mary, continued to pursue her stage career, and it was during one of her jaunts to New York that Bogart met his next wife.

Mayo Metho, apart from having an odd name, was an odd person. She is said to have been the daughter of a sea-faring captain of the Orient and an Oregon-born newspaperwoman. Born in 1904, she went into show business at an early age. Bogart was her third husband, his predecessor being one Percy T. Morgan, of New York. She was blonde, bold and voluptuous, and, although Bogart sensed their marriage would be a mistake, they were wed on 20 August 1938, in Los Angeles. They shared a love of the sea and alcohol, which inevitably brought out the violence which was an integral part of their relationship. Both of them found a perverse pleasure in the passion of their love-hate partnership, and somewhat relished being known as 'The Battling Bogarts'. Their house was known as 'Sluggy Hollow' and their boat was 'Sluggy' too.

Not the least of Mayo's redeeming qualities was her kindness to Bogart's mother, who following the death of her husband had come to live near them, and to Bogart's sister, Pat, who had suffered a nervous breakdown. After the birth of her daughter, Pat Rose became a manic depressive; she insisted that her husband should divorce her, and

Bogart and Ingrid Bergman in the immortal Casablanca *(1942). Warner Bros. had originally planned to cast Dennis Morgan and Michèle Morgan (no relation) in this eventual triple Oscar winner: Best Film, Hal B. Wallis; Best Direction, Michael Curtiz; Best Written Screenplay, Julius J. Epstein, Philip G. Epstein and Howard Kock (for such lines as 'Play it Sam – play " As Time Goes By." '*

then moved to the west coast where Bogart took care of her. His other sister, Kay, had a brief, wild life in the speak-easy days, and died of peritonitis in 1937.

A new turning point arrived when Paul Muni, Cagney, Raft and Robinson all rejected *High Sierra* (1941). Bogart was cast and gave his best performance to date as an ageing gangster. In the same year he again struck lucky when Raft turned down *The Maltese Falcon*, with which John Huston made his directing début. Bogart's understanding of the Sam Spade character, and his sympathy with Dashiell Hammet's sardonic style, gave his performance a flavour which later inspired a cult following that no other actor has equalled. 'Bogey' came into his own at last. This film also led to a lifelong friendship with Huston.

Warners belatedly realized they were handling a star. A new contract was drawn up at $3,500 a week (after *The Big Sleep* (1946) it rose to $200,000 per film with $1,000 a week expenses for location work), and he went into *Casablanca* (1942), with Ingrid Bergman and Paul Henreid. He gave one of his best-remembered, bitter-sweet performances and set the seal of success on the film which won the Best Picture Oscar and made a fortune for Warners.

On the set of *To Have and Have Not* (1945) he met Lauren Bacall, a former New York model, whose photograph on the cover of a 1943 *Harpers Bazaar* magazine had been spotted by Nancy Hawks. She alerted her husband, Howard Hawks, who gave her a screen test. The attraction between Bogart and Bacall was instant and mutual, but it also aroused Hawks's deep disapproval, and Bogart was already in a state of despair over Mayo. She had been diagnosed a paranoid schizophrenic and was on the brink of suicide. He spent Christmas 1944 with her in an attempt to help her through the crisis of their ruined marriage, and it was only his hope that Lauren Bacall would understand and wait for him that kept him together. Mayo and Bogart were divorced in May 1945; he provided her with a generous settlement and she quietly left Hollywood to live with her mother in Oregon. She died there six years later.

On 21 May 1945 Bogart and Bacall were married. He was forty-five, she twenty. Their marriage was an unusual and vivid partnership of two strong characters, which Lauren Bacall has written about with touching candour in her autobiography, *By Myself* (1978). Mary Astor, an admirer and co-worker with Bogart, remarked, 'He hated the marriage trap, being used, being possessed, being made to buckle down as a provider. I think the remarkable Lauren Bacall knew who he was and what he was, and in return, he was at last able to give something no other woman could grab from him – his total commitment.'

They had two children, Stephen Bogart, born 6 January 1949 (named after the character in *To Have and Have Not*), and Leslie Bogart (a daughter), born 22 August 1952 (named after Bogart's early champion, Leslie Howard).

Bogart and Bacall worked together again in *The Big Sleep* (1946), directed by Howard Hawks, *Dark Passage* (1947), and *Key Largo* (1948), directed by John Huston. In 1947 he formed his own company, Santana Pictures, and in 1948 played another of his most memorable parts as the greedy prospector in *Treasure of the Sierra Madre*. In the 1950s he extended his acting range as never before, as shown by *In A Lonely Place* (1950), with Gloria Grahame, *The African Queen* (1952), with Katharine Hepburn, *The Caine Mutiny* (1954), and *Sabrina* (1954).

The African Queen, based on a novel by C. S. Forester, is the story of a love affair between a gin-sodden boatman and an upright but spirited spinster. It was directed by John Huston on location in darkest Africa, and Hepburn's fortitude during the insect-infested filming won Bogart's rare admiration, 'She's got ants in her pants, mildew in her shoes, and she's still cheerful . . . she breezes through it all as though it's a weekend in Connecticut.' Bogart received a well-earned Best Actor Oscar for his performance.

The film was also the basis of a deep friendship between Bogart, Bacall, Katharine Hepburn and Spencer Tracy, to which Miss Bacall pays tribute in her autobiography.

Even in the last painful stages of the cancer which

finally killed him, Bogart still drank, smoked, played host to his friends and never lost his sense of humour. He died on 14 January 1957, aged fifty-eight. At his funeral John Huston commended his craftmanship and his courage, and concluded, 'We have no reason to feel any sorrow for him – only for ourselves for having lost him. He is quite irreplaceable. There will never be another like him.'

LAUREN BACALL
Fourth wife of Humphrey Bogart. Married 21 May 1945

Lauren Bacall, fourth, last and happiest of Humphrey Bogart's wives, was born Betty Joan Perske on 16 September 1924, in New York City.

Her father, William Perske, left home when she was a child, and it was left to her mother, Natalie Bacall, and her mother's family to fill the gap. Her grandmother, uncles and aunts greatly influenced her early years, and Lauren Bacall affectionately recalled the pleasures and pains of growing up in a tightly-knit 'good Jewish family' in her autobiography.

For Bacall, like millions of other adolescent girls of the 1930s, the magic moment of the week was when she stepped into the nearest picture-house and basked in the black and white dreams that flickered in the dark. Her favourite stars were Leslie Howard and Bette Davis. She convinced her mother of her need to act, and succeeded in getting into the American Academy of Dramatic Arts, but her money ran out after one year, and at that time scholarships were awarded only to male students.

Undaunted, she struggled to find work in the theatre, and made her first professional appearance in George Kaufman's 'Franklin Street' in Washington. From being an awkward teenager with large, long limbs, she grew into a strikingly handsome young woman, with beautiful hair, a slightly rasping voice and great presence. Her looks belied her innocence, and when, unable to make a break on Broadway, she found work as a model – most rewardingly for Diana Vreeland on *Harpers Bazaar*.

The discipline required of a photographic model was good for her poise and gave her some much-needed confidence. Her picture on the cover of a 1943 edition changed her life.

Columbia Pictures asked her to be one of the decorative model-girls in support of Rita Hayworth for *Cover Girl* (1944), but she also had the offer of a screen-test with Howard Hawks, and, with admirable foresight, she took a chance and waited for the latter. Hawks struck her as 'a very tall man, with close-cropped grey hair and broad shoulders ... not a demonstrative sort of man ... inscrutable, speaking quietly in a fairly monotonous voice; he seemed very sure of himself.' She was very nervous, but found confidence from the friendliness of Hawks's wife, Nancy, who became one of her closest allies. Perhaps it was she who told Bacall that although Hawks had given Rita Hayworth her first good role in films 'she hadn't listened well enough, so he didn't want to be bothered with her after that.' A useful warning to an apprehensive beginner.

Hawks, who re-named Betty Perske as Lauren Bacall, liked what he saw very much, and was inspired to match her with Humphrey Bogart in *To Have and Have Not* (1945). With Hawks's coaching she developed a style even cooler and more cynical than Bogart himself, which she laced with a studied sexual antagonism. She gave a thoroughly impressive performance, as Slim (incidentally the nickname of Hawks's wife), enjoyed by the critics and public alike. Her characteristic stance of head held low, and sultry, slightly veiled, gaze, was grabbed by the publicists who labelled it 'The Look'. Bacall simply attributed it to her nerves and said she kept her head down in order to stop trembling.

Despite the opposition from her family (including her estranged father), and from Hawks too, Bacall and Bogart were married. It turned out to be a joyful liberation for them both. Bacall didn't try to change him, she even tolerated his excessive drinking and was unmoved by his waspish streak. Bogart upset many of his contemporaries by his gratuitous sarcasm, but with Bacall he found a friend who would stand up to him, and their com-

Humphrey Bogart and Lauren Bacall. Despite much opposition, they married in 1945 when he was forty-five and she twenty, but their partnership was one of Hollywood's success stories. He is a ninth cousin twice removed of Diana, Princess of Wales.

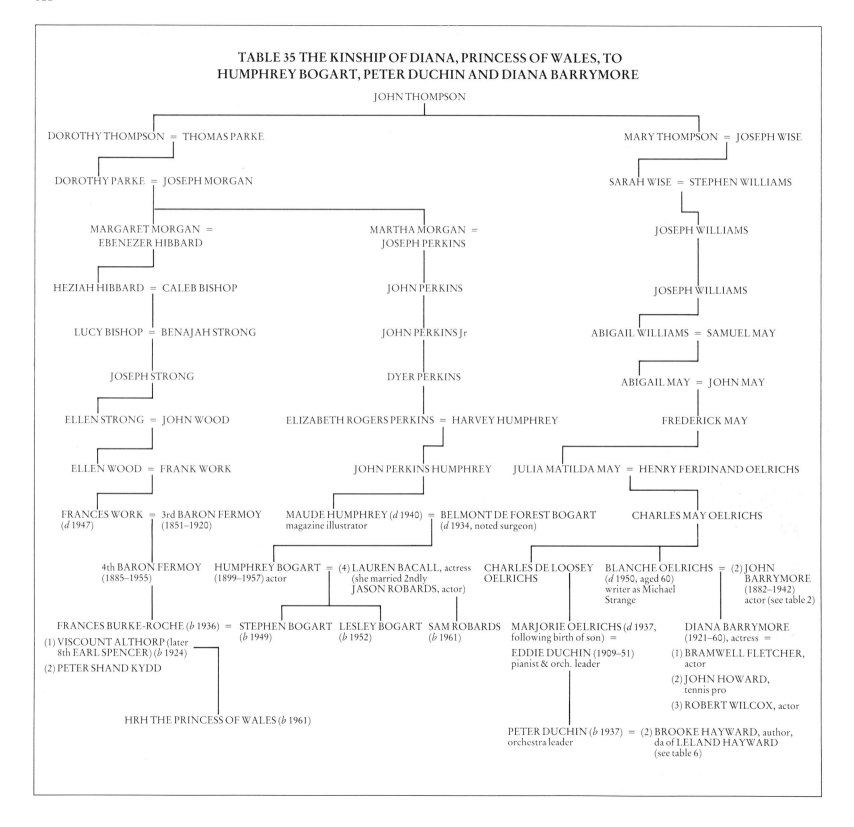

**TABLE 35 THE KINSHIP OF DIANA, PRINCESS OF WALES, TO
HUMPHREY BOGART, PETER DUCHIN AND DIANA BARRYMORE**

JOHN THOMPSON

DOROTHY THOMPSON = THOMAS PARKE

MARY THOMPSON = JOSEPH WISE

DOROTHY PARKE = JOSEPH MORGAN

SARAH WISE = STEPHEN WILLIAMS

MARGARET MORGAN =
EBENEZER HIBBARD

MARTHA MORGAN =
JOSEPH PERKINS

JOSEPH WILLIAMS

HEZIAH HIBBARD = CALEB BISHOP

JOHN PERKINS

JOSEPH WILLIAMS

LUCY BISHOP = BENAJAH STRONG

JOHN PERKINS Jr

ABIGAIL WILLIAMS = SAMUEL MAY

JOSEPH STRONG

DYER PERKINS

ABIGAIL MAY = JOHN MAY

ELLEN STRONG = JOHN WOOD

ELIZABETH ROGERS PERKINS = HARVEY HUMPHREY

FREDERICK MAY

ELLEN WOOD = FRANK WORK

JOHN PERKINS HUMPHREY

JULIA MATILDA MAY = HENRY FERDINAND OELRICHS

FRANCES WORK = 3rd BARON FERMOY
(*d* 1947)   (1851–1920)

MAUDE HUMPHREY (*d* 1940) = BELMONT DE FOREST BOGART
magazine illustrator   (*d* 1934, noted surgeon)

CHARLES MAY OELRICHS

4th BARON FERMOY
(1885–1955)

HUMPHREY BOGART = (4) LAUREN BACALL, actress
(1899–1957) actor   (she married 2ndly
    JASON ROBARDS, actor)

CHARLES DE LOOSEY
OELRICHS

BLANCHE OELRICHS = (2) JOHN
(*d* 1950, aged 60)   BARRYMORE
writer as Michael   (1882–1942)
Strange   actor (see table 2)

FRANCES BURKE-ROCHE (*b* 1936) =

(1) VISCOUNT ALTHORP (later
8th EARL SPENCER) (*b* 1924)

(2) PETER SHAND KYDD

STEPHEN BOGART   LESLEY BOGART   SAM ROBARDS
(*b* 1949)   (*b* 1952)   (*b* 1961)

MARJORIE OELRICHS (*d* 1937,
following birth of son) =

EDDIE DUCHIN (1909–51)
pianist & orch. leader

DIANA BARRYMORE
(1921–60), actress =

(1) BRAMWELL FLETCHER,
actor

(2) JOHN HOWARD,
tennis pro

(3) ROBERT WILCOX, actor

HRH THE PRINCESS OF WALES (*b* 1961)

PETER DUCHIN (*b* 1937) = (2) BROOKE HAYWARD, author,
orchestra leader   da of LELAND HAYWARD
    (see table 6)

patibility was strong enough to withstand the rigours of a top-flight Hollywood career.

When Lauren Bacall was pregnant with her first child, they bought Hedy Lamarr's house in Benedict Canyon. Miss Lamarr offered to give them the place on the condition Bogart made a film with her. This offer was refused. When their second child was expected they moved into a superb house in Holmby Hills.

Bogart's death in 1957 left her bereft. Her children were still very young, and her career had trailed off into indifferent pictures. Some considerable time after her husband's death, she had an affair with Frank Sinatra, who had been emotionally upset by his recent divorce from Ava Gardner.

On 4 July 1961, in Encenada, Mexico, Lauren Bacall married again. Her husband was Jason Robards Jr, the noted film and stage actor. She was his third wife; he was previously married in 1946 (divorced 1958) to Eleanor Pitman, by whom he had two sons and one daughter; and then in 1958 (divorced 1961) to Rachel Taylor, an actress. His father, Jason Robards Sr (1892–1963) was also a stage actor.

By her second husband Lauren Bacall has another son, Sam Prideaux Robards, who was born on 16 December 1961. He is now a film (*Fandango* (1983)), and TV (*Jacobo Tinnerman: Prisoner Without a Name, Cell Without a Number* (1983)) actor.

Miss Bacall's stage career, 'Cactus Flower', on Broadway (1967–9), and 'Applause', a musical version of *All About Eve* (1970), have won her much renewed critical acclaim. For the latter she won a Tony Award, took the show on a national tour and also played in London. 'Cactus Flower' also came to London in 1985.

Bacall's marriage to Jason Robards was dissolved by divorce in 1969.

EDIE SEDGWICK

Edie Sedgwick (see table 36) was a member of a prominent New England family. One of the eight

TABLE 36 WEB CONNECTING HUMPHREY BOGART TO EDIE SEDGWICK, ONE OF ANDY WARHOL'S PEOPLE

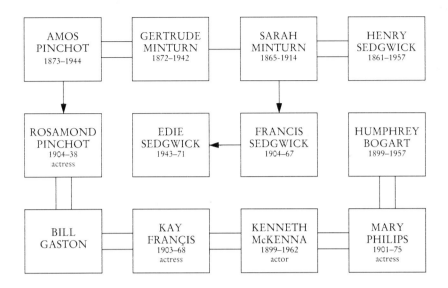

children of a kind but ineffectual mother and a fanatically macho father, she and several of her siblings had severe emotional problems (three of the eight are now dead). Edie was taken up by Andy Warhol and his coterie in New York in the early 1960s. Her short life of drug-addiction and waste was told in *Edie An American Biography* by Jean Stein and George Plimpton (1982).

ROSAMOND PINCHOT

Rosamond Pinchot (see table 36), also linked to the Sedgwick family, was chosen by Max Reinhardt to play the nun in the New York production of 'The Miracle' (1924). He used her again in 'The Eternal Road' (1937), but she despaired of ever achieving real success and was found dead in her car, wearing evening dress and ermine wrap on 24 January 1938, in Old Brookville, Long Island. She died of carbon monoxide poisoning, aged thirty-three.

13 Gloria Grahame: Ancestry and Family

Gloria Grahame is unique in the Hollywood hierarchy as the only film star for whom a Royal ancestry has been established. Equally unusual – although perhaps less distinguished – is the fact that she married her step-son. These two genealogical phenomena, together with her tarnished screen image as 'the other woman' make her an interesting study.

Gloria Grahame's descent from the Plantagenet Kings of England comes through the line of John of Gaunt, Duke of Lancaster, and brings in some of the greatest families of the north of England: Percy, Clifford and Neville. By the eighteenth century her ancestors were typical of the landed gentry, living quietly on their estates in Nottinghamshire. But there suddenly appears on the family tree a dangerous and dashing young man who brought disgrace upon his name.

This was William Parsons, the younger of the two sons of Sir William Parsons. His elder brother, John Parsons, went into the Church, and, as he was unmarried, it seems reasonable to suppose that young William was set to inherit both title and estate. However, country life obviously did not appeal to William and he decided to join the Army. Tiring of army life he took to highway robbery and forgery, for which he was eventually transported. His family was rich and he had married quite well, so it would seem he followed a life of crime out of sheer devilry. On his return to England he resumed his old ways, and he was finally hanged at Tyburn aged thirty-three. His father out-lived him by nine years, and the title passed to William's only son,

Mark, who died 'in great retirement' in 1812, when the title became extinct.

The hanged William Parsons's sister, Grace, married into the Lambarde family of Kent. Her daughter, Mary Lambarde, married the Reverend John Hallward, Vicar of Assington, Suffolk, and she is the ancestress of Gloria Grahame.

Most of the Hallwards went into the Church, but Gloria's great grandfather was a lawyer in London, her grandfather was a well-known artist and friend of Oscar Wilde, and her father, Michael Hallward, was an industrial designer and engineer. He emigrated to the USA. His younger brother, Christopher Hallward, was involved in films, and Christopher's wife was the daughter of Herbert Hampton, sculptor and painter, whose principal public works include memorials of Queen Victoria, King Edward VII and King George V in London, New Zealand and India. His descendants have also gone into the arts.

Michael Hallward married Jeannie McDougall, who acted under the name Jean Grahame on the British stage before the First World War. They had three children, Gloria, born 28 November 1925, in Los Angeles, Joy and Peter.

Gloria began performing on stage at the age of nine at the Pasadena Community Playhouse, and continued to act while at the Hollywood High School. After some experience in stock, she made her Broadway début as Gloria Hallward in 1943 and was signed to a film contract by MGM the following year when she assumed the surname of Grahame. The cynical realism of *film noir* in the

Gloria Grahame, the best of the screen floozies in the 1940s, is nineteenth in descent from King Edward III, and has the rare distinction of having been married to her former step-son.

1940s was perfectly suited to her sultry screen persona and she easily moved up from supporting to leading roles. Her languid manner, seductive voice and pouting lips made her the most memorable screen floozie of the decade.

She married first, in 1945 (divorced 1947), Stanley Clements, an American actor, by whom she had no issue, and secondly, in 1948 (divorced 1952), Nicholas Ray, the American film director, who directed her in *A Woman's Secret* (1949). She then went on to make an excellent team with Humphrey Bogart for *In a Lonely Place* (1950), as the girl who befriends him when he's suspected of murder. By Nicholas Ray she had issue one son, Timothy Ray, born in 1949.

Her divorce from Ray was a serious emotional setback, and she was off-screen for two years. Her next good role was as the sulky moll for whom Jack Palance wants to murder Joan Crawford in *Sudden Fear* (1952). This was followed by *The Bad and the Beautiful* (1952), as a spoilt Southern belle flirting with movie star Gilbert Roland at the expense of her small-time husband Dick Powell. For this performance she won a Best Supporting Actress Oscar.

Somewhat unusually, Gloria Grahame's success did not diminish her subsequent roles, and she was particularly lucky to get *The Big Heat* (1954) – probably her best remembered film – in which Lee Marvin flings scalding coffee in her face. This was directed by Fritz Lang and starred Glenn Ford, and the three of them were brought together again for *Human Desire* (1954), in which she played Broderick Crawford's evil playgirl wife, inciting Ford to commit murder. Barbara Stanwyck was originally offered the part, then Rita Hayworth (who turned it down pleading emotional stress – she was enmeshed in her fourth husband Dick Haymes's problems), and it was then offered to Olivia de Havilland, who also turned it down.

Gloria Grahame married thirdly in 1954 (divorced 1957), Cy Howard, an American comedy writer. He started in radio, writing comedy scripts for Jack Benny, Danny Thomas and Milton Berle, etc; and he later wrote for films including *My Friend Irma* (1949), *My Friend Irma Goes West* (1950), etc.,

and was an executive producer with Desilu TV studios. He made his directorial début in 1970 with *Lovers and Other Strangers*. By Howard, Gloria Grahame had further issue, a daughter, Paulette Howard, who was born in Paris in 1956. Gloria Grahame had fled to France having made a poor film for 20th Century Fox, *The Man Who Never Was* (1956), and infuriated the studio by being uncooperative with the Press.

By 1961 Gloria was once again living in Los Angeles, where she quietly married her former stepson, Anthony Ray (son of Nicholas Ray by his first wife Jean Evans). He was thus a half-brother of her own son Timothy Ray. By Anthony Ray she had two further children, both sons – Tony, born in 1963, and Jim, born in 1965.

She came to Britain in 1978, playing Sadie Thompson in Somerset Maugham's 'Rain' at the Watford Palace Theatre, and in London in 'A Tribute to Lily Lamont', poignantly playing an ageing Hollywood star. She appeared at the Duke's Playhouse, Lancaster (named after her ancestor John of Gaunt) in 1980 as Martha in 'Who's Afraid of Virginia Woolf?' The following year she was in London again to play Amanda in Tennessee Williams's 'The Glass Menagerie', in which her physical decline gave a moving pathos to her role as Amanda. While touring in Lancaster she fell seriously ill and was flown back to the United States. She had been undergoing treatment for breast cancer, and she died soon after arrival in New York, on 5 October 1981, aged fifty-seven.

Of Gloria Grahame's family only sketchy details are available. Her eldest son, Timothy Ray, is a film cameraman living in California. He has no children. Her daughter, Paulette Howard, is a painter and also lives in California; she is unmarried. Her first husband Stanley Clements died in 1981, and her second husband, Nicholas Ray, in 1978. Her third husband, Cy Howard, is now married to Barbara Warner, who, as the daughter of Jack Warner, provides a link with another important film dynasty (see table 29). Gloria Grahame was divorced from her last husband, Anthony Ray, who now lives with their two sons in Maine, where he is a film producer.

TABLE 37 THE ANCESTRY OF GLORIA GRAHAME (I)

EDWARD III, KING OF ENGLAND = 1328, PHILIPPA OF HAINAULT
(1312–77)   (*d* 1369)

JOHN OF GAUNT (4th son), Duke of = (3) 1396, CATHERINE SWYNFORD,
LANCASTER (*d* 1399)   formerly his mistress (*d* 1403)

JOHN BEAUFORT (6th son), Marquess of DORSET = MARGARET, da of THOMAS
and SOMERSET (legitimated 1397 for all   DE HOLAND, 2nd Earl of KENT
purposes save succession to the crown)
(*d* 1410)

EDMUND BEAUFORT, KG (4th son), Duke of = ELEANOR, da of RICHARD BEAUCHAMP, KG,
SOMERSET (*b* 1406; *k* at battle of St   5th Earl of WARWICK, and widow
Albans 1455)   of THOMAS, 9th Baron DE ROS

ELEANOR BEAUFORT (2nd da) = (2) Sir ROBERT SPENCER, of Spencer Court, Devon

CATHERINE SPENCER = HENRY PERCY, KG, 5th Earl of NORTHUMBERLAND
(*d* 1542)

Lady MARGARET PERCY (elder da) = HENRY CLIFFORD, KG, 1st Earl of CUMBERLAND
(*d* 1540)   (*d* 1542)

HENRY CLIFFORD, 2nd Earl of = (1) 1537, ELEANOR BRANDON (*d* 1547), niece of = (2) *c.* 1552, ANNE, da of WILLIAM LORD DACRE
CUMBERLAND (1517–69)   KING HENRY VIII

FRANCIS CLIFFORD, 4th Earl of = 1589, GRISOLD, da of THOMAS HUGHES, and
CUMBERLAND (1559–1641)   widow of EDWARD NEVILL, LORD ABERGAVENNY

FRANCES CLIFFORD (yr da) = 1614, Sir GERVASE CLIFTON, 1st Bt., KB, MP (cr.
                    a Baronet by King James I 1611) (*d* 1666)

Sir CLIFFORD CLIFTON (yr son) (*d* 1670) = FRANCES FINCH

CATHARINE CLIFTON = Sir JOHN PARSONS, 2nd Bt. (*d* 1704)

Sir WILLIAM PARSONS, 3rd Bt. (1686–1760) = FRANCES DUTTON (*d* 1735)
of Stanton le Wold, Notts

WILLIAM PARSONS (yr son), *b* 1717–18, Red = MARY, da of JOHN FRAMPTON,   GRACE PARSONS (only da); = 1747, THOMAS LAMBARDE (1705–69),
Lion Sq, London; Lieut. in Cholmondeley's Foot; of the Exchequer   was left a considerable   of Sevenoaks, Kent
hanged at Tyburn, having returned from transport-   fortune by her aunt the
ation after a conviction for highway robbery and   Duchess of Northumberland;
forgery, 1751   *d* 1778

Sir MARK PARSONS, 4th & last Bt.; *d* 1812, when   MARY LAMBARDE (2nd da) = 1784, Revd JOHN HALLWARD (1750–1826);
the title became extinct   (*b* 1752)   ed. Worcester Coll., Oxford; Vicar of
                                           Assington, Suffolk; son of THOMAS
                                           HALLWARD, gentleman, of Worcester

Revd JOHN HALLWARD (1791–1865) = EMILY JANE, da of CHARLES POWELL LESLIE,
Rector of Shepstone, Leics   of Glaslough, Co. Monaghan

Revd JOHN LESLIE HALLWARD (1823–96), Rector   CHARLES BERNERS HALLWARD (1825–96), lawyer = 1850, ELIZABETH ANN (*d* 1874), da of PETER
of Gilston, Herts   of 18 New Bridge St, Blackfriars   MORGAN, of HM Dockyard, Woolwich

REGINALD FRANCIS HALLWARD (4th son) (1858–1948); illustrator; = 1886, ADELAIDE CAROLINE (*b* 1860), da of Dr ROBERT WILLIAM BLOXAM,
ed. Slade Sch. of Art & RCA Schools; noted for his ceramics and   of Ryde, Isle of Wight (*d* 1868), by his wife, HENRIETTA LOCK
mystical illustrations, also worked with stained glass; he was
acquainted with Oscar Wilde, who appropriated his surname for
the painter in his novel, *The Picture of Dorian Gray* (1891)

(see table 38)

TABLE 38 THE ANCESTRY OF GLORIA GRAHAME (II)

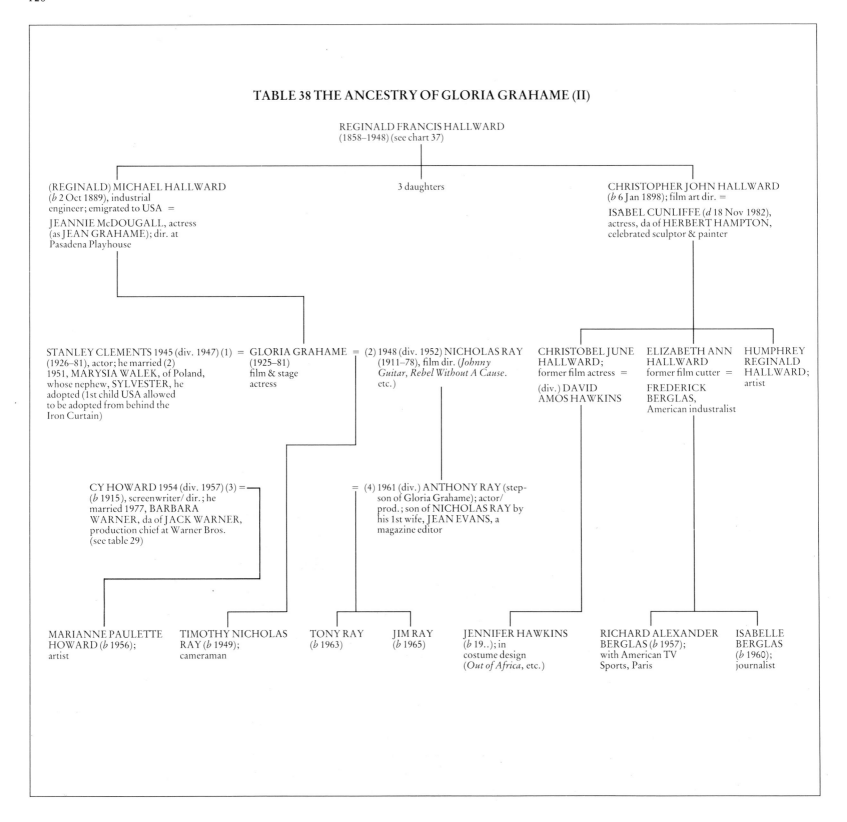

REGINALD FRANCIS HALLWARD
(1858–1948) (see chart 37)

(REGINALD) MICHAEL HALLWARD
(*b* 2 Oct 1889), industrial
engineer; emigrated to USA =
JEANNIE McDOUGALL, actress
(as JEAN GRAHAME); dir. at
Pasadena Playhouse

3 daughters

CHRISTOPHER JOHN HALLWARD
(*b* 6 Jan 1898); film art dir. =
ISABEL CUNLIFFE (*d* 18 Nov 1982),
actress, da of HERBERT HAMPTON,
celebrated sculptor & painter

STANLEY CLEMENTS 1945 (div. 1947) (1) = GLORIA GRAHAME = (2) 1948 (div. 1952) NICHOLAS RAY
(1926–81), actor; he married (2)
1951, MARYSIA WALEK, of Poland,
whose nephew, SYLVESTER, he
adopted (1st child USA allowed
to be adopted from behind the
Iron Curtain)

GLORIA GRAHAME
(1925–81)
film & stage
actress

(2) 1948 (div. 1952) NICHOLAS RAY
(1911–78), film dir. (*Johnny
Guitar, Rebel Without A Cause.*
etc.)

CHRISTOBEL JUNE
HALLWARD;
former film actress =
(div.) DAVID
AMOS HAWKINS

ELIZABETH ANN
HALLWARD
former film cutter =
FREDERICK
BERGLAS,
American industralist

HUMPHREY
REGINALD
HALLWARD;
artist

CY HOWARD 1954 (div. 1957) (3) =
(*b* 1915), screenwriter/ dir.; he
married 1977, BARBARA
WARNER, da of JACK WARNER,
production chief at Warner Bros.
(see table 29)

= (4) 1961 (div.) ANTHONY RAY (step-
son of Gloria Grahame); actor/
prod.; son of NICHOLAS RAY by
his 1st wife, JEAN EVANS, a
magazine editor

MARIANNE PAULETTE
HOWARD (*b* 1956);
artist

TIMOTHY NICHOLAS
RAY (*b* 1949);
cameraman

TONY RAY
(*b* 1963)

JIM RAY
(*b* 1965)

JENNIFER HAWKINS
(*b* 19..); in
costume design
(*Out of Africa*, etc.)

RICHARD ALEXANDER
BERGLAS (*b* 1957);
with American TV
Sports, Paris

ISABELLE
BERGLAS
(*b* 1960);
journalist

14 Richard Greene: Ancestry and Family

In the olden days of Hollywood, any aspiring actor or actress who suddenly got a lucky break was immediately swept up by the well-oiled studio publicity machine. This would churn out reams of fanciful stuff to an ever-hungry film-going public who relished the details of the latest débutante *ingénue*'s glamorous family background, or that of the 'socially prominent' leading man from New York. But most of it was simply gushing trivia, in which the facts were vague and in some cases deliberately obscured.

Ephraim Katz in his authoritative work, *The International Film Encyclopedia* is one of the few film historians to include relevant genealogical details in his entries, and in one of these he notes that the late Richard Greene (Robin Hood) is descended from William Friese-Greene, the pioneer developer of the projection camera. This erroneous information was in all likelihood gleaned from one of the many publicity sheets 20th Century Fox released when Richard Greene first arrived in tinsel town in 1938.

The British Film Institute has an undated Fox publicity release which states, 'He comes from an old theatrical family. His mother, brother, aunts, uncles and grandparents were all in the theatrical profession,' which sounds like a thespian Mafia – but in its way was quite true, as can be seen from table 39. What the publicity didn't say, and kept successfully hidden, was the fact that he was illegitimate. Thankfully, the stigma of illegitimacy has now entirely gone, but in 1918 – when Richard was born – it was considered shocking, and the innocent child often suffered accordingly.

From various certificates of birth, marriage and death, it is possible to put a few facts of Richard's father's life together. Richard Abraham Greene was forty-nine years old when his son was born. He had married in 1889, Laura Randall, a local Southsea girl, when he was a twenty-year-old brewer. They had five children, but the marriage eventually broke up (they separated but never divorced), perhaps when he left his job in order to try his luck on the stage – his younger sister, Evie, had already made a name for herself in musical comedy. He played at some London theatres, but was principally employed as a leading man at the Plymouth Repertory Theatre, where he met a bright young actress from County Durham, Kathleen Gerrard, with whom he lived for the remainder of his life. Their son, Richard Marius Joseph Greene, was born on 24 August 1918, in Plymouth.

He died in 1921, aged fifty-two, when his son was only two and a half years old, leaving a little over £4,000 – all of which he willed to Kathleen. In his will he also specified that in the event of their son being orphaned, he should be placed in 'a Roman Catholic Institution for the training and rearing of children'. (Kathleen was a Catholic.) There was no mention of his wife or their children. Seven years later Laura married again, to one Albert Talbot, a hammerman at the Portsmouth Dockyard, and died in 1949, in total obscurity, aged seventy-eight.

Kathleen gave up acting after Richard's birth, although she continued a lively career in the arts, writing and producing radio plays, and also spent some time in Canada, using her dramatic skills with a group of deaf and/or blind actors. She never married, and Richard was her only child. They remained extremely close all their lives, and she was always on hand to offer advice and support when his own career faltered. She died at Denville Hall, Middlesex, at the grand old age of ninety, and Richard died a little under two years later. Kathleen was survived by her sister, Nina, who was also an actress.

Having been predominantly raised and influenced by independent women, it is not surprising that Richard Greene was drawn to strong-minded females in his adult life. His first marriage, to Patricia Medina, spanned some of his happiest years in Hollywood, and his private photograph album contains some amusing snaps of the young Tyrone Power and Annabella playing croquet, and an even younger Rita Hayworth darting around a ping-pong table.

At the time of his divorce from Miss Medina, Greene was romantically involved with the celebrated heiress, Nancy Oakes, who legally adopted his only child, Patricia Oakes, born in 1951 in Mexico City. Although Nancy Oakes and Richard Greene never married they remained on friendly terms, and she attended his memorial service in London in 1985. His second wife, Mrs Beatriz Summers, from whom he was estranged at the time of his death, also exerted considerable influence over his last years.

It would indeed be a strange coincidence and contradiction if Richard Greene, who was always very sensitive about his past, should have perpetuated his predicament by having his own child out of wedlock, even though the times have changed so radically. Patricia Oakes, who assisted in this search for his ancestors, has contributed this character–career study.

RICHARD GREENE, *by his daughter, Patricia Oakes Leigh-Wood, November 1985*

'I was the saddenest most overnight somebody that ever happened', wrote Richard Greene about his arrival in Hollywood in January 1938,

aged nineteen. The telegramme had arrived on Christmas Eve confirming his contract with 20th Century Fox. A month later he was on the set of *Four Men and A Prayer*, with Loretta Young as his leading lady, David Niven and George Sanders, and John Ford directing. In his attempted memoirs, my father wrote: 'Such things do not happen in real life. To other people, perhaps, but not to you, especially not at the age of nineteen.' But this did happen to Richard, changing not only his circumstances overnight, but also his age. The studio preferred the age of twenty-four, so he aged five years in two minutes. Even his driver's licence was altered! This did not seem so funny when he was being wished a happy fiftieth birthday and he was only forty-five.

Until Richard's return to England in 1940, he made many films for 20th Century Fox; always playing the handsome romantic who gets the beautiful girl. In his second film, *Submarine Patrol* (1938), Nancy Kelly made her screen début. *Kentucky* (1938) followed, with Loretta Young and Walter Brennan. Then the first-filmed Sherlock Holmes's *The Hound of the Baskervilles* (1939). He worked with Sonja Henie, Cesar Romero, Shirley Temple and Anita Louise to name but a few. He had the part of Lord Tyce in Henry King's film *Stanley and Livingstone* (1939), with Spencer Tracy and Sir Cedric Hardwicke in the title roles.

These fun years of Hollywood, where Richard and his friends were young, famous, courted and earning good money, were soon to become a memory for the English stars. The Second World War had been declared so they returned to their homeland to join up. By 1941 Richard found himself in the 27th Lancers, and on Christmas Eve of that year he married the English actress, Patricia Medina.

My father was pleased to be home in many ways. He had been born in theatrical digs in Plymouth in 1918. His father was a member of the Plymouth Repertory Theatre at the time, and his uncles, Frank and Norman were also actors. Frank began his theatrical career at Daly's

Theatre, London, then went to Australia *c* 1909, where he became the leading baritone in the Royal Comic Opera Company, and he finally emigrated to the USA in 1920, where he was in the long-running production of 'Death Takes a Holiday' in New York, 1929–30. Norman was in the London productions of 'The Desert Song', 'Chu Chin Chow' and 'The Chocolate Soldier'. Evie Greene, Richard's aunt, who died the year before he was born, was a musical comedy star of the London stage and also toured in America. On her death at the early age of forty-one, *The Times* wrote, 'She had a salient recommendation that has not always been enjoyed by the musical comedy actress. She could sing, and she had force and considerable talent as an actress as well.'

Richard's grandfather, however, was a navy man. My father shared a love of the sea with his naval ancestor, who had died when Richard was only two and a half years old, leaving his actress mother, Kathleen, and her sister, Nina, to bring the young boy up. Their father, William Wallace Davidson, was an actor and theatrical producer at the Theatre Royal at Crook, County Durham. So when my father got his first part as a spear carrier in 'Antony and Cleopatra' at the age of sixteen, one could only say he was going into the family business. A generous godmother, Florence Sale-Barker, sent Richard to the Cardinal Vaughan School, where he received a classical education which was never forgotten. A great reader and collector of books, he also enjoyed nature, wild-life, fishing, falconry, fox-hunting or just walking in the woods. He had books on all these subjects as well as the classics. But time

Richard Greene at his home in Co. Wexford, Ireland, where he was Master of Fox Hounds. As 'Robin Hood' he was feared by the bad, loved by the good, for 143 episodes on ITV. His grandfather, William Wallace Davidson, was said to have owned one of the first picture houses in Britain.

to develop these interests would come later, for now there was a war to fight and a bride to attend to whenever possible.

During the war years, Richard was twice granted leave to film *Unpublished Story* (1942) and *Don't Take It to Heart* (1944), which co-starred his wife, Pat. After 1944 his health was not good enough for him to go back to France on active service, so he toured the Forces in Shaw's 'Arms and the Man', with Pat Medina and Gordon James. This brought Richard back to the live theatre. His part in Colin Morris's 'Desert Rats' brought him great reviews and he toured in England throughout 1945, eventually coming into London for a successful run. My father had broken away from the matinée idol image with this tough, war-battered character.

In 1947 he returned to 20th Century Fox to resume his contract. Patricia Medina went with him. No longer content to play the dashing hero, he found his return to Hollywood a disappointment because they would not give him the parts he wanted. He ended his contract in 1949, and, sadly, his marriage also ended. He returned to England alone, pausing in New York to do some plays for TV.

From 1953–5 he worked mostly in the theatre, sometimes in TV. Richard got the Robin Hood contract in 1955. After 143 episodes and a feature film, he had enough money to build an ocean-racing yacht, called *Santander*, which gave him great joy. He won several races, including Cowes to Lisbon. He remarried in 1960, a Colombian, Mrs Beatriz Robledo Summers. Together they bought a stud farm in Wexford, Ireland. Within five years he was ranked sixth on the list of top breeders of thoroughbreds in England and Ireland.

All this was wonderful, but also taking time away from his acting career. Richard was also getting older. The *Santander* was sold, and in 1972 the stud farm was also sold. Richard and Beatriz returned to London where they kept a *pied-à-terre*, but the threads of his career were not easy to pick up. Although he made over forty films, countless TV appearances, and many stage productions, he will be remembered by millions as 'Robin Hood'.

TABLE 39 THE RICHARD GREENE DYNASTY

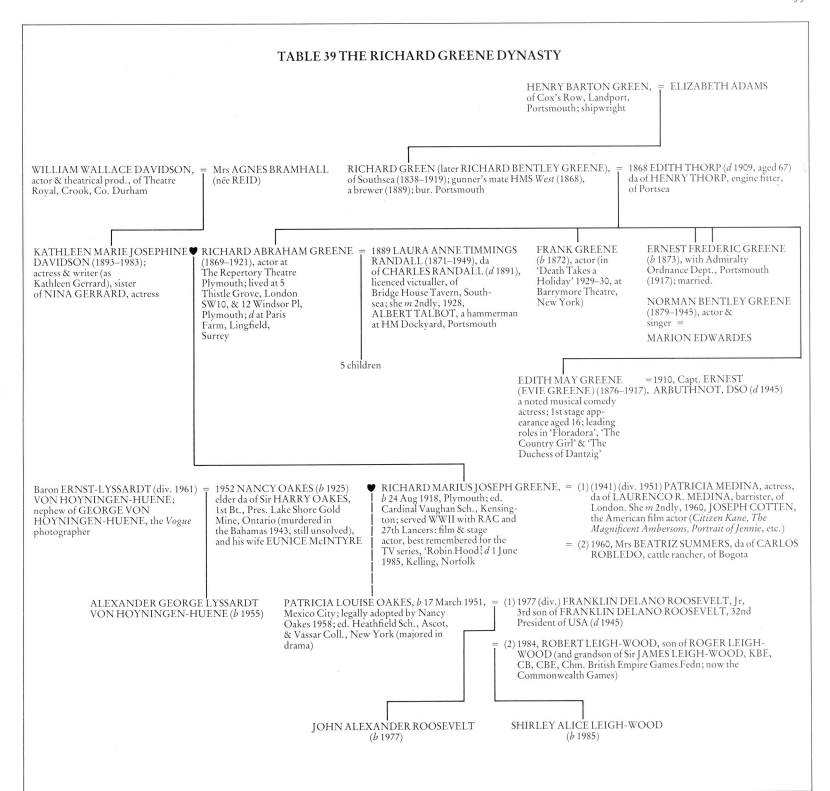

HENRY BARTON GREEN, = ELIZABETH ADAMS
of Cox's Row, Landport,
Portsmouth; shipwright

WILLIAM WALLACE DAVIDSON, = Mrs AGNES BRAMHALL
actor & theatrical prod., of Theatre (née REID)
Royal, Crook, Co. Durham

RICHARD GREEN (later RICHARD BENTLEY GREENE), = 1868 EDITH THORP (d 1909, aged 67)
of Southsea (1838–1919); gunner's mate HMS *West* (1868), da of HENRY THORP, engine fitter,
a brewer (1889); bur. Portsmouth of Portsea

KATHLEEN MARIE JOSEPHINE ♥ RICHARD ABRAHAM GREENE = 1889 LAURA ANNE TIMMINGS
DAVIDSON (1893–1983); (1869–1921), actor at RANDALL (1871–1949), da
actress & writer (as The Repertory Theatre of CHARLES RANDALL (d 1891),
Kathleen Gerrard), sister Plymouth; lived at 5 licenced victualler, of
of NINA GERRARD, actress Thistle Grove, London Bridge House Tavern, South-
SW10, & 12 Windsor Pl, sea; she m 2ndly, 1928,
Plymouth; d at Paris ALBERT TALBOT, a hammerman
Farm, Lingfield, at HM Dockyard, Portsmouth
Surrey

FRANK GREENE
(b 1872), actor (in
'Death Takes a
Holiday' 1929–30, at
Barrymore Theatre,
New York)

ERNEST FREDERIC GREENE
(b 1873), with Admiralty
Ordnance Dept., Portsmouth
(1917); married.

NORMAN BENTLEY GREENE
(1879–1945), actor &
singer =

MARION EDWARDES

5 children

EDITH MAY GREENE = 1910, Capt. ERNEST
(EVIE GREENE) (1876–1917), ARBUTHNOT, DSO (d 1945)
a noted musical comedy
actress; 1st stage app-
earance aged 16; leading
roles in 'Floradora', 'The
Country Girl' & 'The
Duchess of Dantzig'

Baron ERNST-LYSSARDT (div. 1961) = 1952 NANCY OAKES (b 1925) ♥ RICHARD MARIUS JOSEPH GREENE, = (1) (1941) (div. 1951) PATRICIA MEDINA, actress,
VON HOYNINGEN-HUENE; elder da of Sir HARRY OAKES, b 24 Aug 1918, Plymouth; ed. da of LAURENCO R. MEDINA, barrister, of
nephew of GEORGE VON 1st Bt., Pres. Lake Shore Gold Cardinal Vaughan Sch., Kensing- London. She m 2ndly, 1960, JOSEPH COTTEN,
HOYNINGEN-HUENE, the *Vogue* Mine, Ontario (murdered in ton; served WWII with RAC and the American film actor (*Citizen Kane, The*
photographer the Bahamas 1943, still unsolved), 27th Lancers: film & stage *Magnificent Ambersons, Portrait of Jennie*, etc.)
and his wife EUNICE McINTYRE actor, best remembered for the
TV series, 'Robin Hood'; d 1 June = (2) 1960, Mrs BEATRIZ SUMMERS, da of CARLOS
1985, Kelling, Norfolk ROBLEDO, cattle rancher, of Bogota

ALEXANDER GEORGE LYSSARDT
VON HOYNINGEN-HUENE (b 1955)

PATRICIA LOUISE OAKES, b 17 March 1951, = (1) 1977 (div.) FRANKLIN DELANO ROOSEVELT, Jr,
Mexico City; legally adopted by Nancy 3rd son of FRANKLIN DELANO ROOSEVELT, 32nd
Oakes 1958; ed. Heathfield Sch., Ascot, President of USA (d 1945)
& Vassar Coll., New York (majored in
drama) = (2) 1984, ROBERT LEIGH-WOOD, son of ROGER LEIGH-
WOOD (and grandson of Sir JAMES LEIGH-WOOD, KBE,
CB, CBE, Chm. British Empire Games Fedn; now the
Commonwealth Games)

JOHN ALEXANDER ROOSEVELT
(b 1977)

SHIRLEY ALICE LEIGH-WOOD
(b 1985)

15 Elizabeth Taylor's Family Circle

In a sense, every new day in the life of Elizabeth Taylor is a record. For, since the age of eighteen, this is the longest time she has ever remained single; her divorce from Senator John Warner having taken place in November 1982. For the record, her marriage dates are: 1950–1 Nicky Hilton; 1952–7 Michael Wilding; 1957–8 Mike Todd (killed in an aeroplane accident); 1959–64 Eddie Fisher; 1964–74, 1975–6 Richard Burton; 1976–82 John Warner.

This startling chain of unions cannot be accounted for in her immediate lineage, for her parents were comparatively staid. Her father, Francis Taylor, was an American art dealer who lived in London, and her mother was the former Sara Warmbrodt, who hailed from Arkansas City, Kansas. She had been an actress before her marriage, under the name of Sara Sothern. Elizabeth Rosamund Taylor was born in London on 27 February 1932.

The Taylors returned to America shortly before the outbreak of the Second World War, and Francis Taylor bought an art gallery in Beverly Hills. Noting his daughter's theatrical temperament, he succeeded in getting the ten-year-old chit a contract at Universal, through one of their shareholders, but her first conspicuous screen work was for MGM, where she appeared in *Lassie Come Home* (1943), as Roddy McDowall's little chum. MGM rewarded her with a long-term contract which tied her up until the early 1960s. They loaned her out to Columbia where she supported Joan Fontaine, as her saintly, consumptive friend in *Jane Eyre* (1944), and she then starred with Mickey Rooney in *National Velvet* (1944).

MGM were content to watch her grow from a pert child into a dazzling young woman; she did not suffer from the same career cramming that oppressed Judy Garland's youth. She was Amy in the nauseating 1949 version of *Little Women*, and then had her first romantic lead opposite Robert Taylor in *Conspirator* (1949). In the first of many onslaughts, Miss Taylor received the Harvard Lampoon's annual reward 'for so gallantly persisting in her career, despite a total inability to act'. Then she went into *Father of the Bride* (1950), with Spencer Tracy as the doting father, and Joan Bennett as the scatty mother (in a role her eldest daughter says was characteristic in real life); Miss Taylor herself was quite charmless as their tiresome daughter. Later in the same year, *A Place in the Sun* was released, in which director George Stevens elicited an incomparably better performance from Taylor as Montgomery Clift's rich and petulant girlfriend. This was a sign of things to come (and Clift became a very close friend).

By this time Elizabeth Taylor had already married and divorced Nicky Hilton, the young, Catholic heir to the chain of hotels of that name. Her engagement ring of five-carat diamonds began her lifelong love of jewellery. They were married at the Church of the Good Shepherd, Beverly Hills, on 6 May 1950; Miss Taylor wore a £1,500 white satin dress with twenty-five yards of train and was attended by seven bridesmaids. The bride and groom's kiss at the altar was so passionate and prolonged that the priest had to interrupt it. 'I think that's long enough, dear,' he said to the new Mrs Hilton. The marriage lasted only a little longer than

Elizabeth Taylor's devastating violet eyes have seen six husbands and seven marriages come and go, her romantic adventures have received wider press coverage than any other actress.

the kiss – twenty-nine weeks in all. They were both spoilt brats, and Hilton had a weakness for the gambling tables. He also kept a revolver by his crucifix next to the bed.

Miss Taylor's second marriage, 21 February 1952, at Caxton Hall, London, to Michael Wilding (she was twenty, he thirty-nine), was a quieter affair. He had been married before, to a showgirl named Kay Young, but had no children. By all accounts, Miss Taylor fell violently in love with him after they met at a party in London – where she was then filming *Ivanhoe* (1952). He was everything Nicky Hilton wasn't, sophisticated, charming and mature, and was understandably flattered by the attentions of the violet-eyed beauty half his age. They had two sons: Michael Howard Wilding Jr, born 6 January 1953 (in Santa Monica), and Christopher Wilding, born 27 February 1955. While married to Michael Wilding, she made two more noteworthy films: *Giant* (1956), with James Dean and Rock Hudson (which won a Best Director Oscar for George Stevens), and the interminable *Raintree County* (1957), with Montgomery Clift (which won her a nomination for a Best Actress Oscar).

Michael Wilding's infatuated comment upon his marriage, 'Elizabeth wants to be married to someone who will love and protect her,' was a dire misjudgment. If anyone, *he* needed the protection, for it was during this marriage that she started to indulge her coarse streak, and became greedy, high-handed, demanding and shrill. Michael Wilding finally got his cards when they were asked by Mike Todd, master-showman, to share a four-day cruise on his chartered yacht off the coast of California. He was then preparing his momentous adventure saga, *Around the World in Eighty Days* (1956). Todd was a virile and charismatic fifty-two-year-old, Taylor was twenty-five. She freed herself from Wilding, and married Todd on 2 February 1957, in Acapulco, Mexico. They made a flashy and fascinating pair. He gave her a Roll-Royce Silver Cloud, complete with telephones and a 'His' and 'Liz' drinks bar, and every Saturday he gave her an 'anniversary' mink, or diamonds, or sapphires. He also made loud admiring remarks about his wife's sexuality, such as, 'Any minute this little dame spends out of bed is wasted'. Their daughter, Elizabeth (Liza) Frances Todd, was born on 6 August 1957 (in New York).

Just over six months later Todd set out for New York to accept the Showman of the Year award in New York, but his aeroplane, 'Lucky Liz', smashed into the mountains in New Mexico and he was killed. 'This girl's been cruising for trouble all her life – and now she's found someone to give it to her,' Todd had said at the time of their marriage, and they may indeed have spent many years in volatile partnership, for he was surely the most compatible of all her husbands. He also had a shrewd idea of the sort of roles his wife could handle best, and it was his idea she should play Paul Newman's sexually-frustrated wife in *Cat on a Hot Tin Roof* (1958).

The tragedy of Todd's sudden and violent death made an impact on Taylor which lasted for years. She had only just passed her twenty-sixth birthday when he was killed. Unfortunately she turned to Todd's best man, Eddie Fisher, for comfort. He had been a protégé of Todd's, and, with his wife Debbie Reynolds, was very much a part of the Todd–Taylor circle. Fisher's marriage to Debbie Reynolds was unstable, and she had twice filed for divorce – the second time being shortly before the birth of their younger child, a son, Todd Fisher (named after Mike), who was born a mere three weeks before Todd was killed.

With an amazing lack of taste and tact, Fisher and Taylor made no secret of their mutual attraction, and were roundly condemned by the Press. Debbie Reynolds garnered much public sympathy when she was photographed in the doorway of her husband-forsaken house, with nappy pins fastened into the corner of her blouse and holding a baby's bottle bag. Even her mother joined the fray, 'Oh, I hope they blast the living daylights out of that Elizabeth Taylor. Everyone knows exactly what she is.'

MGM released *Cat on a Hot Tin Roof* while the storm was at its height. It became a top box-office hit and won Taylor a second Best Actress nomination

(Susan Hayward won with *I Want to Live*). She then converted to Judaism, the religion of both Todd and Fisher, and married Fisher on 12 May 1959, in Las Vegas. Mike Todd Jr was best man. It was only eleven months since Mike Todd was killed, and six months since Fisher had deserted his wife. Elizabeth Taylor never asked for alimony from any of her husbands, and Eddie Fisher is the only one she spoke disparagingly about after their divorce.

Miss Taylor then went into *Suddenly Last Summer* (1959), from a Tennessee Williams play (he had also written *Cat on a Hot Tin Roof*), with Katharine Hepburn, Montgomery Clift and Mercedes McCambridge. A remarkable cast, but there was continual combat between Hepburn and the director Joe Mankiewicz, and Taylor herself was unable to convey an idea of mental disturbance in her performance. However, it was a financial success, and, for the first time, Elizabeth Taylor entered the top ratings at the box-office (second in 1958). Her last film for MGM was *Butterfield 8*, in which she (reluctantly) played a prostitute.

Walter Wanger signed her up for *Cleopatra* (1963), at 20th Century Fox, for the much publicized fee of $1 million. Even before the filming started, it was clear it would over-run its schedule, and that her final fee would be more in the region of $2 million. Taylor became seriously ill – suffering from pneumonia and anaemia – and was taken to the London Clinic. She was still unwell when the news came she had won a Best Actress Oscar for *Butterfield 8*. Work on *Cleopatra* in London was abandoned, and the project was re-started in Rome. Rex Harrison replaced Peter Finch as Caesar, and Richard Burton replaced Stephen Boyd as Antony. The final and most dramatic cast change was in real life, however, when Richard Burton replaced Eddie Fisher in Miss Taylor's affections.

Cleopatra, dull epic though it was, made dual history as the most expensive film ever made up to that time – $37 million – and as the scene of the most publicized romance of all time. Burton seduced Taylor under Fisher's nose. He was a drunken, boorish lout most of the time, with a thin veneer of arrogance that appealed to the impression-able Miss Taylor. There were endless fights, reconciliations, rebuffs and hysterical scenes. Sybil Burton was eventually driven to file for divorce, Eddie

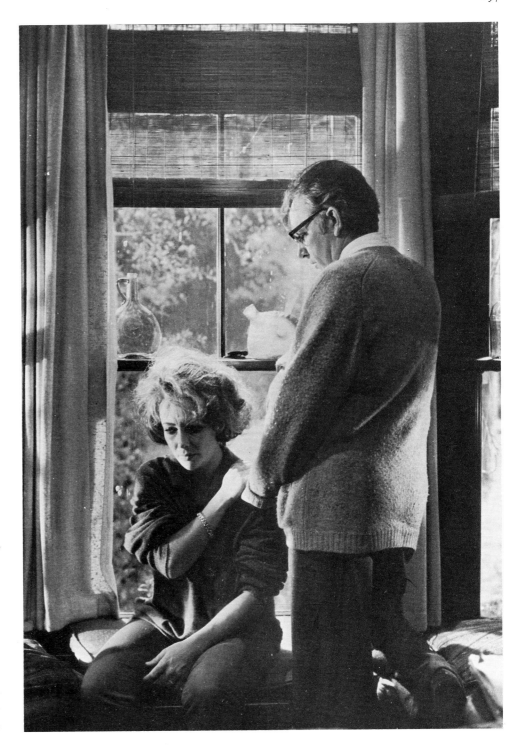

Taylor and Burton were both nominated for Oscars for Who's Afraid of Virginia Woolf?, *but only Taylor won.*

TABLE 40 THE MARRIAGES OF ELIZABETH TAYLOR

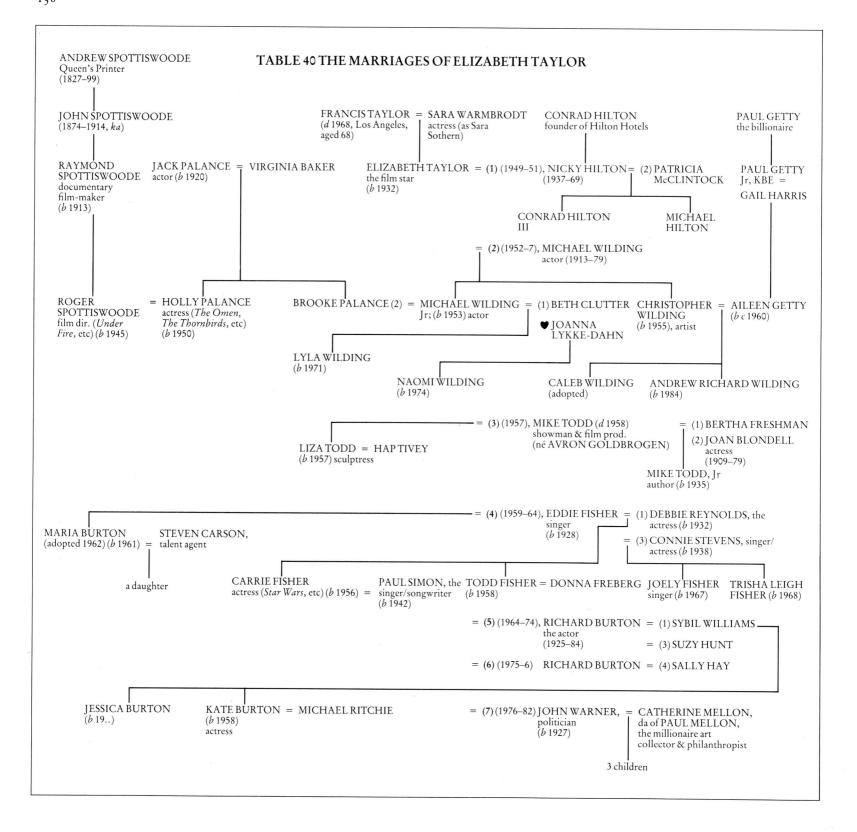

ANDREW SPOTTISWOODE
Queen's Printer
(1827–99)

JOHN SPOTTISWOODE
(1874–1914, *ka*)

RAYMOND
SPOTTISWOODE
documentary
film-maker
(*b* 1913)

JACK PALANCE = VIRGINIA BAKER
actor (*b* 1920)

FRANCIS TAYLOR = SARA WARMBRODT
(*d* 1968, Los Angeles,   actress (as Sara
aged 68)   Sothern)

CONRAD HILTON
founder of Hilton Hotels

PAUL GETTY
the billionaire

ELIZABETH TAYLOR = (1) (1949–51), NICKY HILTON = (2) PATRICIA
the film star   (1937–69)   McCLINTOCK
(*b* 1932)

PAUL GETTY
Jr, KBE =

GAIL HARRIS

CONRAD HILTON
III

MICHAEL
HILTON

= (2) (1952–7), MICHAEL WILDING
actor (1913–79)

ROGER
SPOTTISWOODE
film dir. (*Under
Fire*, etc) (*b* 1945)

= HOLLY PALANCE
actress (*The Omen,
The Thornbirds*, etc)
(*b* 1950)

BROOKE PALANCE (2) = MICHAEL WILDING = (1) BETH CLUTTER
Jr; (*b* 1953) actor

♥ JOANNA
LYKKE-DAHN

CHRISTOPHER = AILEEN GETTY
WILDING   (*b c* 1960)
(*b* 1955), artist

LYLA WILDING
(*b* 1971)

NAOMI WILDING
(*b* 1974)

CALEB WILDING
(adopted)

ANDREW RICHARD WILDING
(*b* 1984)

= (3) (1957), MIKE TODD (*d* 1958)
showman & film prod.
(né AVRON GOLDBROGEN)

= (1) BERTHA FRESHMAN

(2) JOAN BLONDELL
actress
(1909–79)

LIZA TODD = HAP TIVEY
(*b* 1957) sculptress

MIKE TODD, Jr
author (*b* 1935)

MARIA BURTON
(adopted 1962) (*b* 1961) =

STEVEN CARSON,
talent agent

= (4) (1959–64), EDDIE FISHER = (1) DEBBIE REYNOLDS, the
singer   actress (*b* 1932)
(*b* 1928)

= (3) CONNIE STEVENS, singer/
actress (*b* 1938)

a daughter

CARRIE FISHER
actress (*Star Wars*, etc) (*b* 1956) =

PAUL SIMON, the
singer/songwriter
(*b* 1942)

TODD FISHER = DONNA FREBERG
(*b* 1958)

JOELY FISHER
singer (*b* 1967)

TRISHA LEIGH
FISHER (*b* 1968)

= (5) (1964–74), RICHARD BURTON = (1) SYBIL WILLIAMS
the actor
(1925–84)   = (3) SUZY HUNT

= (6) (1975–6) RICHARD BURTON = (4) SALLY HAY

JESSICA BURTON
(*b* 19..)

KATE BURTON = MICHAEL RITCHIE
(*b* 1958)
actress

= (7) (1976–82) JOHN WARNER, = CATHERINE MELLON,
politician   da of PAUL MELLON,
(*b* 1927)   the millionaire art
collector & philanthropist

3 children

TABLE 41 ELIZABETH TAYLOR'S MARRIAGE WEB

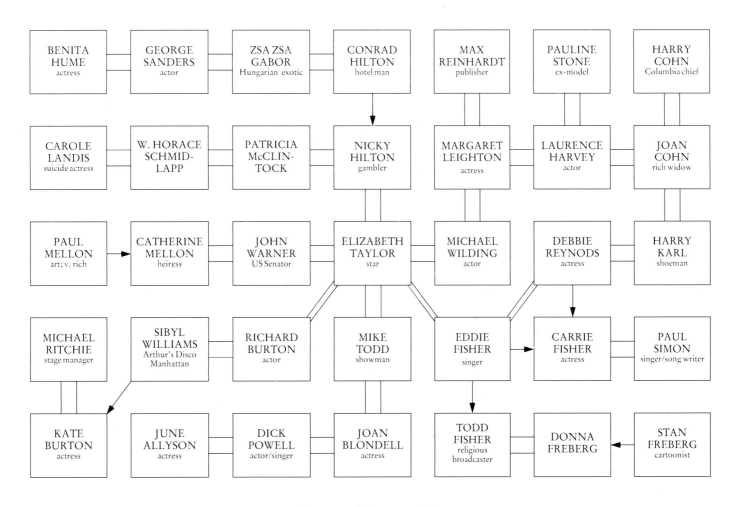

See page 7 for key to symbols.

Fisher was persuaded to let Burton adopt the baby girl he and Taylor had adopted in 1962, and Burton and Taylor were finally married by a Unitarian minister in Montreal on 15 March 1964.

Burton and Taylor made several films together, namely, *The VIPs* (1963), *The Sandpiper* (1965), and *Who's Afraid of Virginia Woolf?* (1966), directed by Mike Nichols, from the play by Edward Albee, and co-starring George Segal and Sandy Dennis. This film contains Elizabeth Taylor's best performance, as Burton's overblown, strident wife, and won her a second Best Actress Oscar, and (co-winner with Lynn Redgrave) the New York Critics' Award. They were also together in the poor *Taming of the Shrew* (1967) *Dr Faustus* (1967), and *Under Milk Wood* (1971).

The Burton marriage faltered in 1974, and they divorced, only to marry again in Botswana, the following year. 'We are stuck for always,' said Elizabeth Taylor, but twenty-six weeks was as long as the action replay could survive. Another divorce, and then Miss Taylor married Senator John Warner, of Virginia and Washington, former Secretary of the Navy; they divorced in 1982.

In 1981 she performed on the New York stage as Regina Giddens in 'The Little Foxes', which came to London the following year. In May 1983 Taylor and Burton opened on Broadway in Coward's 'Private Lives'. *Variety* commented on Taylor, 'The actress is an attractive matronly woman with genuine star presence, but she doesn't begin to suggest a flighty young Englishwoman.' The audience nevertheless flocked to see their tabloid pin-ups. At the very end of 1983 she entered the Betty Ford Clinic, Palm Springs, for the treatment of her addiction to Percodan sleeping tablets and alcohol. She attended group-therapy sessions and lectures, and left after weeks looking radiant. When asked about the living conditions there, she said, with familiar humour, 'It was the first time in my life I'd ever shared a room with a woman.'

In September 1985 she lent her name and considerable support to APLA (AIDS Appeal Project Los Angeles) for a benefit held at the Bonaventura Hotel, Los Angeles. Wearing black lace and emeralds, she looked every inch the last Hollywood star of the Golden Era.

Of her children, the eldest, Michael Wilding Jr, was a musician (trumpet, flute and guitar) with a pop group, Solar Ben, and is now a film and TV actor. He married first, 6 October 1970 (Caxton Hall, London) (divorced), Beth Ann Clutter, daughter of Robert Ian Clutter, an oceanographer, by whom he has issue, Leyla Wilding, born 25 July 1971. He then lived with a Shropshire girl, Johanna Lykke Dahn, by whom he has further issue, Naomi Wilding, born 2 January 1975, in Wales. On 27 August 1982 (in a midnight ceremony in Los Angeles), he married Brooke Palance, younger daughter of Jack Palance, the actor.

Christopher Wilding is an artist. He married in 1981, Aileen Getty, daughter of J. Paul Getty II, KBE (and granddaughter of the fabled billionaire). They have one adopted son, Caleb Wilding, and their own son, Andrew Richard Wilding, born October 1984.

Liza Todd won a scholarship to the Slade School of Art, London, and is now a sculptress. In 1984 she married Hap Tivey, an artist, by whom she has issue, Quinn C. Tivey (a son), born in 1986. Her adoptive sister, Maria Burton, was once a model in London, and on 13 February 1982 (New York) married Steven Carson, a talent agent. They have one daughter.

Selected Bibliography

Burke's Peerge and Baronetage (1970)
Burke's Landed Gentry (various editions)
GEC's Complete Baronetage (1902)
The Dictionary of National Biography
The Dictionary of National Biography of America
Grove's Dictionary of Music
Foster's Alumni Oxon
Who's Who (various editions)
Who's Who in America (various editions)
Who's Who in the Theatre (various editions)

Mary Astor: *My Story* (1959); *A Life on Film* (1971)
Cleveland Amory: *International Celebrity Register* (1959)
Kenneth Anger: *Hollywood Babylon* (1975)
Lauren Bacall: *By Myself* (1978)
Andrew Barrow: *Gossip 1920 to 1970* (1978)
Diana Barrymore: *Too Much Too Soon* (1957)
Joan Bennett & Lois Kibbee: *The Bennett Family Playbill* (1970)
Gerald Boardman: *The Oxford Companion to the American Theatre* (1984)
Frederick Boase: *Modern English Biography (Suppl.)* (1965)
Louise Brooks: *Lulu in Hollywood* (1982)
Zelda Cini & Bob Crane: *Hollywood: Life and Legend* (1980)
Charles Castle: *Joan Crawford, The Raging Star* (1977)
Alistair Cooke: *Douglas Fairbanks, The Making of a Screen Actor* (1940)
James Kotsilibas-Davis: *The Barrymores* (1981)
George Eells: *Ginger, Loretta and Irene Who?* (1976)
Stephen Farber & Marc Green: *Hollywood Dynasties* (1984)
Christopher Finch & Linda Rosenkrantz: *Gone Hollywood* (1979)
Fred Lawrence Guiles: *Tyrone Power, The Last Idol* (1980)
David Halliwell: *Filmgoers Companion* (various editions)
Brooke Hayward: *Haywire* (1977)
Joe Hyams: *Bogie, The Biography of Humphrey Bogart* (1966)

Ephraim Katz: *The International Film Encyclopedia* (1979)
Kitty Kelley: *Elizabeth Taylor, The Last Star* (1980)
Richard Lamparski: *Whatever Became Of . . .?* (various editions)
Anita Loos: *Kiss Hollywood Goodbye* (1974)
Marquis de Ruvigny: *The Plantagenet Roll of the Blood Royal (Mortimer Percy)* (1911)
Samuel Marx: *Mayer & Thalberg* (1976)
Sheridan Morley: *Gladys Cooper* (1979); *Tales From the Hollywood Raj* (1983)
Barry Norman: *The Hollywood Greats* (1979)
Beverly Linet: *Alan Ladd* (1980)
Paul Michael & James Robert Parish: *Movie Greats* (1969)
David Niven: *Bring on the Empty Horses* (1975)
James Robert Parish: *The Paramount Pretties* (1972); *The RKO Gals* (1974); with Don E. Stanke: *The Glamour Girls* (1975)
Roy Pickard: *The Oscar Movies From A–Z* (1977); *The Hollywood Studios* (1978)
Mary Pickford: *Sunshine and Shadows* (1956)
Gary Boyd Roberts & William Addams Reitwiesner: *The American Ancestors and Cousins of The Princess of Wales* (1984)
Bernard Rosenberg & Harry Silverstein: *The Real Tinsel* (1970)
David Shipman: *The Great Movie Stars, The Golden Years* (1979); *The International Years* (1972)
John Springer & Jack Hamilton: *They Had Faces Then* (1978)
Gloria Swanson: *Swanson on Swanson* (1980)
Larry Swindell: *Screwball, The Life of Carole Lombard*
Bob Thomas: *A Biography of Joan Crawford* (1978)
Lyn Tornabene: *Long Live The King, A Biography of Clark Gable* (1977)
Evelyn Mack Truitt: *Who Was Who on the Screen* (1980)
Maurice Zolotow: *Billy Wilder in Hollywood* (1977)

Index

❦